# LILLIPUT FLEET

*In conjunction with Don Newton and available from New English Library:*

TARANTO

# Lilliput Fleet

A. CECIL HAMPSHIRE

NEW ENGLISH LIBRARY
TIMES MIRROR

To My Wife

First published in Great Britain by William Kimber and Co. Ltd., in 1957
© William Kimber and Co. Ltd, 1957

*

FIRST NEL PAPERBACK EDITION JANUARY 1976

*

*NEL Books are published by*
*New English Library Limited from Barnard's Inn, Holborn, London, E.C.1.*
*Made and printed in Great Britain by Hunt Barnard Printing Ltd., Aylesbury, Bucks.*

45002543 8

# CONTENTS

## ACKNOWLEDGEMENTS

I wish to thank the Department of the Chief of Naval Information, the Historical Section and the Records Department of the Admiralty for their invaluable help in making available official records and documents; also the Registrar General of Shipping and Seamen; Chief Skipper Cyril Sutcliffe, R.D., R.N.R. (Retd); the Misses Elsie and Doris Waters for their kindly recollection of those fateful days in 1939 when the world moved towards war, and the Patrol Service most ungallantly requisitioned the Lowestoft theatre at which they were then appearing; Messrs. Brigham and Cowan (Hull) Ltd.; the staff of the Photographic Library at the Imperial War Museum; and the Controller of H.M. Stationery Office for permission to quote from *The War at Sea*, Vol. II, by Captain S. W. Roskill, D.S.C., R.N.

A.C.H.

## ONE OF OUR MINESWEEPERS

SKIPPER GEORGE DUFFY leaned over the bridge rail of the trawler *Daisy Bell* and gazed aft along her narrow deck. His naval peaked cap with its tarnished gold badge was crushed down on to his ears, and his stocky figure was swollen to barrel-like proportions by the heavy duffel coat he wore. A thick woollen scarf was wound around his neck, and his blue uniform trousers were tucked into knee-high seaboots.

The North Sea on this grey winter day was a cold and clammy world. The air was filled with a fine, salt-tasting mist, spindrift whipped from the wave-caps by the lash of a biting easterly wind. The trawler pitched and rolled ceaselessly in the ground swell, and the smoke from her funnel shredded into ragged wisps as her bows plunged deep into the troughs, then soared skywards, mastheads describing wild arcs against the sky.

Under Duffy's watchful eye the crew of the *Daisy Bell*, thickly clad like himself, was working about a pile of gear jumbled on the after deck. One object shaped like a torpedo rested in wooden chocks bolted to the deck. Above its blunt nose protruded a short vertical steel rod with a red-painted metal flag attached. Beside it, draped with heavy chains, lay a pair of square iron frames fitted inside the curved metal vanes, like outsize kites. Festoons of steel wires and chains trailed away to the barrels of the trawler's winch.

Stolidly indifferent to the biting cold the men were rapidly creating order out of the seeming chaos of metal and rope littering the deck, deftly connecting wires and shackles. When their task was completed they stood about silently,

9

balancing themselves easily against the trawler's jerky motion, drawing at cigarettes shielded in their fingers and casting frequent glances up at the skipper on the bridge. The leaden waves smacked against the trawler's sides as she lifted on the swells, and the men hunched their shoulders uncomplainingly as drops of icy water spattered them.

'All right, lads. Out sweep!'

Giving a quick glance around the melancholy expanse of empty sea Duffy bellowed the order through his cupped hands, and the men sprang into renewed activity. Jets of steam spurted whitely from the winch as the engineman worked his levers. While the trawler's engines nosed her ahead in obedience to Duffy's commands, the torpedo-shaped float was manhandled from its chocks and hoisted out on a davit, the men at the rail shoving it away whenever the clumsy object threatened to crash against the trawler's plates at each roll. The float splashed into the water and the davit hook was deftly uncoupled; one of the kite-like objects followed it over the side and the winch clattered and trembled as the wire went reeling out until the metal float with its red flag was bobbing like a sportive porpoise 500 yards astern of the trawler's quarter. Shackled to the float wire the second kite was hoisted out, the action of the flowing water on its curved vanes forcing it beneath the surface. Then the winch brake gripped to keep float, wire and kites steadily pulling.

From the trawler's bridge wing a duffel-coated signalman bent two black canvas spheres on to the halyards and hoisted one to the masthead, the other to the end of the starboard yardarm. As the vessel increased speed the grubby square of bunting at her gaff streamed and flapped in the wind. It was a White Ensign, for the year was 1940 and the steam trawler *Daisy Bell*, now transformed into one of his Majesty's minesweepers, was about to commence her daily task of clearing the seas of the deadly menace sown so assiduously by the enemy.

This was fishing of a different but perhaps more rewarding kind for Skipper George Duffy, R.N.R., who, before the war, had earned more than £2,000 a year from the catches he had brought back from Arctic waters. It was also history repeating itself, for his father had gone minesweeping in World War I. He had been a Skipper in the old R.N.R. Trawler Section, as it had been called, and it was only natural that George should follow in his footsteps and join the renamed R.N.R. Patrol Service as soon as he, too, qualified as a 'Deckie'.

Like most fisher folk, the Duffys could boast a long connection with seafaring. Had not an ancestor, Andrew Duffy, been press-ganged into the Navy 150 years back? He had served his time, received an honourable discharge and returned to fishing. Now there was no longer need for a Press Gang. The fishermen of Britain volunteered in time of peace for their own special task in war, one at which they were unrivalled experts.

As the trawler forged steadily ahead the sweep float plunged and curveted in the waves, its direction indicated to other ships by the black ball at the vessel's yardarm. Aft the engineman remained by his winch, his pipe gripped between his teeth as he scanned the taut wire surging through the fairlead, ready to ease the brake if the wire should suddenly pull and 'sing', indicating that the sweep had encountered a mine mooring. Another seaman perched himself on the stern grating, alertly watching the antics of the spray-wreathed float as it bounded through the waves.

The rest of the trawlermen went off about their daily duties. One small group climbed up on to the whaleback forecastle and began to clean the 12-pounder gun, most formidable weapon in the trawler's slender armoury. At the extremity of port and starboard bridge wings a single Lewis gun swung on its pedestal, ammunition pans fitted ready for instant action. On a circular steel platform built abaft the funnel the Oerlikon gunner wriggled inside his shoulder grips and began training the muzzle of his weapon, squinting through his sights at the imaginary foe. Seated in the doorway of the tiny galley the cook began to peel potatoes into a bucket, a damp cigarette-end clinging to his lower lip as he hummed gently to himself. The ship's cat, a large tabby, picked her way delicately over the Carley raft on the trawler's port side and settled down to doze inside a coil of rope.

Suddenly there came a yell from the watchers aft as the taut wire began to vibrate, and all hands turned to stare at the grey ocean astern. Away on the quarter the float had buried its nose deeply in the waves and was ploughing up a feathery plume of spray. A moment later a glistening black object, rounded and studded with horns, broke surface a bare fifty yards from the trawler's stern.

While Duffy slowed engines, two steel-helmeted trawlermen carrying rifles made their way along the heaving deck and carefully wedged themselves against the ship's roll. They began to fire deliberately at the mine, the bullets kicking up tiny spurts of water close to the bobbing sphere. Again they aimed and fired, and then, with the lightening rapidity of a pantomime demon disappearing from the stage in a puff of smoke, the mine vanished in a towering column of foam, flame and green water. A lucky shot had hit one of the horns. The *Daisy Bell* shuddered as if she had been struck by an invisible hammer. But before the ragged mushroom of spray could subside the burly skipper had rung down for the engines to go ahead. With satisfied grins on their faces the riflemen walked slowly forward easing their magazines, and the signalman crossed the engine-room casing and solemnly added another chevron to the sixteen already chalked around the base of the trawler's funnel.

But death now lurked beneath the patch of water over which the *Daisy Bell* was steaming, and her crew went about their work with a dour nonchalance tinged with a keen alertness. At any moment the reeling bows of their vessel might crash down on one of those menacing spheres, or one might get tangled in the sweep and bob up immediately under her counter. Either way disaster would result, sudden, swift and final. Strapped around their chests outside their heavy winter clothing the narrow inflated Navy lifebelts seemed less of a mere obstruction to movement.

Again the sweep wire tautened, and its frenzied jerking was followed by another thudding hammer blow as the sea astern boiled again into a monstrous swelling. A mine had detonated in the sweep and the signalman chalked up another victory on the funnel. Soon afterwards a second mine exploded with a mountainous heave of the water surface, and then a third, as if in sympathy with its fellows.

Patiently, hour after hour, the *Daisy Bell* steamed up and down a wide stretch of sea, dropping dan buoys at intervals to mark her passage, each swath of swept water overlapping so that no lurking mine should escape the searching sweep wire. Normally at least two trawlers would be on the job together with two skippers in each vessel, one to act as first lieutenant. But enemy air attacks had so depleted the small Minesweeping Group at her base port that the *Daisy Bell* was the only vessel left undamaged. Although his 'Number One' was ashore suffering from influenza Duffy knew that at all costs the port must be kept open, and had taken his ship to sea by himself to do the job.

Once a small armada of ships loomed out of the grey haze and there was a sudden coruscation of signal lamps. But the humpy vessels resolved themselves into a friendly coastal convoy of colliers and small tramp steamers plodding southwards. Steaming steadily onwards, like a flock of grey sheep rounded up by the lean destroyer pack snapping at their flanks, they passed through the trawler's swept channel and disappeared over the horizon, leaving the minesweeper to her lonely task.

As the meagre daylight began to fade Duffy decided to haul in his sweep and pick up the bobbing dan buoys. Six mines had been detonated, a good bag for one day. Each represented a ship saved from possible destruction, and he was satisfied that the port approaches were once more clear for traffic. As soon as the sweep gear and buoys were inboard and stowed the *Daisy Bell* could head for harbour.

Sipping a mug of hot sweet tea in between quick surveys of the horizon Duffy suddenly cocked an attentive ear to a new sound, a faint uneven drone which vied with the whistle of the wind through the funnel stays. The sound was the throbbing of aircraft engines, which presently grew louder. The men paused in their work, an unspoken question in their searching eyes as they anxiously scanned the clouds. Then abruptly from the mist the plane emerged heading for the small vessel. It was a twin-engined machine flying low, not more than eight hundred feet above the waves.

Duffy grasped a rocket pistol and fired the challenge, his

gaze straining for a glimpse of the plane's wing markings. But as it roared overhead his reply came in a burst of machine-gun fire. When the aircraft banked the sinister-looking swastika on its dorsal fin left no doubt as to its identity.

'Action stations!' The skipper hurled himself at the nearest Lewis gun; the men dropped wires and gear and raced for their weapons. But the big Heinkel was already upon them. Two black objects leisurely left its belly and then swished downwards, curving into the sea and exploding twenty yards from the *Daisy Bell*. As the bombs whistled past Duffy swung his gun, hose-piping a jet of coloured tracer at the enemy plane, and was answered by a stream of fire from her gunners.

The bullets plunked viciously into the little ship, clanging hollowly as they ricocheted off the steel funnel casing and showering up wood splinters as they tore into her deck. The Oerlikon gunner was now at his weapon, and the 12-pounder's crew were frenziedly loading and firing their gun at maximum elevation. Two men lay where enemy bullets had caught them, one writhing, the other face downward and still, his head cradled in his arms as if asleep. But from the outflung skirt of his oilskin ran a thread of scarlet.

The aircraft made a tight turn and raced again, undeterred by the hail of fire spouting up from the trawler. Looming larger and larger like a swooping bird of prey, the enemy plane roared into the attack, the trawler's gunners struggling to keep it in their sights. Again two bombs left the fuselage and whistled downwards, while tracer stabbed the air with fiery spears. One bomb struck the *Daisy Bell* with a metallic thud, the other missed and exploded in a gout of flame and smoke beyond the trawler's port side.

But the fishermen had hit back with deadly aim, and the enemy aircraft was now losing height, thick smoke pouring from the fuselage as it juddered away into the mist. A mile from the trawler, the Nazi pilot already a sightless corpse in the shattered cockpit, the plane dived steeply into the sea and sank almost immediately. The minesweeper men relaxed their tense and sweating bodies and grinned shakily at each other.

Duffy barked an order through the voicepipe to the helmsman in the wheelhouse below and, as the vessel's bows began swinging towards the distant land, he shinned down the bridge ladder and clambered aft. Amidships a jagged hole in the engine-room casing showed where the bomb had passed through and, with a brief glance at the twisted steel, he descended to the engine room.

'Where'd it go?' he asked the steel-helmeted Chief Engineman standing unemotionally by his throttle.

The engineer jerked his thumb towards the sinister-looking cylinder wedged in the buckled grating a few feet away from him and spat contemptuously.

'Och, it were a dud,' he explained.

'Gie us a hand, Jamie,' ordered the skipper, and together the two men worked the unexploded bomb free from its resting-place and hefted it on deck, where they staggered to the ship's side and dropped it unceremoniously overboard.

'What happened to yon aircraft?' asked the Chief Engineman, glancing round and mopping his forehead with a grimy sweat rag.

'We got the bastard,' said Duffy and went off to examine the casualties.

One man was dead, his chest a bloody pulp where the Heinkel's bullets had caught him. The other had sustained a flesh wound in the leg, and when the skipper reached him he was sitting up and puffing at a cigarette lit for him by the cook, who combined first aid with his culinary duties.

With the men still at action stations, the *Daisy Bell* steamed steadily back to port. Duffy prowled restlessly up and down the tiny bridge, his keen eyes striving to pierce the gathering gloom. He hoped they would reach harbour without further trouble. Also he wanted to get down to his cabin and write out the report of their recent action before he forgot the details. That blasted Nazi had killed Geordie Thompson, one of his best men. He knew Geordie's wife and family, for most of his crew came from the same fishing port and they had sailed together in peacetime. Below the wheelhouse the signalman carefully chalked a swastika on the funnel.

The chill winter dusk was swiftly closing in when a dark

shape suddenly loomed ahead. 'Convoy,' muttered Duffy to himself as he put the trawler's engines to half speed and peered over the bridge rail. In a moment he'd be in the middle of them if he didn't watch out. But as the strange ship sheered past something unfamiliar about her dim out-lines roused his suspicions, and he flashed the recognition signal. For several tense seconds nothing happened; then the world seemed to explode in his face as guns opened fire on the trawler at point-blank range.

Other dark shapes slid past on both sides of the little *Daisy Bell*, and a hail of flashing tracer poured into her as the enemy craft glided rapidly into the mist. Duffy gave a roar of fury. Minelaying E-boats sneaking in to lay more of their rotten eggs right under his nose!

The Germans, discovering that their opponent was but a solitary trawler, spun their helms and returned to the attack. A long burst of fire at close quarters silenced the *Daisy Bell's* Oerlikon gunner and knocked out two of the 12-pounder's crew. Firing his Lewis gun grimly the skipper, unaware that he had somehow lost his steel helmet and that blood was running down his face from a wound in his head where a splinter had gashed him, saw with satisfaction his tracers plunking into the stern of an E-boat, to be followed by an iridescent glow. A sharp bark from for'ard told him that the trawler's 12-pounder had opened up again. A direct hit, too, for the glow on board the enemy craft blossomed suddenly into a vast red rose.

With fumbling fingers Duffy shipped a fresh pan of ammu-nition, but the enemy had had enough and sheered off into the gloom. Rain was falling and, leaning dazedly on the bridge rail, the skipper became aware that the *Daisy Bell* was yawing aimlessly about the darkening ocean. He pulled himself together, wiped the blood from his cheek with the back of his hand, and went into the wheelhouse.

A shell entering by one of the shattered windows had turned the place into a shambles. The Second Hand, who had been at the helm during the action, lay slumped in a corner. He was badly wounded but faintly breathing. Oddly, the crazy gyrations of the ricochet had left unscathed the brass bulkhead clock which still ticked stolidly.

16

For'ard two of the crew of the 12-pounder were dead, their places at the gun having been taken by the cook and the signalman to fire the last round of the battle. Aft the Oerlikon mounting had received a direct hit but the gunner was alive, having been blown bodily from his platform with a crash that knocked the breath out of him. The decks were torn and splintered and the funnel was riddled with jagged holes. But the engines still maintained their rhythmic beat under the steady eye of the old Chief Engineman, and the trawler had sustained only superficial damage along the waterline.

An hour and a half later the *Daisy Bell* limped into port and secured alongside the naval base. Warned by the skipper's laconic signal as he entered harbour, an ambulance with masked headlights was waiting on the jetty. Under the shaded glare of a yardarm cluster the dead and wounded were borne away. Then, while the rest of the minesweeper's crew relaxed before a meal on their tiny mess deck, Duffy, with a patch of sticking plaster showing beneath his cap peak, trudged over to the office of the Commander (Minesweeping) with his written report of the day's events.

Next day the Official Admiralty communiqué included a brief and rather dull item of home news. 'Yesterday afternoon,' it said, 'H.M. Minesweeper *Daisy Bell*, Skipper G. Duffy, R.N.R., shot down a Heinkel 111. Later the same vessel encountered a number of E-boats laying mines off our east coast. In the brief action which followed at least one of the enemy vessels was severely damaged. H.M.S. *Daisy Bell* sustained some casualties but only minor damage. The next of kin are being informed.'

## CHAPTER II

## BIRTH OF A FLEET

ONE DAY in the early summer of 1939 Captain J. U. P. Fitzgerald, the Director of Torpedoes and Mining, sat at his desk in the grey Admiralty building at the top of Whitehall. Before him lay a file of papers to which he had just added a fresh minute. He was about to start the file on yet another round of Admiralty staff departments with the Treasury as its eventual objective. For even with a dire emergency threatening the country the ultimate decision to add even a single rowing boat to the Fleet still rests with those black-coated, striped-trousered gentlemen who constitute the permanent officials of H.M. Treasury. Captain Fitzgerald's minute, which was firmly backed by the Naval Staff, asked for one hundred ships to be added to the Royal Navy.

But even at that late stage in the march of world events the Director of Torpedoes and Mining was not seeking anything so ambitious as the immediate construction of a special fleet of warships costing millions of pounds to build. Backed by professional foreknowledge of the shape of things all too obviously to come, he pleaded yet again that the 300 trawlers already earmarked for requisitioning from the fishing fleet as a vital expansion of our naval strength in the event of war be increased to 400.

'It is known,' ran Captain Fitzgerald's minute in effect, its sombre urgency dictated by the mass of ominous evidence garnered by British naval intelligence, 'that the potential aggressor has planned a heavy programme of minelaying and submarine attacks against this country if England should be involved in hostilities.'

Furthermore, he reminded all concerned, if the Far

Eastern member of the Rome-Berlin-Tokyo Axis should choose to enter such a war her aims would also be directed against Great Britain, which would then be faced with a global threat menacing not only the country's seaborne communications but its very existence and that of the Commonwealth and Empire. Against such a threat the Navy could deploy an ageing Fleet of which the anti-submarine element would at once be strained to the utmost, while the minesweeping element was so meagre as to be almost non-existent.

In the event, this renewed Admiralty request was finally granted. A total of 400 trawlers was approved to be taken up by the Navy in emergency: 200 for anti-submarine duties, and 200 for minesweeping.

But by then Hitler had invaded Poland.

*    *    *

The practice of requisitioning vessels from the fishing fleet to serve with the Navy in a war dates back in modern times to the year 1910 when a Trawler Section of the Royal Naval Reserve was brought into being. But the origin of this organisation goes back still further when, in 1907, at the suggestion of Admiral Lord Charles Beresford, then commanding the Channel Fleet, the Admiralty purchased a number of fishing trawlers to use as experimental vessels for minesweeping. Admiral Beresford also considered that the fishermen themselves could play a very useful part in the Fleet in time of war. Accordingly after its successful trials the newly constituted trawler minesweeping flotilla began to pay a regular series of visits to the various fishing ports throughout the country with the idea of interesting fishermen in the Navy, and to give them elementary instruction in the kind of work they would be required to do.

When the trawler Section was created the rank of Skipper, R.N.R., was instituted for its officers as being the most appropriate. Equivalent to the then Warrant Officer in the Royal Navy, entry was open to fishing skippers between the ages of twenty-five and forty-five who were in possession of a Board of Trade certificate of competency as such and had held command for not less than two years. They could serve in the R.N.R. for periods of five years at a time up to a maximum of twenty years, receiving an annual retainer and the full pay of their rank when called up for service or training. The top rung of promotion for them would be the rank of Skipper Lieutenant.

Entry into the Reserve of the necessary ratings was open to experienced fishermen as certificated Second Hand, Engineman, Deckhand and Trimmer. Ratings were also required to serve for periods of five years at a time up to a total of twenty-five years, with a yearly retainer; and when called up for service or training received the same rates of pay as naval personel of equivalent rating. All were put through a course of minesweeping training.

At the same time arrangements were made between the Admiralty and the trawler owners for the charter of eighty trawlers in an emergency. Later this number was increased to 150. The sole task then visualised for these 'minor war vessels' was minesweeping. But the mines of those days were nothing like as complicated in mechanism, nor did they become as varied in design, as the formidable array of devilish contrivances that appeared in World War II. In fact, in 1914 there was but one type of sea mine, the moored contact variety which could only be exploded by a vessel brushing against one of the detonating horns with which it was studded.

Before the 1914–18 conflict was more than a few weeks old, however, it became painfully obvious that our mine-sweeper force was completely inadequate in numbers. German U-boats continually laid mines in the waters around Britain and particularly in the entrance to the Moray Firth, then the Grand Fleet's main anchorage. In addition German surface minelayers ranged the seas planting their deadly eggs in the ocean traffic lanes from the White Sea to the North American coast. One enemy armed raider, the *Wolf*, in a daring sortie as far as the Pacific and back, scattered a total of 450 mines in the focal shipping areas of the South Atlantic, the Indian Ocean, north and south Australia, around New Zealand, and as far as Fiji. Thus minesweeping organisations were soon needed on a global scale.

By the time the Armistice was signed, the R.N.R. Trawler Section, originally a force of some 1,200 officers and men, had expanded to 39,000, manning more than 700 vessels at home and abroad. The bulk of these ships were deep-sea trawlers and drifters, and their crews were representative of every fishing port in the United Kingdom, from the Hebrides to Brixham. More than two hundred of them were sunk during the war by mine explosion, surface attack or heavy weather, nearly half the sinkings taking place in east coast waters, and casualties among their crews were high.

But the minesweeper men, free and easy sailors who did not take kindly to naval discipline, did a splendid job of work in their own element. Tough and hardy, used to the bitter conditions and wild seas of the northern fishing grounds where in three minutes a chilly breeze can become a howling Force 10 hurricane, they went out daily in all kinds of weather to sweep the war channels clear of the bobbing spheres of death scattered so assiduously by the enemy. During the four years of war the Germans laid a total of 43,636 mines. More than half this number were sown in and around British coastal waters. Every harbour of consequence, every fairway, channel and anchorage was laced with them again and again. Throughout the year 1917, for instance, more than seventy mines a month were laid in the Dover area alone, and up to a score a day in the approaches to Harwich. In six months one flotilla of minesweepers swept a distance equivalent to steaming three times round the world.

Nor did the task of the trawlermen come to an end with the cease-fire on November 11th, 1918. For another weary twelve months the little ships went out with their sweeps to clear not only the enemy-laid minefields but those of the Allies as well. Of these, nearly seventeen thousand British and American mines had been sown in a vast belt stretching for two hundred and thirty miles between the Orkneys and the Norwegian coast. Known as the 'Northern Barrage', the object of this lethal underwater fence was to deter U-boats and surface raiders from breaking out into the Atlantic by the northern route.

21

But at the end of 1919 the trawlers were at last returned to their owners and their crews resumed their normal business of wresting a living from the sea under more peaceful conditions. Along with the other naval reserves the R.N.R. Trawler Section was reconstituted. It was renamed the R.N.R. Patrol Service, for in addition to minesweeping a large percentage of the vessels had in fact been employed during the war on a variety of duties ranging from harbour defence to coastal convoy escorts. Its personnel dwindled, and a mere handful of trawlers were retained to continue to wear naval grey paint and the White Ensign. This tiny flotilla was eventually based on H.M.S. *Boscawen* at Portland, and to them the post-war entries into the R.N.R. Patrol Service went for their biennial training.

Also situated at Portland and close neighbour of the *Boscawen* was H.M.S. *Osprey*, a training establishment of special importance. Its work was concerned with the new and potent weapon which had been added to the Navy's anti-submarine armoury, the Asdic device. Since trawlers both could be, and had been, used as convoy escorts, an essential part of whose task is the hunting and destruction of U-boats, it was eventually decided to allocate some of the vessels due to be taken up from the fishing industry in any future emergency to anti-submarine work; to train a percentage of the R.N.R. Skippers as anti-submarine specialists, and Patrol Service ratings as Submarine Detector Operators.

The strength of the permanent R.N.R. Patrol Service at the time when the Director of Torpedoes and Mining was endeavouring to obtain approval for the increase to 400 of the number of trawlers to be taken over from the fishing fleet, was 454 Skippers and 3,733 ratings. But the overall size of the Patrol Service is based on a minimum complement of officers and ratings required to man each individual vessel in wartime, this figure then being multiplied by the number of ships the Service is allocated. To the total thus arrived at a further percentage of the whole must be added to allow for wastage due to sickness and other causes. And at the outset of World War II the R.N.R. Patrol Service, even though based on the original approved figure of 300 ships, was in fact considerably under strength both for officers and men.

* * *

While in 1939 the director of Torpedoes and Mining was asking for additional trawlers to be requisitioned for the Patrol Service another important question concerning this section of the R.N.R. was being considered by the Admiralty. This was the selection of a wartime assembly base for the Patrol Service crews, where they could be brought under naval discipline and given any training necessary while waiting to be formed into crews for drafting to the ports where their ships would have been sent for conversion into warships.

A brief explanation of the constitution of the Royal Naval Reserve and its call-up arrangements will clarify the necessity for such a base. This force, the Navy's first professional reserve after its own Fleet Reserve, is divided into two sections; the General Service[1] and the Patrol Service. The former is composed of officers and men drawn from liners and other ocean-going vessels belonging to the Merchant Navy. In peacetime these officers and men undergo periodical spells of training in the general depots at Portsmouth, Chatham and Devonport, and in addition are given the opportunity to specialise in the gunnery, torpedo, antisubmarine, signal and navigation schools. Thus in wartime these 'big ship' sailors are qualified to be drafted direct to vessels of the main fleet and can take their places alongside the regular Navy man.

In emergency the General Service are called up by the local Registrars of the R.N.R., resident in their own districts, who for mobilisation purposes are affiliated to one or other of the three main naval depots. Thus when he receives his call-up notice the Reservist dons his naval uniform, which he is required to retain in his own possession at all times, and departs for the naval barracks at Portsmouth, Chatham or Devonport, there to await absorption in due course into the expanding Fleet.

But R.N.R. Patrol Service personnel, drawn exclusively

[1] R.N.R. ratings' section now disbanded.

from the fishing industry and for whom no warships are immediately available either in commission or reserve, have little to do with the main fleet since they are not trained for service in the larger units. Their presence in the general naval depots at a time of mobilisation would in fact be something of an embarrassment; it would be difficult to provide accomodation for them, and there is no administrative organisation in being to deal with their special requirements.

Amid the welter of more important problems occupying the attention of the Admiralty consequent upon Britain's belated rearmament following Munich, then, all that could be contemplated for the Patrol Service was a temporary assembly point at which its personnel could be concentrated to await drafting to their ships. A small staff of officers and men drawn from the general naval depots could be sent down to deal with the initial mobilisation documentation of the trawlermen, get them away to sea and then hasten back to their normal duties. The questions of subsequently maintaining the ships of the Lilliput Fleet, bearing its crews for pay and victualling, keeping necessary records, dealing with casualties and replacements, and the hundred and one duties of a normal naval depot had to be shelved for later consideration.

The principal requirement was to earmark a suitable assembly point. Originally an east coast port had been decided upon. Then when the threat of air bombing began to assume an exaggerated importance, a west coast port was thought to be preferable. Finally considerations of rail travel and general accessibility sent the searching finger back to the east coast. This time Lowestoft was chosen, a fishing port itself, central and reasonably accessible by train from all parts of the country. Representatives of the Admiralty Surveyor of Lands went down to Lowestoft and eventually decided to requisition a municipal pleasure park on the seashore known locally as Sparrow's Nest. This place had, in fact, been the original choice.

Sparrow's Nest (the name refers to a man and not to a bird) was originally a country estate, sometime the home of the Marchioness of Salisbury, which had later been ac-

24

quired by the municipal authorities for use as a public park. In 1939 it comprised a manor house with thatched roof in a dubious state of repair, several conservatories, a concert hall and an open-air stage, the whole contained within some seven acres of grounds. Under the temporary ship name of H.M.S. *Pembroke X* Sparrow's Nest had formed the concentration area for the men of the R.N.R. Patrol Service at the time of the Munich crisis mobilisation a year earlier. It was then that Lowestoft had first suggested itself as a convenient future assembly centre, as it, in fact, had been in World War I.

In the department of the Admiral Commanding Reserves at the Admiralty arrangements were accordingly set in train to despatch a temporary staff to the new base when required, for the supply of stationery, books of regulations, stores, provisions, clothing, bedding and all the necessary equipment for the functioning of a naval depot and drafting centre. A number of retired naval officers resident in districts adjacent to Lowestoft were given dormant appointments by the Admiralty appointing them to key jobs in the assembly base if and when mobilisation should be ordered. Selected for command of the base was Captain Basil H. Piercy, a retired naval officer whose home was not very far away from Lowestoft.

At the same time the other retired naval officers living within easy distance of more than a hundred ports and harbours throughout the country had similarly received orders appointing them to take over in emergency in those ports as Naval Officers in Charge or Resident Naval Officer, depending on the size and importance of the place. At dozens of private shipyards arrangements had been finalised for the work of converting deep-sea fishing trawlers into minor warships to be put in hand immediately when required. The Trade Division of the Admiralty was ready to commence requisitioning the earmarked trawlers and despatching them to these yards whenever the order should be given. The local Registrars of the R.N.R. stood by with their mobilisation notices ready for posting. The whole of this complicated machinery could be set in motion immediately the Admiralty should give the signal.

\*   \*   \*

Meanwhile the war clouds were piling up over Europe. On March 19th, 1939, Nazi troops invaded Czecho-Slovakia, and two days later Hitler announced that the country had ceased to exist and would henceforth become a Protectorate of the German Reich. The Führer then turned his attention to Danzig and the Polish Corridor. Soon afterwards Danzig went the way of Czecho-Slovakia, and almost before the world could draw breath Hitler was screaming to his jack-booted troopers that his patience with Poland was almost exhausted.

In Britain the Reserves and Auxiliary Forces Act was passed, following which some 15,000 naval reservists were called up. In batches from June onwards R.N.R. General Service men were mobilised and sent to join the destroyers and cruisers of the Reserve Fleet as these were brought forward and put into commission. By early August the Reserve Fleet was fully manned and under its flag officer, Vice-Admiral Sir Max Horton, was inspected by King George VI in Weymouth Bay on August 9th.

On the 23rd a coded telegram went out from the Admiralty, and Captain Piercy and his designated staff officers packed their bags and departed for Lowestoft. At Sparrow's Nest concert hall that week two famous stage and radio personalities were appearing with their own company in a seaside revue called *Road Show*. Twice nightly Lowestoft's summer visitors were rocking with laughter at the humorous sallies of Elsie and Doris Waters in their act as those well-known Cockney ladies 'Gert and Daisy'. But abruptly in mid-week the Navy appeared at the stage door to hand Elsie and Doris not a bouquet but the unwelcome news that Sparrow's Nest, its concert hall, open air stage and all its grounds and buildings would be required the very next day for sterner purposes. In fact the last-performance audience had scarcely left the building than workmen began stripping the theatre of its gay trappings. Sadly Gert and Daisy paid off their company which then broke up and went its several ways.

That evening the two sisters who were staying in an hotel at Beccles hired a launch and went for a leisurely cruise up the river. The weather was glorious and as the sun sank

26

slowly towards the west a great hush enfolded the country-side. But behind the warm beauty of that summer evening there lurked the icy chill of foreboding. 'This is the last peace we shall know for a long time,' mused Gert propheti-cally, and Daisy, for once lacking her usual cheery quip, nodded in gloomy agreement.

Miles away from peaceful Suffolk under that same sum-mer sun Nazi panzers stood massed on the Polish border. On nearby German airfields the engines of death-loaded Luftwaffe bombers were warming up. And in a Danzig an-chorage the captain of a Nazi battleship checked over his charts of Gdynia's harbour defences.

Seventeen U-boats had already sailed from Kiel for the Atlantic, and a group of smaller submarines lurked beneath the smiling surface of the North Sea ready to unload their cargoes of mines in our estuaries and harbour approaches. Before the end of August two German pocket battleships and their attendant supply vessels had slipped secretly out to the open sea, and nearly forty U-boats were poised to strike at our seaborne lifelines.

At 4.38 p.m. on the 29th August, the order went out for a general mobilisation in Britain. On the 31st all naval re-serves were called up, and the Home Fleet sailed for its war station. At Lowestoft the White Ensign now floated over Sparrow's Nest. Naval sentries with rifles and fixed bayonets began a vigil at its gates which was to continue for seven years.

Then at a quarter to five on the morning of the 1st of September the storm broke. Nazi legions swarmed over the Polish border, and Warsaw erupted in the flame and smoke of Luftwaffe bombs.

At Lowestoft and at other ports around the coast the mobilisation machinery for the R.N.R. Patrol Service had already begun functioning. From the 24th August onwards, as the trawlers earmarked for naval service returned home from the fishing grounds their cargoes were unloaded even more speedily than usual. Workmen swarmed aboard the rusty, salt-caked craft and began their work of transforma-tion. 'They threw the fish out and threw us in,' complained an R.N.R. skipper afterwards with pardonable exaggeration. But there was much to do and little time to do it.

*     *     *

In 1939 the average British fishing trawler was a sturdily built vessel of anything from 275 to 590 tons gross. Her dimensions ranged from a 115-foot length with a 22-foot beam to 170 feet in length and a beam of 28 feet in the largest craft. She had a short and often whalebacked forecastle, one or two masts and a single funnel placed immediately abaft the bridge and wheelhouse. On the well-deck below the bridge structure was a powerful steam winch for working the trawl and, extending beyond this almost to the break of the forecastle, a capacious fish-hold running the full width of the ship. The ships were coal burning and their speed ranged from seven to ten knots, sometimes more.

In pre-war days British fishing trawlers were built for the primary purpose of catching fish and returning with it as soon as possible since they were not then equipped with a refrigeration plant. Little space was squandered on the provisions of crew amenities in the shape of spacious cabins and luxurious mess rooms, although these were comfortable enough. Periodically throughout the season the vessels sailed for the fishing grounds which might be anywhere from Iceland to the White Sea, trawled until their holds were full, and then hastened back with their cargoes spurred on by the knowledge that the catch of the first ship home would fetch the highest price. Back in port and the fish disposed of, skipper and crew packed their gear and went to their homes until they should be required again, leaving their vessel without a backward glance to be taken over by their owner's ship-fitters. These men, engineers, carpenters, shipwrights, joiners, painters and riggers, carried out all the maintenance work required. This included routine boiler cleaning and any necessary engine repairs; periodical drydocking, hull cleaning and painting; overhaul of radio and navigational instruments; renewal of rigging, test and overhaul of anchors, cables and trawl gear, and general refitting.

This system has long been the custom in the fishing fleets. but it was to cause a certain amount of heartburn in the early days of the mobilisation of the Patrol Service, since the Navy requires individual ships' companies to carry out their own minor refits.

To transform the trawlers into men-of-war hull frames and deck beams had first to be strengthened to enable them to carry guns. The largest weapon, usually a 12-pounder or a four-inch if one was available, was mounted on the fore-castle; an Oerlikon, Bofors or a pair of point five-inch machine guns on a special mounting aft of the funnel, and Lewis or Hotchkiss guns in the bridge wings for defence air attack. In ships destined for anti-submarine duties, Asdic gear was installed and depth-charge throwers and rails fitted.

The trawl winch was removed from the fore well-deck, and the fish-hold became the ship's company mess deck. Wooden mess tables and stools were provided, and if the normal crew bunks were not left in position, hammock hooks fitted in the overhead beams. Ammunition for the ship's guns and small arms was stowed in a magazine speci-ally constructed beneath the mess deck. The officers' quar-ters below the wheelhouse usually comprised an all-purposes cabin some twenty feet square. This compartment contained two bunks, a table, and two upright and two easy chairs, for at least two Skippers would be appointed, one to act as First Lieutenant; sometimes, in fact, up to as many as four officers were carried in vessels acting as Group Leaders. There was a cupboard for stationery and a small safe for the confidential books and cash needed for local disbursements. In a little coal-fired galley in the after-deckhouse, the meals for both officers and men were cooked, and here, too, was the provision store. Luckier vessels had a small domestic re-frigerator installed.

All in all, life on board was cramped and anything but comfortable. Due to the peculiar motion of a trawler in a seaway, since she rides the waves instead of punching through them like a heavier vessel, the normal functions of daily existence are often apt to be severely curtailed in bad weather. Provided cooking can be carried on, eating a meal is no easy feat; washing is difficult, shaving is impossible, and bathing out of the question. There was no recreation space as such, a mere few feet of deck upon which to stretch the legs, no canteen, and not even the modest domestic comforts of a corvette or destroyer.

Yet these sturdy little ships and the crews who manned them were destined to spend weeks at sea at a time, often under the most appalling weather conditions, and many of them were cheerfully to undertake and successfully accomplish in the face of extreme hardship and adversity deep-sea voyages of thousands of miles over submarine and mine-infested waters.

From the 24th of August onwards, then, each train arriving at Lowestoft brought its quota of trawlermen from every fishing port in the kingdom. From Fleetwood and Shoreham they came; from Grimsby, Hull, Falmouth and Brixham; from Milford Haven, the Isle of Man and the Inner and Outer Hebrides; from Buckie, Fraserburgh, Aberdeen and Peterhead; some in civilian clothes and humping their Navy rig in sea bags; others in uniforms still redolent of the moth balls in which they had been stowed away by wives and mothers. In a babel of dialects, Scots, Welsh, Lancastrian, Yorkshire, West Country and East Anglian, but all talking the same kind of fisherman's jargon, the men of the R.N.R. Patrol Service streamed into Sparrow's Nest.

Working without respite at tables set up in bathing huts hastily converted into temporary offices, the naval staff from the main depots at Portsmouth, Chatham and Devonport dealt rapidly with the incoming trawlermen. They were medically inspected, given a meal, issued with a month's advance of pay and arrangements made for them to send regular allotments from their pay to wives and families. Kits were checked over and deficiences made up, and bedding and gas masks issued. As each man passed through this joining routine he was allocated to a trawler undergoing conversion. Within a matter of hours from the initial time of arrival at Lowestoft many of the skippers and ratings had been formed into crews and were entraining once more for the ports at which their ships awaited them. By the 3rd of September a hundred Patrol Service vessels were actually in commission.

* * *

From the outset it was evident that the pattern of the sea war would be repeated by the enemy even more ruthlessly than in 1914-18. On the evening of the 3rd of September, 1939, the 13,581-ton Donaldson liner *Athenia,* with 1,418 passengers and crew, was torpedoed without warning and sunk some 250 miles west of Ireland. U-boats laid mines off the Tyne, Humber and in the Thames Estuary.

Too small to be worth a torpedo, the Patrol Service trawler with its scanty weapons, lack of armour and slow speed stood very little chance in a straight fight against the guns of a surfaced U-boat. The same considerations rendered the average minesweeping or anti-submarine trawler little more than a sitting duck for the swooping dive-bombers of the Luftwaffe; swift and powerfully armed E-boats could brush these lumbering escorts contemptuously aside in their darting attacks on our coastal convoys; larger hostile surface units could blast the average Patrol Service craft out of existence like a giant swatting a fly. Nevertheless time was to show that the enemy was by no means going to have things all his own way with the little ships.

Sublimely indifferent to the hazards they were about to face, the men of the Navy's Lilliput Fleet sallied forth to do battle.

CHAPTER III

# NO PHONEY WAR

BECAUSE of the comparative absence of activity on land during the early months of hostilities this twilight period was dubbed 'the phoney war'. But there was never anything phoney about the war at sea.

The first enemy mines to be laid were of the moored contact type, of which the Germans were known to possess some 100,000 in September, 1939. But soon Hitler's first 'secret weapon' appeared in the form of the magnetic mine. The principle of this device was no secret to the Admiralty but it complicated matters very considerably, for although British mining experts were aware of the possibility of its appearance no adequate counter-measures could be prepared until it was known what sort of firing unit the Germans were employing. The minesweepers could do little to combat the menace since they were all equipped to deal only with the moored contact variety.

When, however, one of the new mines was recovered intact in the Thames Estuary in November, 1939, stripped down and its secrets bared, the de-gaussing antidote was at once put into production. But in the meantime the threat had become very grave, and many ships fell the victim to magnetic mines. H.M.S. *Adventure*, the Navy's only cruiser-minelayer, was one of the first, to be followed a few hours later by the destroyer *Blanche*. In three days nine merchant ships were sunk by the same agency, among them the 8,000-ton Dutch liner *Simon Bolivar* with the loss of 138 lives; the Yugo-Slav *Carica Milica* and the Danish *Canada*. Off Harwich the minesweeping trawler *Mastiff* went up in a gout of flame and smoke, and the destroyer *Gipsy* was towed in with her back broken. More neutral merchant ship victims were claimed, including the Japanese liner *Terukini Maru*, 11,000 tons, and the Dutch *Spaarndam*, 8,800 tons. Congestion in the Downs and Thames Estuary was such that at one time 186 merchant vessels were lying trapped in the anchorage; twenty of them were mined or in collision.

When it seemed likely that the Thames Estuary might be closed to shipping altogether, special measures were taken by the Admiralty. A radio appeal was broadcast for wooden-hulled trawlers and drifters with volunteer crews to man them. Using a mock-up sweep, which consisted largely of a magnetised iron bar towed at the end of a line, dubbed not inappropriately 'the Bosun's Nightmare', it was hoped to keep vital channels open until ships could be degaussed and an effective sweep devised.

In a speech in the House of Commons some time afterwards Winston Churchill, First Lord of the Admiralty, told of these measures. 'We have deemed it necessary to call upon a large number of trawlers to assist in the dredging of our harbours,' he said. 'The effect of these serious dangers was sufficient to bring forward an overwhelming response from fishermen and trawler crews who were called upon to give their country assistance for, I imagine, only a short time. The offices at some of the fishing ports which remained open during the night were crowded and thronged out, and in a very short time the full complement was made up by these fisherfolk eager to serve their country in a manner which they felt would be really effective.'

It was the appearance of the magnetic mine, in fact, which was responsible for the Lilliput Fleet being given its own special badge, a badge that was eventually to be worn by some 70,000 officers and men who, by 1945, comprised the Royal Navy Patrol Service. Yet, oddly enough, its introduction was almost certainly due to a misunderstanding.

Due to the urgent need for setting the newly requisitioned wooden-hulled minesweepers and their crews to work clearing the mine-choked channels there was no time to put the men into naval uniform. In any event many of them were well over the normal recruiting age and would not be required after the emergency had been overcome. The captain

3

of each vessel was simply given an Admiralty Warrant appointing him a Temporary Skipper in the R.N.R. The crews wore their own civilian clothes with an arm brassard.

Somehow this came to the notice of the First Lord and the possibility mentioned that if any of the crews should be captured while doing mine clearance work in civilian dress the Germans would shoot them as *france-tireurs*. It is probable, however, that Mr Churchill was told merely that these temporary naval volunteers had been given no distinguishing insignia to wear and not that they lacked a uniform. At all events a typical Churchillian minute was soon winging its way to the Fourth Sea Lord, the Admiralty Board member responsible for such matters. 'I am told that the minesweeper men have no badge,' ran the minute. 'If this is so it must be remedied at once. I have asked Mr Bracken to call for designs from Sir Kenneth Clark within one week after which production must begin with the greatest speed, and distribution as the deliveries come to hand.'

Whatever Mr Churchill had in mind was not clear to the Fourth Sea Lord's department, who minuted the paper to the Admiral Commanding Reserves for action, with the suggestion that some form of woven arm badge would probably suffice. Almost equally in the dark as to the First Lord's purpose, but noting that action was undoubtedly being taken by Sir Kenneth Clark, the officer concerned on the staff of Admiral Commanding Reserves drew a rough sketch of a badge he thought might adequately represent the functions of minesweeper men in case this should after all be needed, which was duly despatched to the Board. But the paper was soon returned with a fresh complication introduced by the Second Sea Lord, who asked: 'What about the anti-submarine men?'

At this stage the office of the Admiral Commanding Reserves pigeon-holed the paper, for by now a suggestion for a comprehensive badge covering the activities of both sections of the Patrol Service had been produced at the request of Sir Kenneth Clark by the late Mr Kruger Gray, a well known artist and medal designer. His design took the form of a shield upon which was depicted a sinking shark transfixed by a marline spike, against a background formed by a fishing-net containing two trapped German mines, the whole surrounded by a rope embellished with two examples of the nautical knot known as a 'fisherman's bend' and surmounted by a naval crown. Below was a scroll bearing the letters 'M/S-A/S' (Minesweeping Anti-Submarine).

The shark, it was explained, had been chosen as being the most characteristic of U-boat activities, and depicted down by the head to show this pirate of the seas not only wounded but foundering. The marline spike as the weapon implied that the death wound had been inflicted by the Merchant Navy; the net and mines signified the labours of the minesweepers, and the knots to indicate the element of the fishing fleet within the Patrol Service.

Made of silver about the size of a shilling, with a pin at the back so that it could be attached to the sleeve, several examples of the finished badge were struck off by the Mint and sent to the Board of Admiralty for approval and subsequent submission to the King. Royal assent was duly given and action to produce the badge directed in another crisp Churchillian minute, 'Approved, press on.'

Officers and men employed in minesweeping and anti-submarine duties in the Patrol Service were to be eligible for award of the badge after six months service afloat. But for meritorious conduct in the face of special danger or difficulty it could be awarded after a shorter period.

Thus, although the question of a uniform for those who had volunteered to serve temporarily in the wooden-hulled minesweepers seems to have dropped from sight altogether, the Lilliput Fleet gained a unique distinguishing badge. Never before had one section of the Royal Navy been similarly honoured, if one excepts the large silver arm badge specially issued to the men of the Mine Clearance Service which operated for some twelve months after the end of World War I.

In addition to their surface and submarine minelayers the Germans laid mines by aircraft on a tremendous scale. Something like one third of the Luftwaffe's entire bomber force was for a time employed in minelaying against the United Kingdom.

While the trawler minesweepers were hard at work clearing safe channels, merchantmen employed in vital coastal traffic were formed into convoys and escorted by anti-submarine trawlers, backed up by destroyers and other vessels which could be spared from the Fleet and from the more important ocean convoys.

Both escort and minesweeping trawlers were formed into groups of from four to six vessels each and based on ports all round the country under the Flag and Naval Officers-in Charge. Specialist officers of the Royal Navy, the Royal Naval Reserve and the Royal Naval Volunteer Reserve took over as Group Commanders, and in some cases as commanding officers when R.N.R. Skippers with the appropriate specialist qualification were not available.

Port minesweeping groups were responsible for keeping the swept channel clear of mines in their own area, while the escort trawlers shepherded their flocks of merchantmen up and down the coastal sea lanes, guarding their plodding charges against the constant threat of air, surface and underwater attack. Between the Faeroes and Iceland a small group of anti-submarine trawlers operated as armed boarding vessels with the cruisers of the Northern Patrol in enforcing our contraband control.

Life afloat was grim indeed in an A/S or minesweeping trawler in those early days of the war. Adequate air cover over the sea was impossible to maintain at all times, and many of the little ships fell victim to the continual swooping attacks of the Luftwaffe. Their attackers from the air were usually Heinkel bombers which worked in pairs.

The Heinkel 111 of later marks was a twin-engined machine with stubby wings, a large tail and a perspex nose. It had a crew of six, and was armed with from six to eight 7.7 mm. machine-guns. These weapons were usually sited in the nose, above and below the fuselage pointing forward and aft, and one each to port and starboard firing through side windows. In addition it could carry a bomb load equivalent to eight 550 lb. bombs and a large number of incendiaries for dropping by hand. Top speed was some two hundred and seventy miles an hour. Altogether the Heinkel constituted a very formidable menace indeed.

The trawlermen fought back magnificently. But lacking

the speed, the armament and the manoeuvrability of larger Fleet units they stood much less chance of survival against determined assault from the air.

*　　*　　*

On a bleak February morning in 1940 four minesweeping trawlers were busy clearing the war channel some twenty miles north-east of Aberdeen. In peacetime they had been the Hull fishing vessels *Thomas Altoft* and *Ohm*, the *Robert Bowen* of Milford Haven, and the *Fort Royal* of Aberdeen. Now they prefixed those names with the letters H.M.S., and their crews, all trawlermen, were representative of a dozen British fishing ports. The *Robert Bowen* and *Thomas Altoft* were ageing vessels of 290 tons, built in 1918 and 1919 respectively; the *Ohm*, a 300-ton craft, was even older, being of 1915 vintage; largest and most modern of the four was the *Fort Royal*, built in 1931, and of some 350 tons gross.

The *Ohm* was commanded by Skipper Edmund Chilton, R.N.R.; the *Thomas Altoft* by Skipper Thomas Lowery, R.N.R.; and the *Fort Royal* by Chief Skipper William Craig, R.N.R., with a young R.N.V.R. officer as his first lieutenant; whilst the *Robert Bowen* carried the Group Officer, Lieut.-Commander E. King, R.N., with Skipper Lieutenant John Clark, R.N.R., in command.

An extension of wood and painted canvas had been erected over the top of the original wheelhouse of each trawler to provide her captain with a tiny compass plat-form, or 'monkey island', from which he could oversee operations when engaged in minesweeping, and con the ship and fight her in action. A 12-pounder gun was mounted on the forecastle, and Lewis guns were fitted in the port and starboard wings of the wheelhouse. Protection for the bridge stucture was provided by a number of splinter-proof mattresses. Above the wheelhouse windows the vessels flaunted, like their gallant sisters throughout the Patrol Service, a wooden plaque on which was carved and painted the ship's badge, more often than not home-made both as to design and motto.

All four trawlers had their sweeps out and were steaming

in H formation. Each ship had her lookouts posted, the Lewis guns were fitted with their ammunition pans, and the 12-pounder projectiles were ranged handily so that the gun could be brought into action in a matter of seconds from the moment the alarm bells sounded. Duffel coats or great-coats and oilskins, scarves and balaclava helmets were the rig of the day for officers and men, for the sky was grey and overcast and a chill wind blew.

A few minutes before noon when the trawler cooks were busy in their tiny galleys preparing to dish up the midday dinner, two aircraft suddenly streaked out from the barely visible shoreline and headed for the little group of ships. Almost before their appearance had been reported by the lookouts, and certainly before their identity could be established, the Nazi planes, for they were Heinkel 111's, were diving to the attack. The trawlermen raced for their guns, while axes were hurriedly wielded aft as the sweep wires were ruthlessly severed. In the duel of death about to commence no ship, least of all a small, slow-steaming trawler, could afford to be hampered by a load of heavy gear trailing over the stern.

Tearing in from a height of only fifteen hundred feet, the Heinkels slammed their bombs down at the *Fort Royal* which had the inshore position. Instinctively Skipper Craig and his men ducked as they glimpsed the missiles curving towards them. The first bomb screeched over the trawler and exploded harmlessly in the sea a few yards beyond her. The second struck the little *Robert Bowen*, which was to sea-ward but abreast of her consort. The bomb tore into her fair and square amidships, and the agonised shriek of her disintegrating was drowned in the roar of the bomb's explosion, for the *Robert Bowen* broke in half and sank immediately. In a split second her ship's company were blasted into eternity; not a soul survived.

But their comrades could spare no more than a fleeting glance towards the spot where a moment before the *Robert Bowen* had been bravely steaming. With their cannon spitting flame the two Heinkels zoomed upwards, while beneath them the trawlers' 12-pounders banged away desperately and their Lewis guns sprayed the air with streams of bright, deceptively slow-moving tracer. Hawk-like the Nazi planes wheeled sharply and snarled downwards again, their perspex noses aimed at the *Fort Royal*. This time their intended victim was not to escape, for their bombs, dropped simultaneously, struck together and shattered the whole of the trawler's forepart. When the spray and flying debris fell back into the sea the *Fort Royal* was sinking fast. In less than three minutes the ex-Aberdeen trawler had lurched beneath the waves, her survivors clinging to a Carley raft they had managed to launch.

Now only the *Thomas Altoft* and the *Ohm*, the ex-Hull trawlers, were left. Warily their skippers eyed the circling Heinkels, whose black-crossed wings stood out starkly against the drab backcloth of the unheeding sky as they banked. At the helm of each vessel her Second Hand stood gripping the spokes of the wheel, ready to spin it to port or starboard as the trawlers dodged and swerved under the lashing attack. Faces pale and grim beneath their steel helmets, the trawler gunners hugged their weapons and waited for the next onslaught.

This time, as if by preconcerted arrangement, the Heinkel pilots split formation. Whereas previously they had dived together on their target, now they came in separately, the first making for the *Ohm*, the second for her consort. But the trawlermen were burning to avenge the slaughter of their comrades and with their guns they sought frantically to impale the streaking Heinkels on the flying spears of lead and steel they cast up. If the curtain of fire hurled skywards was miraculously evaded by the jinking aircraft, at least it spoilt the aim of the Nazi pilots.

One bomb, missing the *Thomas Altoft* by a razor's edge, exploded alongside her, heaving the straining vessel bodily upwards out of the water and starting her plates fore and aft; five others fell near the *Ohm* and damaged her stern. But the Heinkels were to claim no more victims that day. After two more vicious attacks during which a total of fifteen bombs were hurled at the swerving, hard-steaming trawlers, the planes wheeled sharply and streaked away seawards.

Early the following afternoon H.M. Trawlers *Thomas*

*Altoft* and *Ohm* entered Aberdeen harbour, their hulls and upperworks dented and scarred by bomb fragments and explosive bullets. Since their wireless transmitters had been wrecked by the concussion of near misses at the commencement of the air attack their battle for life had gone unheeded, unknown at the naval base. Four officers and eighteen ratings died, and two gallant little minesweepers vanished from the Navy List in an obscure action that netted a bare six lines in the day's war communiqué on the Home Front.

\* \* \*

A few days later two grey-hulled warships flying the White Ensign of the Royal Navy were steaming southwards some seventy miles east of Copinsay, one of the smallest of the Orkney Islands. From their size and shape they appeared to be sister ships. A glance at Lloyd's List would have proved the supposition correct, for in the issue of that invaluable work of reference for the year 1939 they appeared as the fishing trawlers *Ayrshire* and *Fifeshire*, and for twelve uneasy months since Munich they had been working the distant-water fishing grounds out of Grimsby. Launched in 1938, they measured 175 feet in length with a 28-foot beam, their gross registered tonnage was 540, and they had been equipped with all modern refinements for the more efficient catching of fish. Then their brief peacetime careers had been interrupted to fulfil a sterner requirement.

The trawlers now both belonged to the 11th A/S Striking Force which had its base at Rosyth, to which port they were now making their way in company. But despite their Navy grey paint and the White Ensigns fluttering bravely from their gaffs, they were warships yet in little more than name. For until their main armament should be fitted their sole offensive weapons comprised merely a pair of Lewis guns apiece.

The *Ayrshire* was commanded by Sub-Lieutenant Nigel Dixon, R.N., and the *Fifeshire* by another youthful gunroom officer of the Royal Navy, Acting Sub-Lieutenant J. V. Searles-Wood. The crews of both ships were trawlermen belonging to the R.N. Patrol Service.

The day was cold and unpleasant. Low clouds were scudding across the sky driven by a strong to gale-force southeasterly wind, there was a high sea running and visibility was down to about a mile. The trawlers were steaming in line abreast about half a mile apart and making a bare eight knots, for they were bucking into the weather and at times taking green seas over their high bluff bows.

Hunched over the upper bridge of his command, Sub-Lieutenant Dixon was scanning the horizon with his binoculars when, without warning, the *Ayrshire*'s hull trembled to the concussion of three loud explosions. Startled, he glanced hurriedly around the deck below and then over at his consort. To his horror he saw that with gouts of smoke and flame pouring from her she was rapidly disappearing beneath the waves. In a moment, it seemed to Dixon, she had gone, sunk, and in the next instant that the *Ayrshire* herself was fighting for her own existence.

Almost sub-consciously he had given the order to alter course towards the stricken *Fifeshire*, and the trawler was heeling over under the pressure of her rudder. Then with a triumphant flirt of their wings at their success in so speedily disposing of one of the trawlers a brace of Heinkels came hurtling at the *Ayrshire*.

Sub-Lieutenant Dixon may have been young in years for command, but he was a natural-born tactician. On the instant that the situation became clear to him his brain began swiftly and icily planning his strategy. The only weapons available to counter the forthcoming onslaught were a single Lewis gun, the other being unserviceable, and the speed of reaction to his orders of the experienced Second Hand now at the helm in the wheelhouse below.

As the Heinkels lined up for their bomb run Dixon began edging the *Ayrshire* round. Then as the glinting leading edge of the wings of the first plane loomed larger and larger he swung the trawlers bow until it pointed straight at the enemy. With a target now reduced to the bare 28 feet of the trawler's beam the Heinkel pilot was abruptly presented with an unexpectedly greater margin of error. His bombs and those of his companion crashed into the sea ten yards at either side of the labouring *Ayrshire*. As the Nazi planes thundered over at near masthead height their gunners pumped cannon shells into the little ship. Then with the thin wavering stream of tracer from the trawler's single Lewis vainly clawing after them they were gone, zooming upwards at full blast to gain altitude for the next swoop.

Four times the Heinkels pressed home fresh attacks, their bullets and cannon shells ripping into the *Ayrshire*'s bridge and wheelhouse, her deck planking and hull plates, the solitary lifeboat on its davits and the wireless cabin. Time after time Dixon, clinging grimly to the splintered upper bridge structure, zigzagged his vessel, wrenching her almost bodily around at the last moment to comb the arrow-like dives of the swooping aircraft. And each time their bombs shot harmlessly into the sea.

The little fighting trawler trembled and shook continuously from the concussion of near misses. Bridge windows splintered, glass and crockery below decks shivered to fragments, bulkhead fittings jarred loose amid showers of dust and flaking paint, hatch doors blew off or flapped wildly from their broken hinges; aft in the rudder glands steel bolts started and loosened; the needle of the magnetic compass jumped to thirty degrees out of true and remained there; the echo-sounding transmitter collapsed.

Pumping burst after burst into the air from their solitary Lewis gun, the trawlermen cheered hoarsely when they saw a few, at least, of their tracers sink home in the oil-streaked bellies of the enemy planes.

Then, as suddenly as it had begun, the attack was over. With their bomb loads expanded the Heinkels circled briefly then formated on each other and made off eastward; their score an ill-armed British minor war vessel and all but one of her company. Seaman Albert Blowers was the sole survivor of H.M. Trawler *Fifeshire*, late of Grimsby.

\* \* \*

On the same bleak February day that the *Fifeshire* and *Ayrshire* were attacked off the Orkneys, H.M. Minesweeping Trawler *Solon* was patrolling the swept channel near Great Yarmouth. The *Solon* was a little ship of no more than 350 tons gross. She had been built in 1931 by Cook, Welton

42

and Gemmell for the Standard Fishing Company of Grimsby. She was 140 feet long with a beam of 24½ feet and she could steam all out at about 11 knots.

Since being taken over by the Navy the *Solon* had been hastily fitted out with minesweeping gear and armed with a 12-pounder. For secondary armament she boasted only one Lewis gun, for these light automatic weapons were temporarily in short supply and the Navy had a great number of urgent commitments to fulfil.

She was commanded by Lieut.-Commander Gillett, a retired Royal Navy officer called back for service, and her R.N.R. Patrol Service crew also included a general service signalman, Pensioner Alfred Wells. Although she normally worked with three other minesweepers she belonged as yet to no particular numbered trawler group but came within the Nore Command. Her accounting base was at Sheerness.

Keenly alert for trouble, for the trawlermen were only too well aware that poor visibility and low overhang favoured the darting attacks of the Luftwaffe, the crew of the *Solon* were nevertheless taken by surprise when a pair of He. 111's suddenly shot out of the mist and came hell for leather towards them. But Gillett had trained his men well and in double quick time they had manned their 12-pounder, the Lewis gunner had grabbed his weapon, and they stood ready to let rip.

At a height of only two hundred feet the Heinkels flashed over the little trawler, their bombs hurtling down and their guns streaming fire. Explosive bullets smashed the trawler's Lewis gun and crumpled the gunner into a bloody heap. Gillett on his fragile upper bridge was sent reeling under the impact of a bullet.

But there was only one thought in his mind: to fight off the enemy and bring his ship through safely. Since the solitary Lewis gun was now out of action he ordered those of his men not serving the 12-pounder to grab rifles and post themselves where they could best hit back. When the Heinkels came in for their second run, in addition to bombs and machine-gun bullets, they now showered the swerving, heeling *Solon* with incendiaries. They meant to get her, for Hitler had planned to strangle our sea-borne trade with his

Luftwaffe-sown mines; and every minesweeper that could be destroyed aided the plan of forcing Britain to capitulate through starvation.

In the next attack bomb fragments and machine-gun bullets accounted for the *Solon*'s 12-pounder gunlayer, and shattered the leg of Second Hand George Shaul. The trawlermen, lowered their smoking rifles, kicked and threw the incendiaries overboard as they rained down. One bomb which, had it exploded, would have sent her to the bottom crashed on to the engine-room casing and bounced off over the side, leaving a huge ugly dent in the steelwork.

Like the gallant *Ayrshire*, the *Solon*, too, somehow miraculously survived the fiercely pressed-home attacks. But she looked a shambles. Her hull and upperworks were torn and scarred by bullets and slivers of flying steel, her plates jarred and leaking due to the near misses; spent bullets and unexploded incendiaries littered her deck. Then at last with ammunition and bomb loads expended the baffled Nazis made off into the North Sea mists.

Second Hand Shaul, whose battle station was at the wheel, was unable to stand. Gallantly he tried to steer the ship from a sitting position, but from this posture he found it impossible to see the compass. Although the seamanship he had learned as a boy in the Service had long grown rusty from disuse, Pensioner Signalman Wells took over in the wheelhouse. Under his guidance the battered little trawler came safely back into Yarmouth.

In addition to the thousands of machine-gun bullets aimed at her, the *Solon* had for over an hour withstood a hail of more than a score of high-explosive bombs and some two thousand incendiaries. She survived the war as she deserved.

Farther south the trawler minesweeper *Benvolio*, Chief Skipper Aldred, R.N.R., and the A/S trawler *Peridot*, Skipper Burgess, R.N.R., both victims of mines, added their shattered hulls to the growing pile of sunken ships along Britain's east coast.

## CHAPTER IV

# THE V.C. TRAWLER

NAMSOS is a small Norwegian town with a population of
some three to four thousand inhabitants, whose neat wooden
houses shelter in a fold of the mountains at the head of
Namsen Fjord. The fjord lies about halfway up the deeply
indented coastline of Norway, and the snow-capped hills
which cradle it are neither as precipitous nor ruggedly pic-
turesque as those farther south. The town itself, most of
whose adult population is engaged in fishing or the timber
business, is a quiet little place, even dull, offering few attrac-
tions for the tourist.

Seldom normally does anything happen to disturb the
peaceful serenity of Namsos. Fishing craft lie off the pier,
their crews overhauling their gear or mending their nets, and
the bubbling wake of an occasional timber-laden steamer
furrows the glassy blue surface of the fjord. Certainly it is
not a port on the normal visiting list of fishing trawlers from
Hull and Grimsby.

Yet in the spring of 1940 more than a score of the crack
ships from these two famous British fishing ports were to
visit Namsos. But neither they nor the little Norwegian town
and its once peaceful fjord bore the slightest resemblance to
normality. The sturdy hulls of the trawlers, their superstructures, masts and funnels were painted battleship grey or
daubed with camouflage. Guns poked ugly snouts from fore-
castles and bridge wings, and the White Ensign of the Royal
Navy fluttered from their gaffs.

On shore a pall of smoke hung over the town. Many of the
wooden houses were wrecked or in flames, those of their
inhabitants who had not been killed or injured having fled
to the hills, and the fjord echoed to the ugly crump of ex-

ploding bombs, the whine and crack of shells, the rattle of machine-gun fire, and the breath-stopping scream of dive-bombers. The war in Europe, the 'phoney war', had suddenly burst into savage eruption. Almost in a single night Norway had been invaded and Denmark overrun by the Nazis.

The Germans had landed troops at Oslo, the capital; at Arendal, Bergen and Krisiansund in the south; at Trondheim, ninety miles from Namsos, and at Narvik in the north. A British Expeditionary Force had been hastily despatched to the aid of the resisting Norwegians, and was landing at Narvik, and at Namsos and Aandalsnes, north and south of German-held Trondheim with the intention of assaulting the latter by a pincer movement. To provide anti-submarine protection for the British warships and transports spearheading the landings and to ferry the troops inshore twenty-nine trawlers of the Lilliput Fleet had been sent to Norway.

They comprised the 11th A/S Striking Force, made up of the trawlers *Cape Siretoko, Argyllshire, Northern Pride,* and *Wisteria*; the 15th A/S Striking Force, comprising the *Cape Passaro, St Goran, St Kenan* and *St Loman*; the 16 A/S Striking Force, comprising the *Aston Villa, Gaul, Angle* and *Arab*; the 12th A/S Group, composed of the *Stella Capella, Cape Argona, Cape Chelyuskin* and *Blackfly;* the 21st Striking Force, which included the *Daneman, Lady Elsa, Man of War,* and *Wellard*; the 22nd A/S Group, which comprised the *Warwickshire, Hammond, Larwood, Bradman* and *Jardine*; and the 23rd A/S Group comprising the *Indian Star, Melbourne, Berkshire* and *Rutlandshire*. Of these ships, those which bore the names of famous cricketers would never again return to the fishing grounds; and the shattered hulls of the *Gaul, Melbourne, Aston Villa, Cape Passaro, St Goran, Rutlandshire, Cape Siretoko, Warwickshire,* and *Cape Chelyuskin* would join them, to lie rusting where they had been wrecked and driven ashore, or sunk beneath the chilly uncaring waters of the fjords or the North Sea along with the corpses of many of their gallant crews.

For by the suddenness of their treacherous attack the

Germans had captured the principal airfields, and with practically no ack-ack guns for their defence, the Allied ships were subjected to ferocious air attacks. Every minute of the day they were assailed by high level and dive bombers, and sudden swooping machine-gun attacks at masthead height. To move about the fjord in daylight was sheer suicide, and since there was little room in its narrow waters to dodge the incessant rain of bombs and bullets the trawlers were obliged to camouflage themselves with evergreens and lie up where they could under the shelter of overhanging cliffs, emerging to carry out their patrols only after dark.

Commenting afterwards, the Third Sea Lord, then Admiral Sir Bruce Fraser, said that the trawlers 'went through the devil of a time'. Later in his despatches the Commander in-Chief, Home Fleet, Admiral of the Fleet Sir Charles Forbes, paid tribute to the magnificent morale and gallantry of their officers and men.

*     *     *

On the 28th of April, 1940, the trawler *Arab* was on patrol in Namsen Fjord along with her sister ships of the 15th and 16th A/S Striking Forces. Commanding the *Arab* was thirty-eight-year old Lieutenant Richard Been Stannard, R.N.R. Son of a master mariner, Stannard was himself a 'big ship' man. He had been educated at the Royal Merchant Navy School, and served his cadetship at sea in the old C and D Line. Ten years before the outbreak of World War II Stannard joined the Orient Line as a First Officer and the Royal Naval Reserve as a Sub-Lieutenant. He was perfectly at home in a trawler, however, having been trained by the Navy both in A/S work and minesweeping.

As his first lieutenant Stannard had a young Australian Naval Reservist, also an A/S specialist, Sub-Lieutenant Ernest Lees; his other watchkeeping officer was Temporary Sub-Lieutenant R. F. Ellis of the R.N.V.R. The Second Hand and Coxswain was David George Spindler who with the rest of the crew belonged to the R.N.R. Patrol Service.

The *Arab* was a vessel of some 530 tons gross, built by the Smith's Dock Company of Middlesbrough in 1936, and owned by Hellyer brothers of Hull. She was a modern trawler with a cruiser stern, 170 feet long with a beam of 28 feet, and had been equipped with the latest echo-sounding gear, and wireless direction-finding apparatus. One of the 400 trawlers earmarked to be taken up from the fishing fleet, she had also been requisitioned by the Admiralty in September, 1939, and fitted out as an anti-submarine escort vessel.

Some 5,000 Allied troops had been landed in Namsos, and supply ships were arriving with ammunition, petrol and heavy equipment. But none remained longer than could be helped in the inferno that was Namsen Fjord. Stores were dumped on the pier or anywhere along the waterfront where room could be found. With their steel-helmeted crews closed up at the guns, the little trawlers weaved about among the bigger vessel lending aid and protection where they could. Dodging the sticks of bursting bombs that fell almost without ceasing and fighting off the diving Stukas, they nudged store ships alongside, ferried troops from transports, and went to the aid of vessels that had gone aground in the chaos.

Events happened with such speed and unexpectedness that it was almost impossible for any senior officer to exercise control. If some task was seen to require attention the nearest available warship was detailed to deal with it. Yet despite the overall confusion ships were somehow brought in, anchored or secured alongside if there was room, their cargoes unloaded, and sent off on their way as quickly as possible.

The 28th of April, 1940, was a Sunday, but there was no let-up in Namsen Fjord. No Sunday Divisions for the ships' companies of the warships as in peacetime, with the church pendant at the yardarm and Divine Service on the quarter-deck afterwards. No let up for the transports and supply vessels, whose winches continued to spurt steam and their derricks to swing back and forth as loads were hastily hoisted from the holds and dumped ashore. The airfields at Trondheim and elsewhere in German hands were busy, too, bombing up and arming the Stukas which, with their white-edged black crosses standing out starkly on oil-streaked wings and fuselage, came swooping down on to the harried ships in *Geschwaders* of six, nine, and twelve at a time. The whistle and thud of bombs, the crack of 4-inch and 12-pounders and the constant hammering of machine-guns continued unabated.

At about that time in the forenoon when the sailors of the figting British trawlers would normally have been welcoming the traditional pipe of Up Spirits a particularly vicious air-raid developed over Namsos. Droves of high-flying Dorniers drenched the Fjord with high explosive, to be followed by the inevitable swarms of dive-bombers. When the last of these had finally jinked over the hills in the direction of Trondheim, a huge column of smoke arose from stricken Namsos. Adding their quota to the darkening pall rising high above the fjord were flame-shot gouts of smoke from a fire raging amid the piled-up stores on the pier. Close by lay a dump containing many tons of hand grenades. In addition to other damage the Luftwaffe bombers had wrecked the town water supply beyond repair, and fire-fighting from shore resources was out of the question.

But there were a host of other troubles clamouring to be dealt with afloat. In the immediate vicinity of 16th A/S Group's senior officer, Lieut.-Commander Sir Geoffrey Congreve, R.N., in the trawler *Aston Villa,* the transport *Saumur* was badly aground and, to make things worse, she had managed to get a wire wrapped firmly around her propeller. She would be a sitting duck for the next attack, and transports were valuable. Congreve ordered the *Angle* and *Arab* to go to her aid.

As senior ship with a Royal Navy Lieut.-Commander in command, the *Angle* went in first to tackle the job. She soon had the situation well in hand, so Stannard went off to see if he could be of help elsewhere.

There was one place where assistance was urgently needed, the worst in the whole crowded fjord, the fire on the pier which was now raging furiously. If it were not checked many hundreds of tons of vitally needed stores would be destroyed, while the grenades and other ammunition nearby might go up in a colossal explosion. Stannard ordered hoses to be rigged on the forecastle, and steamed at full speed towards the pier. As the trawler nosed in the heat of the flames caused the paint on her sides to blister and curl.

When the trawler's stem finally bumped against the pier uprights, Stannard ordered her to be kept in that position with the engines going slow ahead. Then he turned the bridge over to his first lieutenant and shinned down to the foredeck. Accompanied by two of the crew and ordering the rest of the men to remain aft, he climbed on to the forecastle and began directing water into the blaze.

For two hours he stood facing the searing heat as the trawler's pumps sucked up the icy water of the fjord and sent it spurting through his copper branchpipe. Frequently Stannard and his men had to duck to avoid flying fragments from bursting grenades. Occasionally his helpers soused him to prevent his clothes from charring. Soon, however, their hair and eyebrows became singed, their faces blackened, their throats parched and dry and their lungs full of the choking smoke. And their efforts were having about as much effect as a cup of tea poured into the erupting crater of a volcano. Just as Stannard realised the hopelessness of the situation another air raid developed.

Circling above the smoking fjord to select their victims before screaming down to the attack once more, the Nazi airmen noted the British trawler lying pressed against the blazing pier and quickly divined her purpose. No fewer than sixteen Stukas pointed their spinners at the valiant little *Arab*. But Stannard and his First Lieutenant, the young Australian, Lees, were ready for them.

The trawler shot astern from the pier, crew back at their guns, and made for an overhanging cliff, spouting streams of tracer as the Ju. 87s slammed their bombs at her from every point of the compass. But they failed to hit her. With her hull plates starting from the concussion of near misses, the *Arab* slid safely beneath her rocky shelter. Frustrated, the Stukas zoomed away in search of an easier target.

The next day, Monday was no different from Sunday. Warships and merchantmen jostled each other in Namsen Fjord and heavy-scale air attacks continued throughout the daylight hours. Ashore things were going badly for the Army and there was talk of evacuation.

With the coming of dawn on Tuesday, the 30th April, the Luftwaffe were back in force. The familiar pattern of bursting bombs and diving Stukas began to be repeated almost before the heavy-eyed trawlermen in the *Arab* could drink the mugs of hot tea and munch the corned-beef sandwiches brought to them at the guns by the cook. Soon the sloop H.M.S. *Bittern* was in trouble as the Ju.87s marked her down for their special target.

The valiant little *Arab* promptly sailed in to add her small quota of gunfire to the heavier armament of the 1,190-ton sloop. In the narrow crowded anchorage the *Bittern* was unable to dodge and manoeuvre under the persistent attack of her enemies. For a while, aided by the trawler's guns, she was able to fight them off. But later on the planes returned, and this time they left the luckless sloop a mass of flames. The men of the *Arab* took off her smoke-blackened survivors, and the blazing warship was later sunk by her sister ships.

As the day wore on Stannard took his trawler to the aid of other ships of the Group whenever they were hard pressed, although the *Arab* herself had been damaged. But it was obvious to him that in their present situation the battle could have only one eventual outcome for the ships. There were no anti-aircraft guns on the heights around the fjord to drive off the bombers. Those same snow-capped hills effectually masked the ships' radar sets so that they could gain no prior warning of the approaching enemy.

Tried to the limit of endurance by incessant air raids and the necessity for constant vigilance against the threat of a night attack by enemy surface craft or submarines, the trawlermen were verging on collapse from fatigue. In four days the *Arab* alone had undergone thirty-one enemy air attacks during which more than a hundred and thirty bombs had been aimed at her.

Stannard made up his mind. He took his ship beneath the exiguous shelter of an overhanging cliff and secured her head and stern. He found a cave nearby and stocked it with blankets and provisions. Lewis guns from the ship were taken ashore and set up around the cave for defence. At the top of the cliff the lieutenant established an air raid lookout post and equipped it with machine-guns. Then, remaining on board himself, he sent his crew ashore to the cave to snatch some much-needed rest. Next day the *Gaul* and *Aston Villa* joined the *Arab* at her anchorage under the cliff, and their crews joined up with that of Stannard in the cave shelter and took turns at manning the lookout post.

Whenever enemy aircraft approached the trawlers Stannard opened fire on them and spoilt their aim. At dusk he left the guns and, with the earphones on in the asdic cabinet, kept anti-submarine watch throughout the hours of darkness.

In daylight the dive bombers came over in flights of twelve at a time, concentrating their efforts against the little group of trawlers huddled in the lee of the cliff. Others screamed down to beat up the sailors' lookout post. The *Gaul* took a direct hit amidships which damaged her so badly that she later had to be sunk. Next a bomb slammed into the *Aston Villa* and started a fierce fire on board. Only a handful of her crew had remained in the ship and the uninjured got ashore. Promptly Stannard boarded the *Arab* with two of his men, for the blazing *Aston Villa* only a few yards away constituted a menace as the flames licked nearer to her magazine and depth charges. Cooly he cut the trawler's moorings and manoeuvred her away to a safe distance. Miraculously the *Aston Villa* did not blow up. Her crew managed to extinguish the fire, and her engine-room staff laboured so mightily and to such good effect that she could actually steam at six knots by the time that Namsos had to be evacuated. Despite the pleadings of her captain the trawler had to be sunk by our own forces, for as a lame duck she could never have cleared the coast before the dive bombers found her again.

Evacuation now became the order of the day, and at Namsos and Aandalsnes the weary, defeated men of the Expeditionary Force and their Norwegian comrades clambered aboard warships and transports hastily sent to bring them away. Overhead the triumphant Luftwaffe planes circled and swooped ceaselessly.

Torn and scarred by bomb fragments and cannon fire, her plates leaking, her available living spaces crowded with survivors from other ships and from the shore, the gallant little *Arab* at last turned her battered bows towards the mouth of

Namsen Fjord and the open sea. For five days Stannard, almost single-handed, had maintained his weary men in their cave shelter ashore and fought off all attempts to sink his ship. So well planned had been the defences of his look-out post that despite the incessant bombing and machine-gunning only one man had even been wounded. Now at last they were leaving behind this hell on earth.

But, like clouds of enraged hornets, the Junkers attacked the departing ships again and again with reckless fury. As the trawler steamed towards the open sea columns of spray soared skywards from near misses, almost blotting her from sight. Dive-bombers swooped with chattering cannon, to be met and deflected by the steady barrage flung up by the *Arab*'s gunners.

One Nazi pilot, cocksure that the tiny British warship could not escape, circled her signalling with a hand lamp. 'Steer east or be sunk,' ordered the winking light peremptorily. Stannard was icily furious. 'Hold your fire until I give the word,' he told his gunners. Then, as the *Arab* forged onwards, he watched the bomber carefully. After orbiting round to see if his order was being obeyed, the German pilot lined himself up and came in to the attack.

The needle of his altimeter spun round as he went into the dive. 1500 feet – 1200 feet – 1000 feet – 800 feet. And then Stannard roared the one word, 'Fire!' Instantly jets of tracer spat from the *Arab*'s guns, to converge on the oil-streaked fuselage of the diving bomber. Impaled on the fiery spear of shells and bullets, the Junkers suddenly gushed smoke and reeled away like a stricken bird. Then it crashed into the fjord and disintegrated.

A few days later H.M. Trawler *Arab* berthed safely in an English port.

In the *London Gazette* of the 16th August, 1940, Lieutenant Richard Been Stannard, R.N.R. was cited as having been awarded the Victoria Cross, 'for outstanding valour and signal devotion to duty at Namsos.' It was the second naval V.C. of the war. At the same time Sub-Lieutenant Ernest Lees, of the Royal Australian Naval Volunteer Reserve, was awarded the Distinguished Service Cross; Engineman James Nicholson and Seaman Charles Newman of the R.N.R., the Distinguished Service Medal, and Seaman Charles Hassock was mentioned in despatches. 'For daring, resource and devotion to duty,' the *Arab*'s Second Hand, David George Spindler of the R.N.R.' was awarded the Conspicuous Gallantry Medal.

\* \* \*

Farther north the little ships had also been in the thick of things. Patrolling off the entrance to Narvik Fjord while the troops of the Expeditionary Force slogged it out with the German defenders, was the trawler *Northern Gem*. Her captain was Chief Skipper L. F. Scarlett, R.N.R., later to earn a D.S.C. for gallantry, and his first lieutenant, Temporary Sub-Lieutenant L. Head, of the R.N.V.R.

The *Northern Gem* was a fine little ship. Of 655 tons gross, she was one of fifteen trawlers built at Bremen in 1936 for the firm of Northern Trawlers, Ltd., of London. Turbine driven, she had a cruiser stern and a raking stem, was 188 feet long with a beam of 28 feet, and had boasted the most up-to-date navigational and technical equipment for her peacetime function. She was one of the first ships of the fishing fleet to be taken over by the Navy at the outbreak of war.

Fitted out as an anti-submarine and escort vessel, the *Northern Gem* had spent the early weeks of her naval service on escort duties and was later sent to join the Northern Patrol as an armed boarding vessel. Her crew of ex-fishermen had received a brusque introduction to the war at sea. They were used to bad weather and tough conditions while out on the fishing grounds. But there was a limit to the longest and toughest fishing trip. Eventually you made port, the catch was unloaded and you went home for a well-earned spell.

In the Navy in wartime things were different. All that could be hoped for was a bare twenty-four hours in harbour, scarcely long enough to get the chill out of one's bones, and then off again to face the rigours of the Denmark Strait.

After days and nights on patrol in the heavy grey wastes

the whole ship's company would be drooping with weariness. Joints were stiff from constant soaking, faces sore and burning fom the lash of frozen spindrift, and the deadly cold chilled to the marrow. For these were the early days before many of the little ships were adopted by kind-hearted clubs and communities ashore, whose womenfolk spent all their spare time knitting warm woollen socks, scarves, mittens, gloves, jerseys, and even quilts and blankets for sailors they would never see.

In peacetime the Navy rarely sent its ships into Arctic waters, and there was then no special cold-weather clothing and equipment in the victualling yards. The trawlermen considered themselves lucky to get an official issue of a pair of seaboot stockings each, and perhaps a scarf and balaclava helmet.

Christmas, 1939, had been the grimmest any of them could remember. For forty-eight hours the *Northern Gem* had battled against a screaming hurricane. While the stout little trawler was forced to heave to, those of her men who were off watch stumbled below to wedge themselves into odd corners of their crazily reeling mess deck to eat their Christmas dinner. It was bully beef and hard tack, since cooking was out of the question and there were no fresh provisions, washed down with a mug of rum-laced tea so strong that a mouse could have walked across the surface without wetting its feet. Eventually they had struggled back to their base in the Orkneys to find themselves chalked up as overdue.

For the base staff remembered the fate that had overtaken the *Rawalpindi*, one of the armed merchant cruisers with whom the trawlers shared the northern Patrol. Out of the dusk one evening a few weeks earlier had loomed the great grey shapes of the *Scharnhorst* and *Gneisenau*. With her guns defiantly blazing, the gallant *Rawalpindi* had been sent to the bottom by the German ships in less than fifteen minutes.

Now the *Northern Gem* was doing sentry-go off the little iron-ore port where the Allied troops were struggling to obtain a foothold. The Germans were thrusting up through Norway to reinforce their garrison at Narvik. Since the sea was denied to them, they were sending in troops by air.

As the trawler began to swing her bows round preparatory to starting another leg of her patrol, her lookouts spotted a German aircraft apparently intending to land on a snow-capped hill nearby. But either the pilot misjudged the height or the Junkers had already been damaged by ack-ack fire, for the plane landed heavily, cascading snow and earth in all directions as it slithered to a standstill. Even as it crash-landed Skipper Scarlett ordered away an armed party to round up the Nazi airmen.

Steel-helmeted and carrying rifles and bayonets, a handful of trawlermen swung themselves into their lowered boat and began pulling ashore. Scarlett watched them through his binoculars as they landed and started to trudge up the hill towards the crashed Junkers. Then as the trawler moved away on her patrol they were cut off from his view.

Seeing no one near the crashed aircraft the landing party incautiously lowered their rifles as they approached. Suddenly a rasping shout of 'Hande hoch!' halted them in their tracks. Seeming to spring from the earth around them, a number of figures wearing camouflaged jerkins and grasping tommy guns and machine pistols surrounded them. Other armed Nazis poured out of the Junkers, and the grim realisation dawned on the bemused trawlermen that they were now to become the captives instead of the captors. The plane was a troop-carrier and the enemy far outnumbered the sailors. Cursing eloquently, they dropped their useless rifles and raised their hands above their heads.

But they were to be humiliated still further. In passable English the Unteroffizier ordered them to strip. They gaped at him unbelievingly. 'We can't do that, Fritz, it's too bloody cold,' they protested.

'Do not argue,' snapped the Unteroffizier, gesturing meaningly with his Luger. 'Strip, and be quick about it.'

Further argument in the face of levelled guns was obviously pointless. Fuming with rage, the trawlermen began slowly to divest themselves of their clothing. Then they squatted while they removed their seaboots and the thick stockings. Next came their jumpers and finally their trousers. The Nazis roared with laughter as their victims stood

shivering in their undergarments and bare feet, already turning blue with the cold.

'Goot,' grunted the officer. 'Now pick up our equipment
and march.'

Weighed down beneath the machine guns, grenades, rifles
and ammunition they had been forced to unload from the
troop-carrier, the shivering sailors began trudging through
the snow surrounded by the jeering Nazis. 'Blimey,' whis-
pered one trawlerman to his leading hand, 'where are they
taking us with this bloody lot?'

'Don't ask me,' growled the leading seaman. 'I'm too
blasted cold too worry.'

Then without warning, there was a sudden ear-splitting
crash, and a shell burst a hundred yards away. As one man
the sailors dropped their loads, fell flat and tried to burrow
into the snow while earth and debris showered around them.
The shell was followed by a second, and then a third in
rapid sucession. Unknown to them the party of Nazi troops
and their captives had been spotted by another British
trawler on patrol in the fjord and she had promptly opened
fire. Her gunnery was too accurate for the nerves of the
Germans for, after one startled look towards the fjord, they
turned and fled.

Finding themselves alone, but feeling far too exposed for
comfort, the trawlermen scrambled to their feet and between
shellbursts dashed away down the hill. Spotting a small hut
which appeared to be deserted they rushed inside and
slammed the door. After trying to rub some semblance of
life back into their bare feet, and flapping their arms against
their half-naked chests in an effort to get warm, the leading
hand put his head round the door and peered outside. Then
he slammed it again with a cry of alarm. For charging towards the hut with bayonets gleaming at the end of their
levelled rifles was a file of steel-helmeted men.

Another trawlerman leaped to the door and peered out.
Then he jerked round with a grin of relief on his bearded
face. 'They're not Jerries,' he yelled. 'They're bloody Marines!' Promptly the sailors hurled themselves out into the
snow waving their arms frantically. 'We're not Germans,'
they howled, 'we're British matlows!'

Later when Narvik was finally evacuated the trawler *Northern Gem* was one of the last British warships to leave. She reached home safely, and we shall meet her again in another episode of her wartime career.

\* \* \*

Despite the worst the Luftwaffe could do the British Navy transported, maintained and eventually evacuated all arms of the ill-fated Expeditionary Force to Norway with the loss of only thirteen troops killed and nine wounded. Forty-one gallant airmen who, though they had never before landed on an aircraft carrier, had flown their planes on to the *Glorious* rather than destroy them, died when the carrier and her destroyer escort were sunk by the German battleships *Scharnhorst* and *Gneisenau* and the heavy cruiser *Admiral Hipper* on the way back to England.

One other unit of the Lilliput Fleet also died under the guns of the big German warships. Like the destroyers *Ardent* and *Acasta* who had tried to defend the *Glorious,* she went down fighting to the last to protect her charge, an oil tanker.

H.M. Trawler *Juniper* was not, like so many of her sisters, an ex-fishing vessel. She had been built specially for the Navy. Along with nineteen others, the *Juniper* was a 'Tree' class trawler, built to Admiralty specification under the 1939 Naval Estimates. These trawlers, which all bore the names of trees, were laid down in British yards soon after the war began. Later they were joined by hundreds of other Admiralty-designed trawlers, built in the United Kingdom, America, and Canada, bearing the names of Shakespearian characters, of dances, islands, lakes, hills, fish, and even Knights of the Round Table. And these, along with thousands of other small craft destined for the Lilliput Fleet, were to emerge from the shipyards in a continual stream throughout the war years.

The *Juniper* was built by Messrs Ferguson Brothers, and had been commissioned for service as an anti-submarine and escort trawler in March, 1940. She was of 600 tons displacement, had a speed of 12 knots and was armed with one four-inch gun and a number of smaller weapons. After a quick work-up she was attached to the 19th A/S Striking Force under the Admiral Commanding the Orkneys and Shetlands. Her captain was Lieut.-Commander G. S. Grenfell, an officer on the Emergency List of the Royal Navy. His officers were Temporary Lieutenant R. C. B. Daniel and Temporary Sub-Lieutenant N. L. Smith, both of the R.N.V.R., and the crew were all R.N.R. Patrol Service men. Grenfell had gone up in February to stand by his ship while she was building until finally ready for him to take over.

On the 7th June, 1940, the Juniper sailed from Tromso escorting the 5,666-ton tanker *Oil Pioneer*, operated by her owners, the British Oil Shipping Company of London, on behalf of the Ministry of War Transport. Although Grenfell did not know it, German surface forces were out in strength.

Three days previously the *Scharnhorst*, flying the flag of Vice-Admiral Marschall, and accompanied by the *Gneisenau*, *Admiral Hipper* and four destroyers had left Kiel with the intention of attacking British and Allied shipping and shore installations in the Narvik area. At half-past five on the morning of the 8th June Grenfell sighted the German ships.

There was little he could do with one 4-inch gun against the massive armament of the enemy. Nor could either of the British ships hope to escape. But the *Juniper* might be able to delay the inevitable long enough to ensure that the Germans would meet worthier opponents before they got back to harbour. Accordingly he wirelessed an enemy sighting report, ordered the tanker to act independently, hoisted his battle flags and sailed in.

Just ninety minutes later the gallant little trawler and her consort slid beneath the waves, battered to wreckage by a couple of contemptuous salvoes from the *Hipper*. Twenty-five survivors of the tanker and four only from her tiny escort were fished out of the sea by the enemy, to spend the rest of the war behind barbed wire.

CHAPTER V

# WHITE ENSIGN SUPERIOR

ON May 10th, 1940, the great German blitzkrieg was launched against the West. Backed by lorried infantry, panzer divisions lanced swiftly through the Netherlands, Belgium and Luxemburg. In less than three weeks they had reached the Channel coast, and the remnants of the blitz-shocked British Expeditionary Force were rolled up and penned into Dunkirk and a few small enclaves to the south. Holland and Belgium capitulated, and a few weeks later the French signed an armistice at Compiègne on Hitler's terms.

But before the collapse of France had come the epic of Dunkirk. Much has already been written about the evacuation under the noses of the Nazis, and despite the worst the Luftwaffe could do, of more than 338,000 British and Allied troops by little ships from Britain. But some fragment of the part played in this great withdrawal by the Patrol Service might well be related here.

Of the 250 large and small British warships which transported troops from the beaches of Dunkirk to this country more than half were trawlers and drifters belonging to the Lilliput Fleet. One third of these were sunk. Patrol Service skippers and crews also manned some of the hundreds of other miscellaneous craft which took part in Operation Dynamo.

There was, for example, Skipper Jack Wayman of Fleet-wood. He was a Second Hand in the R.N. Patrol Service when the B.E.F. was being swept back to the French coast by the triumphantly onrushing panzers. He had been blooded in Norway when his trawler ferried toops to Trondheim in that short-lived and ill-fated campaign. In the fjords they had been bombed by the Luftwaffe and shelled from the shore by advancing Germans. For three whole days their little ship had been the target of savage and unremitting air attacks. Finally they had got away, still, by some miracle, afloat.

Directed from an office in London specially set up for the purpose by the Admiral Commanding Reserves, the Flag Officer of the Patrol Service, to deal with the provision of experienced crews for the armada of small craft being assembled for Operation Dynamo, Second Hand Wayman found himself given command of a Thames sand barge. The barge was motor-driven and could make four knots, but since she was intended only for river work she boasted no navigational instruments, not even a compass. Guided for part of the way over by the stream of traffic passing between Dover and the French coast, and for the rest by the huge wavering pall of smoke that hung like a funeral pyre over Dunkirk, Wayman brought her to the beaches.

His job then was to take his clumsy scow as close in to the long, patiently waiting queue of soldiers as he could, embark the maximum number possible and ferry them to one of the larger vessels waiting farther out. On his first trip he managed to cram 400 troops on board. Then as he slowly worked the barge's blunt stern to seaward and began swinging her round the Luftwaffe appeared. In waves of up to one hundred and fifty at a time, the dive-bombers zoomed and swooped overhead. Cataracts of spray from near misses drenched Wayman and his sardine-packed passengers.

Crawling across the bomb-riven water like a labouring beetle, the sand barge finally bumped alongside a paddle steamer, and the khaki tide washed swiftly inboard to the larger ship. Then Wayman cast off and went back for more. If a Ju.88 swooped too close for comfort he spat back at it with his only weapon – a rifle.

With another 300 troops aboard the sand barge again wrenched herself free of the beach and started working laboriously round to aim for the nearest transport. But of course the luck could not hold. A Junkers streaked over and released its bomb load. The bombs fell close to the slowly moving barge and their explosions overthrew it, tossing

61

the soldiers into the water like a pile of fruit from a suddenly upturned coster's barrow. As the dazed and weary men began swimming, with Wayman cheerfully encouraging them, other Nazi airmen swept in low and machine-gunned the bobbing heads.

Dodging bullets and flying bomb fragments the trawler-man eventually waded ashore a mile or so from Dunkirk. Ignoring the bombing and shelling, the small-arms fire and the rumbling tanks of the enemy, Wayman walked calmly back into the stricken town, made his way down to the docks and thumbed a lift back to Britain in a destroyer. Then he found himself another ship and went back to carry on where he had been forced to leave off.

There was, too, H.M.S. *Fisher Boy*. Built at Yarmouth as a herring drifter in 1914, this little 40-ton craft was already a war veteran. For four years in World War I she had patrolled the anti-submarine boom across the entrance at Taranto harbour in Italy. Then she had returned home to fulfil for the next two decades her proper function of catching her-rings for British meal tables. In November, 1939, the *Fisher Boy* was called upon for service once again.

This time, with four of her sisters, the ex-Yarmouth herring drifter formed a special unit known as 'Vernon's Private Navy'. The scientists of H.M.S. *Vernon*, the Navy's torpedo and mining establishment and headquarters of Britain's anti-mining campaign, needed all the information they could get on the nature and design of enemy mines and the lethal obstructions the Germans were adding as deter-rents to sweeping their minefields. It was the dedicated task of the little drifter flotilla to go out and look for and en-deavour to recover intact for laboratory dissection new types of enemy mines as these were reported.

Chief Skipper George Brown of the R.N.R. Patrol Service, a veteran fisherman from Great Yarmouth who commanded the *Fisher Boy* for much of her war service, summed up the hazardous task of mine recovery in a typical sailor's under-statement.

'Searching for the mines was the most nerve-racking part,' he said. 'When we had actually got one in the trawl we were too busy with the delicate job of recovery to worry about the risks. But of course we did have some anxious moments recovering new types of mines when we hadn't the slightest idea how they were going to behave.'

Temporarily released from her important work to help in the Dunkirk evacuation, the little *Fisher Boy* and her sisters joined up with the remainder of the rescue armada. Like Jack Wayman's sand barge, the *Fisher Boy* ferried waiting soldiers from the bomb- and shell-torn shallows where they stood waist deep to the destroyers farther out in batches of a hundred and fifty at a time. Then when the larger ships were full she collected two hundred more troops, packed them somehow below and about her meagre deck space and steamed off to Ramsgate with them.

On one of her cross-Channel trips she encountered the fiercely blazing and listing hulk of the troopship *Scotia*. Rolling over under the savage impact of five direct bomb hits the liner dragged many of her company down with her. When the *Fisher Boy* and her consorts arrived on the tragic scene the water was black with the heads of struggling soldiers over which Nazi planes were skimming with machine-guns blazing. The ex-herring drifters rescued all the swimmers alive and brought them back to safety.

In all '*Vernon*'s Private Navy' ferried no fewer than 4,085 British and Allied troops from the beaches at Dunkirk to the shores of Britain. Of this number Skipper Brown and his men carried no less than one-third in the *Fisher Boy*.

\* \* \*

For the purpose of cloaking their war moves in secrecy the Allied Chiefs of Staff Committee arbitrarily plucked a huge block of words from the English dictionary, put them into safe storage and issued selected chunks of them to the Commanders-in-Chief of the fighting services for use as code names to cover all important offensive and other wartime operations planned to take place within their commands. No subordinate officer was allowed to use a word of his own choosing for any independent or other type of action he might plan against the enemy. He was officially allocated to that command or go without.

Naturally these code names bore not the slightest relationship to any of the operations they were designed to screen, although it occasionally happened that a word appeared to be singularly appropriate for the operation to which it acted as a cover. Such a code name was 'Retribution', applied by the British Naval Commander-in-Chief, Mediterranean, in 1943 to the final liquidation of the Axis forces in North Africa. Since the enemy was then faced with a choice of surrender in Cape Bon or of endeavouring to escape by sea, where British naval forces hopefully awaited such an attempt, the Navy remembered Dunkirk and applauded the aptness of the code word.

Later on some of these code names became so well known that they are remembered almost more readily than the actions they veiled. 'Dynamo', 'Husky', 'Torch', and finally in 1944 the majestic 'Overlord'.

But it is unlikely that many people have heard of Operations 'Quentin', Quidnunc', and 'Quixote'. Certainly in the spring of 1940 they remained unknown to all but a handful of civilians and naval personnel. Of the latter the commanders of three British destroyers and six trawlers of the R.N. Patrol Service knew about the projected operations these names concealed and what they entailed.

The destroyers were the *Jackal* (Commander T. M. Napier, R.N.), *Jaguar* (Commander A. F. Pugsley, R.N.) and *Javelin* (Lieut.-Commander J. H. Hine, R.N.), new and powerful 1,760-ton ships, launched in 1939, armed with six 4.7 in. guns and able to steam at 36 knots. Three years later two of them, the *Jackal* and *Jaguar*, were to end their brief careers in battle in the Mediterranean.

The trawlers were the *Grampian, Pelton, James Lay, Milford Queen, Cape Melville* and *Milford Princess*, all formerly well known on the distant-water fishing grounds. The *Grampian* was commanded by Lieutenant Albert Longmuir, R.N.R., a minesweeping specialist, and the remainder by Skippers belonging to the R.N.R. Patrol Service, also trained in minesweeping. In general charge of the three operations, which were in fact really one, was Commander Napier in the *Jackal*. Accompanying the expedition was the corvette *Puffin*, and air cover was to be provided by Blenheim bombers from No. 16 Group, Royal Air Force.

The task of the trawlers was to sever the submarine tele-communications cables between Britain and Germany. After all there was nothing further we wished to say to any German privately, and we were unlikely to transmit messages to any other European country which still enjoyed neutrality on lines passing through enemy territory.

Six of these cables were to be hauled up, cut and sealed. They ran from Mundesley and Bacton on the Norfolk coast some ten miles south of Cromer, to Nordeney and Borkum in the East Frisian Islands, from Lowestoft to Nordeney, and from Lowestoft to Borkum. The cuts would be made at a spot about halfway across the North Sea.

Now undersea cable work, as the crew of any Post Office telegraph ship will testify, is in normal times a difficult and highly specialised job. The cables themselves are usually of massive construction, comprising in their make-up a thick and intricate core of copper wire sheathed in substantial layers of gutta percha, brass binding tape and iron armouring wires or lead sheathing, and they weigh something like thirty tons per nautical mile. Pinpointing the exact position of a cable on the sea bed at depths of a hundred fathoms and more requires navigation and plotting of a very high degree of skill. Add to these difficulties the continual threat of air bombing, attack by surface or submarine, and cable work appears to be a very disagreeable task indeed.

Their captains thoroughly briefed for the job, the little group of trawlers, each of whom carried a special cable party of one officer and two cable hands from H.M.S. *Osprey*, the Asdic Training Establishment at Portland, sailed from Great Yarmouth on the night of the 18th May. It was a clear night with a bright moon and the sea was calm. With the sharply etched outlines of the destroyer ahead and on either beam and the corvette astern, the trawlers proceeded steadily out towards the centre of the North Sea. Overhead droned the watchful Blenheims.

After several hours' steaming the trawlers paired off without fuss, each accompanied by one of the destroyers, and moved away in different directions. The corvette sailed off by herself to cruise round in a wide circuit. With one officer on the bridge of each trawler poring over a chart folded back to focus attention on the area around Latitude 53 degrees 36 minutes North, Longitude 2 degrees 53 minutes East, the vessels gradually crept up to previously pencilled positions.

At half-past three on the morning of the 19th they stopped engines. Special grapnels were lowered over the side, and with the cable officer sitting on the inboard end to act as a 'feeler', the search for the mud-and slime-covered cables lying buried somewhere in the murky fathoms below commenced.

Eight hours and a great deal of hard work later the *James Lay* hooked the first of the cables, Lowestoft to Nordeney. Laboriously the heavy dripping snake was hauled up from the depths. It was secured with chains by seamen lowered over the bows on bosun's chairs and the cable party went to work. The armour sheathing and its sensitive core were hacked through, then both severed ends were carefully sealed. When all was finished the holding chains were slipped and the now separate cables splashed back into the sea and sank.

While this and similar actions were going on aboard the other pairs of trawlers, the destroyers were continually circling round and round. A number of aircraft were sighted from time to time and the guns' crews eyed them warily. But none came in to attack the little group of ships. There was hazard enough for the trawlermen already, for the area had been mined by the Germans and the grapnel parties had to grope for the objects of their search with infinite care and delicacy.

Once the *Jackal* sighted a ship and with guns trained she sped towards the strange vessel. But when the destroyer steamed up to her the ship was found to have not a living soul on board, her crew having apparently abandoned her. She was the Dutch salvage tug *Hector*. The *Jackal* put an armed party on board and the *Hector* was towed back to Britain.

The *Javelin*, too, discovered a distraction to enliven the monotony of patrol. Her lookout sighted a rubber dinghy in which he thought he could see signs of movement. To the great relief and delight of the dinghy's feebly waving occupants the big destroyer was soon alongside their bobbing craft. They were five members of the crew of a shot-down Whitley bomber.

When night at last fell on the 19th May, 1940, the North Sea in the area of Latitude 53 degrees 36 minutes North, Longitude 2 degrees 53 minutes East was empty of ships. The trawlers had gone and were safely berthed again in harbour at Great Yarmouth, the destroyers and corvette had turned their attention to other business. Operations 'Quentin', 'Quidnunc', and 'Quixote' had been successfully completed and telecommunications with Nazi Germany had been severed. They were not to be re-connected until Operation 'Overlord', still far in the future, had become history.

\* \* \*

A month later, on the 19th June, H.M. Trawler *Moonstone* was on anti-submarine patrol off Aden. Nine days previously, with the British Expeditionary Force driven from the Continent and a Nazi invasion of Britain seemingly only a matter of time, Mussolini had climbed on to Hitler's band wagon and declared war against Britain and France. The Italians boasted a large fleet which included a considerable number of submarines, of which at least eight were known to be based at Massawa in the Red Sea. Thus these at once became a threat to our sea route to India and the East. But as yet the fighting qualities of Mussolini's Navy were an unknown quantity. The men of the Lilliput Fleet were to be among the first to put these qualities to the test.

H.M.S. *Moonstone* had begun her active life as the fishing trawler *Lady Madeleine*. Built by the well known firm of Cook, Welton and Gemmell of Beverley in Yorkshire for Jutland Amalgamated Trawlers Ltd, of Hull, she was launched in 1934. Before conversion for naval service she was of some 390 tons gross, but the fitting of guns and other warlike equipment had brought her gross tonnage up to about 600. She was 150 feet long with a beam of 25 feet, she had a cruiser stern and a straight stem and could steam at a top speed of 12 knots. Along with four other fishing trawlers, she had been purchased by the Admiralty early in

1939 for use in anti-submarine training and renamed *Moonstone*.

Her sister ships had also been re-christened on conversion, and now appeared in the Navy List as H.M. Trawlers *Amber*, *Beryl*, *Coral* and *Jade*. Thus they brought the total of 'Gem' class trawlers owned by the Admiralty up to fifteen, for ten others had been purchased from the fishing industry back in 1935. All were similar in appearance and tonnage in their new role as minor warships, and at the date of the outbreak of the Second World War none was more than seven years old. They were armed with one 4-inch gun and a number of smaller weapons, and each was fitted with depth-charge rails and throwers.

Since all the 'Gems' had been commissioned prior to the outbreak of war they were not manned by the R.N.R. Patrol Service but by Royal Navy ratings and commanded by a Boatswain of the Royal Navy. When hostilities began a young Reserve officer had been added to the compliment.

Early in 1940 the *Moonstone* was operating as one of the units of the 4th Anti-Submarine Group based at Malta. Her sister ships in the Group were the *Beryl*, *Coral* and *Jade*. Subsequently she had been transferred to Alexandria where she was employed on escort duties between that port and Aden. Her captain was Boatswain William Moorman, R.N., and as First Lieutenant he had with him Midshipman Matthew Hunter of the R.N.R. Most of the crew came from the Chatham port division and were what the Navy calls 'general service' ratings.

Already the Italian submarines from Massawa were on the job, although this was not yet known to the naval authorities at Aden. What the latter did know, however, was that the Norwegian tanker *James Stove* had been sunk by torpedo on the 18th June in the vicinity of Aden, and that the Yugo-Slav ship *Drava* had been stopped by gunfire from a submarine in the same area soon after noon on the same day but afterwards allowed to proceed. They had also received a report from one of the fighter pilots attached to the nearby R.A.F. base that he had spotted a U-boat insolently cruising on the surface in the Straits of Bab-el-Mandeb and had gone down to attack her with bombs. Unfortunately his bombs had missed and the submarine had dived.

A thorough sweep of the area was promptly ordered. The destroyer *Kandahar*, the sloop *Shoreham* and three smaller vessels not fitted with asdic were despatched to cruise in an area some twenty-six miles from Aden around the position where the U-boat had last been reported. The idea was to force the vessel to remain submerged while as an inner screen the *Moonstone* would be patrolling in an area from seven to twenty-five miles from the approaches to Aden in case her commander should decide to close the coast.

That night while the six British ships cruised watchfully through the tropic darkness the U-boat quietly surfaced to charge her batteries. Her lookouts carefully scanned the horizon all round, but there was nothing to be seen. Presently she began transmitting by wireless the story of the day's activities to her base at Massawa. But this was a foolish thing to do for, a few miles away, the *Kandahar*'s direction-finding apparatus quickly picked up and pinpointed the transmission. Swiftly the big destroyer began to knife through the phosphorescent water towards the submarine.

But the U-boat commander suddenly became alive to the danger. The morse key in the ship's wireless office fell silent, the crew went to diving stations, the conning-tower hatch was closed down, and the submarine sank once again beneath the quiet waters.

At dawn next day a squadron of Blenheim bombers took off from Aden to search a ninety-by-one-hundred-mile stretch of the Gulf of Aden in the hope of catching the pirate cruising on the surface. But as each plane came back in to land at base the crew shook their heads gloomily. They had nothing to report.

At about half-past eleven in the forenoon of the 19th Able Seaman Tom Brown, who was on duty in the *Moonstone*'s asdic cabinet, reported a strong submarine echo almost dead ahead. Moorman checked on this and at once sounded off Action Stations. Midshipman Hunter, who was also the A/S officer, doubled off to his place by the depth charges. The sun was shining, a light breeze was blowing from the south-west and there was a moderate swell. It was, in fact, a perfect day.

With the crew alert at guns and depth-charge positions the little trawler gradually overhauled her prey who at first appeared to be unaware of the stalking hunter. Steaming hard, the *Moonstone* at length moved into a favourable firing position, and the depth charges were set ready for release. Tense seconds dragged by as the contact passed slowly beneath the trawler's straining hull, then the young midshipman received from the bridge the executive signal for which he had been impatiently waiting. Down flashed his upraised arm in the firing order, and the first pattern left the throwers. All eyes were turned aft to the *Moonstone*'s bubbling wake as the death-laden canisters sank swiftly into the green depths.

Split seconds later the water astern boiled in a furious upsurge, and the tremendous concussion of the exploding depth charges thudded against the trawler's hull plates. As she continued to forge ahead the asdic echo faded and then died altogether. It was obvious to Moorman that during the last few minutes of the trawler's approach the U-boat commander had detected the sound of her throbbing screw and dived deep.

For seemingly endless disappointing minutes Brown heard nothing but maddeningly abortive pings as the asdic's supersonic beam probed vainly in a wide arc about the depths beneath. More than half an hour crawled by, but no one took account of the passage of time in the tropic heat of that June day in the approaches to the Straits of Bab-el-Mandeb. Somewhere beneath the glittering sunlit surface of the sea lurked the slinking shape of a U-boat, and the trawlermen were determined to find and destroy her.

The 4-inch gun was ready loaded, gunlayer and trainer tensed to swing their weapon round in any direction to cover the submarine if it should suddenly surface. All hands scanned the sea with particular keenness for at any moment the bubbling track of a torpedo might come lunging at them.

Then at twenty minutes past noon Brown regained contact. This time the submarine was closer, a bare three hundred yards off and moving away from them. Ordering special settings to be made, Moorman carefully dropped two depth charges with a short interval between them and steamed slowly ahead, scanning the sea around through his binoculars.

Suddenly someone gave an excited yell: 'There she is!' All eyes swivelled aft in the direction of the pointing finger. Half veiled in a mist of fine spray, a dripping conning-tower and whaleback had heaved itself from the depths almost a mile astern.

'Full ahead. Hard a' starboard!' came Moorman's barked commands, and the trawler began to heel over as she swung in a 180-degree turn. Then he leaned over the bridge rail and shouted to the men on the for'ard gun platform: 'Open fire as soon as you bear!'

Through his glasses the Boatswain had time to observe that their quarry was a big ocean-going submarine, and that she mounted two guns, one forward and one aft of the conning-tower. Her nationality stood revealed, too, for from a short pole above the conning-tower there streamed the green, white and red of Fascist Italy.

Already she had opened fire with automatic weapons from her bridge, and Moorman kept his bows towards her so as to present the smallest possible target while leaving his own main armament with a good field of fire. From one of the trawler's bridge wings a staccato hammering began as Leading Signalman Halliday opened up with a Lewis gun, pouring a withering stream of tracers at the enemy.

With eyes glued to their sighting telescopes Petty Officers Quested and Ellis, gunlayer and trainer respectively of the *Moonstone*'s 4-inch gun, had waited impatiently for the submarine's long black hull to swim into their crosswires. Steadily the range closed, and then at last the trawler's big gun spat flame. A column of spray rose and flowered briefly before collapsing back into the sea just beyond the submarine. An over. 'Down 200. Shoot!' Again the trawler's gun banged. Short. 'Up 100. Shoot!' This time her aim was true. The fifth round was another hit, and now the range was almost point blank.

Forward of the trawler's bridge young Matthew Hunter, the R.N.R. midshipman, efficiently organised a supply party

71

so that ammunition for the 4-inch passed from magazine to forecastle in a steady stream. There was a sudden crash as a pom-pom shell from the submarine found its mark somewhere on board the relentlessly advancing trawler. But a swift check-up confirmed that damage was slight and that no casualty had been caused. So far the enemy had not manned their 3.9-inch guns and, this, Moorman determined, they must be prevented from doing. For if they could get those weapons into action they would be able to knock seven bells out of the little *Moonstone*.

He ordered rifles to be got up. Then with the youthful First Lieutenant directing them the spare hands on deck became snipers, positioning themselves behind the trawler's bulwarks. At five hundred yards range they opened a steady and deliberate fire at the hesitant Italians. Over the heads of the riflemen streams of tracer from the Lewis guns converged on the greasy whaleback as the submarine lay wallowing. Only later did Moorman discover that his gunfire had caused the submarine's helm to jam hopelessly. Ignoring the enemy fire Quested and Ellis at the 4-inch laid and trained their weapon with care and deliberation. Their seventh and eighth rounds were also direct hits.

A gout of flame and smoke mushroomed abruptly from the base of the submarine's conning-tower. As it eddied in the light breeze another sprouted above it. A four-inch shell had burst within the constricted area of the steel-walled bridge, killing every man who stood there.

It was this bullseye that heralded the end of the battle. Braving the streams of lead hurled at them by the approaching trawler, a number of the submariners began frantically waving white garments over their heads in token of surrender. Others clambered over the wrecked conning-tower and started to haul down their flag. Unbelievably the action was over, and the *Moonstone* had defeated an opponent three times her own size.

As the trawler surged alongside the submarine, rifles and Lewis guns still trained on the gesticulating Italians in case of treachery, Moorman shouted to them not to make any attempt to scuttle their vessel or he would open fire on them again. But these representatives of Mussolini's Navy had had enough of fighting and were only too embarrassingly ready to scramble aboard the *Moonstone* and demonstrate the fact. But since they outnumbered his own men Moorman was not to anxious to have them in the trawler. Accordingly he sheered off and took up a position some distance away until a bigger vessel which could cope should arrive.

He had not long to wait, for before commencing his first depth-charge attack Boatswain Moorman had informed the *Kandahar* by wireless that he was in contact with the enemy, and the destroyer was steaming at top speed for his position. Soon after the Italians had surrendered the *Kandahar* appeared on the scene and took over. After embarking the prisoners the destroyer commander endeavoured to take the big submarine in tow, but the task was too difficult while the latter's helm was still jammed. The *Kandahar*'s engineer officer and several of his men then boarded the submarine, and after some hard work managed to free the helm and get the engines going. With a prize crew on board the submarine, which was found to be 1,230-ton *Galileo Galilei*, then set out for Aden.

But the little trawler which had fought so bravely was not to be deprived of the full glory of her victory. For, some hours later, spectators in the warships and merchantmen at Aden and the townspeople on shore turned out to cheer a stirring sight. Steaming perkily down the middle of the deep-water channel with her ship's company properly fell in on forecastle and well-deck at their stations for entering harbour came H.M. Trawler *Moonstone*. Following submissively astern of her tiny captor glided the long snaky whaleback of a submarine. On a jury-mast rigged above the battered conning-tower of the U-boat flew two flags. Lowermost was the green, white and red of Italy, and superior to it proudly flaunted the White Ensign.

As had been the custom with vanquished ships in the days of the French and Spanish wars of past centuries the captured submarine was later absorbed into the Royal Navy. At first renamed 'X 2', she later became H.M. Submarine *P.711*.

\*     \*     \*

Meanwhile, with the invasion threatening at home, past history had been revived. Just as Nelson in 1801 had commanded a special squadron of light craft cruising in the Downs for the defence of our coasts against invasion by Napoleon, so in August 1940 a similar flotilla was formed to give early warning of any invasion attempt by Hitler. In addition to powerful forces of cruisers and destroyers held ready to pounce upon the enemy landing craft should they appear, an Auxiliary Patrol was formed from the trawlers and drifters of the Lilliput Fleet together with other small craft hastily requisitioned for the purpose.

Their duty was to patrol in the Channel and North Sea and keep constant watch to seaward, for at Trondheim in Norway and in the Cherbourg area of the French coast the Germans had assembled strong concentrations of barges and merchant vessels. Anti-submarine trawlers and such minesweeping trawlers as could be spared were diverted from their vital duties to join the Auxiliary Patrol. For weeks the little ships maintained the vigilance, while twice daily the Admiralty transmitted to them a special code word, 'Deluge'. 'Deluge 1' signified that the weather was favourable for small-craft operations; 'Deluge 2' that small-craft operations were possible; and 'Deluge 3' that the weather was unsuitable. But until all danger of invasion was officially considered to be past the men of the Auxiliary Patrol maintained their unsleeping watch.

And every night Luftwaffe bombers droned overhead, bringing a fresh load of mines to clog the approaches to Britain's ports. Rosyth, the Tyne, Newhaven, Plymouth, the Bristol Channel, Milford Haven and Liverpool were all at times completely closed to shipping due to enemy minelaying. Recorded Winston Churchill: 'that was a dark and dangerous hour. We were alone and had to face single-handed the full fury of the German attack seeking to strangle our life by cutting off the entry to our ports of the ships which brought us food and the weapons we so sorely needed.'

## CHAPTER VI

## *EUROPA* BECOMES A MOTHER

By February, 1940, all the personnel of the R.N.R. Patrol Service had been mobilised and the majority of skippers and ratings were serving at sea. But Sparrow's Nest at Lowestoft was busier than ever, for 'Hostilities Only' personnel were beginning to stream in. Since entry into the permanent Reserves ended automatically on the outbreak of war conscripts under the National Service (Armed Forces) Act were therefore enrolled in the newly titled R.N. Patrol Service. Fishing skippers called up received the rank of Temporary Skipper, R.N.R. Entry into the Patrol Service for ratings was still confined as far as possible to personnel from the fishing fleet and others with practical experience of small craft.

Since a great many liners had been taken over by the Director of Sea Transport for service as armed merchant cruisers, troopships and landing ships, many of their former chefs and stewards whose jobs had thus disappeared found their way into the Patrol Service. There was a growing demand for both categories. Some early and very welcome arrivals from overseas were a number of Newfoundlanders, tough, hardy and superb small-boat seamen. Then there were men from countries which had been overrun by the Nazis: Poles, Norwegians, Danes, Dutch Belgians and Free French. Most of these were either fishermen or sailors from the merchant marine of their own countries. There was room for a good many of them in the Patrol Service as we shall see later.

The group of officers and men from the general depots who had been sent down to Lowestoft to run the assembly base until the converted ships of the Lilliput Fleet were manned and in service, had become a well-knit team. They were now experts at coping with the special problems and difficulties of fishermen. But once the R.N.R. Patrol Service was mobilised their task, strictly speaking, was at an end. Obviously, however, the Patrol Service would continue to grow both in ships and personnel, and some central establishment to deal with drafting, promotion of officers and advancement of ratings, casualty records and all the usual functions of a port division became an urgent requirement.

To attach Patrol Service personnel arbitrarily to the port divisions at Chatham, Portsmouth and Devonport was out of the question for a variety of reasons. Not least of these was the fact that these three divisions already had their work cut out to deal with the ever increasing flow of H.O. entries into the R.N. general service. The Admiral Commanding Reserves at the Admiralty, who was also considered to be the Flag Officer of the Patrol Service, naturally wished to retain in being the team of officers and men now at Lowestoft, and suggested the creation of a special port division for the Lilliput Fleet. This was agreed to by the Admiralty, but in view of the aerial bombing and the possible threat of invasion where, they asked, could such a depot most conveniently be sited. Shrewsbury was seriously considered as a likely spot and some naval stores were actually despatched there in readiness while the question was still being debated. But it was finally decided that Lowestoft was no more vulnerable than Chatham, Portsmouth and Devonport: it was a fishing port, was conveniently central and the nucleus of a depot staff was already on the spot. Sparrow's Nest was accordingly raised to the status of a port division for the whole of the Lilliput Fleet.

In May, 1940, the new Patrol Service Central Depot, as it was called, was formally commissioned with the ship name *Europa* and Captain Basil Piercy became its first Commodore. For its badge and motto the new depot used the design of the silver M/S-A/S badge, and added a scroll above and below, the upper bearing the name H.M.S. *Europa,* and the lower the words 'R.N. Patrol Service'. The motto, a triumph of aptness in view of the two most important tasks performed by the majority of its ships, was *In Imis Petimus* which translated, means 'We search in the depths (of the sea).'

But a naval port division is more than just a couple of offices containing a number of filing cabinets. It is a large establishment able to provide adequate living and messing accommodation for the thousands of officers and ratings constantly passing through. It boasts capacious administrative buildings to house pay, victualling and drafting offices; it has gunnery, torpedo and seamanship instructional schools; large up-to-date galleys for the preparation of meals, store rooms for provisions, clothing, tobacco and rum; armouries for weapons and ammunition; a canteen, a parade ground for drilling, living accomodation for the Commodore, and other necessary appurtenances.

None of these was present at Lowestoft nor likely to be, since neither money, materials nor labour could be spared for building a barracks that might be bombed flat before it could be completed and in any case would not be required after the war. Faced with the problem of creating all this out of very little Commodore Piercy and his officers began to look round Lowestoft itself.

Sparrow's Nest with its existing buildings and hutments would form the heart and core of the new depot. Here was a parade ground and a grassy 'quarterdeck' from a mast in the centre of which flew the White Ensign. Here were offices already functioning and a certain amount of storage space all centralised on the seashore, fenced in and guarded.

The first and most important requirement was living accommodation for both the permanent and floating population. Fortunately the children of Lowestoft and in some cases whole families had long since been evacuated from what had early been scheduled as a probable danger area. The town contained many small boarding houses and private residences whose owners had made a practice in peacetime of taking in a few summer visitors. Landladies and householders were sounded out and readily expressed their willingness to take in as many sailors as they could accommodate and feed. At the peak period of the war no fewer than 963 of these courageous women braved the twenty thousand

77

bombs which were showered on Lowestoft to feed and billet in far greater comfort than they might otherwise have enjoyed the men of the Patrol Service in their brief spells ashore between ships. Each week the Paymaster at Sparrow's Nest paid out thousands of pounds in billeting allowances to the landladies of Lowestoft. But it was worth every penny.

Skippers under training or awaiting appointments as well as the depot staff officers were accommodated in a number of small hotels along the front. Their main mess was set up in a large house called Briar Clyffe.

As a training centre for seamanship, anti-submarine and gunnery the Oval cricket ground was taken over and hutted accommodation erected on the sacred turf. Newly entered Skippers received their initial training in a similar though smaller instruction establishment set up on the municipal bowling greens. Both were conveniently close to Sparrow's Nest.

The Patrol Service Central Depot could find plenty of use for the Lowestoft schools which were standing idle and empty. One at St John's Road became a navigational training establishment for Skippers and Second Hands. To ensure the steady promotion of officers and ratings whose normal Board of Trade examination for fishing certificates had been interrupted by the war the curriculum was drawn up to Board of Trade (now Ministry of War Transport) requirements. Periodical examinations were held under the aegis of the Ministry and certificates awarded. Since many petty officers were required to take command of various miscellaneous small craft a special Patrol Service rating of 'Second Hand (Small Craft Only)' was created. Whenever possible these uncertificated Second Hands were given the opportunity to take courses and sit examinations for their 'tickets' at the Patrol Service Navigational School.

New entries were flooding into Lowestoft, some 22,900 joining by the end of 1940. More accommodation was required and the Roman Hill Council School was taken over as a barracks. St Nicholas Orphanage became the depot Sick Quarters, while St Luke's Hospital, a large building on the sea front, was turned into a self-contained engineering barracks. Workshops and a training centre for Patrol Service enginemen and stokers were established out at Oulton Broad. Here hundreds of trawler enginemen who in peacetime had been accustomed to leave such details as boiler cleaning and other maintenance work to shore staffs when their ships returned from the fishing grounds learned to run and maintain their department at sea efficiently under all conditions of service. Not least of the considerable achievements of the naval engineer officer in charge of this establishment was the preparation and printing of a Patrol Service engineering manual specially devoted to the care and maintenance of the machinery of a small ship which, with the approval of the Admiralty, became the engineman's *vade mecum* in every vessel of the Patrol Service.

The Patrol Service Central Depot also produced another wartime wonder – a naval cookery school entirely run and staffed by civilian women. The majority of trawler cooks in the fishing industry are men aged between fifty and sixty. Since a sailor floats on his belly just as much as a soldier marches on his and a well-fed mariner is a contented one, the trawler cook is required to be an expert at his job and is paid accordingly. Thus in addition to the standard wage of a qualified deckhand he also receives a substantial bonus on the catch.

When the trawlers due for requisitioning from the fishing industry were taken up by the Admiralty on the outbreak of war most of the trawler cooks serving in them were, of course, over the age for call-up. Furthermore, the rate of pay laid down for the Patrol Service cook was too low to attract those individuals – most of them married men with families – who might otherwise have volunteered to serve. In consequence the vacancies for cook had to be filled by young conscripts who either volunteered to serve as trawler cooks or were drafted willy nilly to sea as such. Not only had most of them very little notion of cooking at all, but in anything of a seaway were completely flaked out and useless.

This was a very serious state of affairs, for if a trawler cook cannot do his job the crew cannot eat. So grave in fact did the situation become at one time that Captain Creasy, then Director of Anti-Submarine Warfare at the Admiralty, informed the Board unequivocally that if remedial action was not promptly taken all his anti-submarine trawlers would be out of action due to starvation!

Arrangements were thereupon made for numbers of Patrol Service cooks to be sent to the general naval depots for training under the experienced Chief Cooks in the big modern galleys at those establishments. But this was soon found to be of little use. The barracks staffs were far too busy coping with their own routine work to spare the time to teach green youngsters anything more about the culinary arts than how to peel potatoes. Furthermore, cookery classes held in the spacious well-equipped electric galleys in the depot could not hope to transform ham-fisted amateurs into expert small-ship chefs capable of producing varied and appetising meals on a two-by-four coal-fired range in the tiny galley of the average trawler whose unpredictable motion at sea necessitates the most skilful juggling of pots and pans.

It was at this psychological moment that Miss Grace Musson appeared on the scene like an angel from Heaven. Peacetime Head of Lowestoft Technical College, this grey-haired, twinkling-eyed expert suggested to Commodore Piercy the establishment at Lowestoft of a cookery school for his men. Piercy jumped at the idea and without bothering to obtain higher approval authorised her to go ahead. The good results were soon apparent and subsequently with Admiralty blessing the Lowestoft Church Road School was requisitioned to become the R.N. Patrol Service Cookery School.

Miss Musson gathered about her eleven domestic science teachers as instructresses, and a number of coal-fired ranges as used in the average fishing trawler were installed in the classrooms. Each stove was sited in a small compartment no larger than the galley of a trawler and upon it the pupils were required to prepare and cook a complete daily set of meals under conditions which almost exactly simulated those they would find at sea, with the exception, of course, of the motion of the vessel in a seaway.

Courses lasting five weeks were instituted, the embryo cooks being accommodated in the school while under instruction and being required to eat what they cooked! Miss Musson and her band of ladies worked miracles with their unpromising material. They ran their establishment with the smooth efficiency of an assembly line in a factory. At one end of the factory there entered young men to the number of 160 at a time, many of whom had never in their lives before even boiled an egg. At the other there emerged trained cooks whose culinary creations could bear comparision with the products of the most highly trained hotel chef.

New entries joining the Patrol Service Central Depot underwent courses of instruction in naval routine and discipline, hygiene, seamanship, and a certain amount of square-bashing, followed by short courses in mine-sweeping and the use of depth charges. Later the depot instituted its own gunnery school wherein were trained selected men for special non-substantive ratings of Patrol Service Seamen Gunner, Small Vessel Gunlayer, and Anti-Aircraft Gunner Third Class.

Meanwhile on the Service Certificates of the men of the Lilliput Fleet, wherever their ships were serving, the letter 'L' for Lowestoft was added to the official numbers, just as for general service ratings of the Royal Navy the letter 'C', 'P' or 'D' indicated a man's home port. For the officers and men of the Patrol Service now had their own depot which would draft them to and from ships, arrange for their promotion and advancement, look after their general welfare, and inform their next of kin if anything untoward should happen to them. Not only had *Europa* joined the Navy: she had also become a mother with a vast and widely scattered brood.

\*   \*   \*

All through the sun-drenched summer of 1940, one of the finest for weather on record, Luftwaffe bombers with fighter escorts smashed at our coastal convoys. Other German aircraft hammered away at ports around the coast. Attacks on the little minesweepers became so fierce and concentrated that in order to conserve losses the Admiralty was compelled to order the routine daylight sweeps to be abandoned between the Thames Estuary and Beachy Head. Minesweepers were ordered to sweep ahead of convoys in that area only at night. Such of the Navy's heavy units as were still in the dockyards at Portsmouth and Plymouth were hastily moved up north out of harm's way.

Day after day the bombs rained down unceasingly on Dover, Skegness, Portland, Devonport, Southampton, Ramsgate, Cardiff, Portsmouth, Wrabness and the London Docks. On one blazing August day the whole of Dover's twenty-three barrage balloons were shot out of the sky by the darting German fighters. Scarcely had a second batch been hauled up than twelve of them were sent crumpling to the ground in flames under a hail of incendiary bullets.

And the mining of ports went on continuously. From the Kyles of Bute to Avonmouth and from Fowey to Sunderland the minesweepers laboured to keep open the vital channels through which we received our sustenance. As in World War I enemy minelayers were out ranging the oceans, for mines were reported off Cape Agulhas in the South Atlantic, off Egypt and the Libyan coast and in the Suez Canal. In consequence the Commander-in-Chief, Mediterranean, asked for minesweeping trawlers to be sent out to him.

In this furious phase of the war with the Battle of Britain to follow, thirty-four ships of the hard-pressed Lilliput Fleet were sunk by mine and bomb. Among them were the *Cape Finisterre* which, when overwhelmed off Harwich by four enemy aircraft, took one of them with her to the bottom and sent the others reeling home damaged; off Dover the anti-submarine trawler *Kingston Galena* and the minesweeping trawlers *Rodina* and *Fleming*; in London docks the minesweeping trawler *Abronia* and off the Nore two of her sisters, the *Tamarisk* and *Pyrope*; at Falmouth the *Resparko*.

Now, too, began the long-drawn-out battle of the Atlantic with the growing development of the notorious U-boat wolf-pack tactics. In August twenty anti-submarine trawlers were withdrawn from their duties on the Northern Patrol and based at Belfast for convoy escort work. Ocean convoys were now ordered by the Commander-in-Chief, Western Approaches, to be accompanied by escort groups comprising two destroyers two sloops or corvettes and two trawlers.

\* \* \*

In the accounts already published about the Battle of the Atlantic and the long struggle against the U-boats, attention is not unnaturally focused more upon famous destroyer captains and the dashing individuals who later commanded the fast, well-equipped ships of the specially formed submarine-hunting groups, such as Walker of Western Approaches. Little of the limelight falls upon the anti-submarine trawlers of the R.N. Patrol Service.

Yet these humble, unglamorous little ships with their slow speed, limited armament and comparatively untrained crews were to prove just as much of a headache to the Nazi U-boat fleet as their bigger sisters in the Navy's general service. One of the first units of the Lilliput Fleet to make her mark in this respect was the A/S trawler *Visenda*.

This little ship had begun her fishing career in 1937, having been built by Messrs. Cook, Welton and Gemmell for the Atlas Steam Trawler Company of Grimsby. She displaced 455 tons, measured 175 feet overall from her trim cruiser stern to her high bluff stem, and swelled out amidships to a 27-foot beam. Taken over by the Navy at the beginning of the war, she had been armed and fitted for her new job as an anti-submarine trawler and attached to the Orkneys and Shetlands Command for duty as an armed boarding and escort vessel. She operated from Kirkwall and her normal beat lay between that port and Reykjavik in Iceland. In command was Lieutenant Ralph Winder, R.N.R., and her crew hailed from the Patrol Service Central Depot.

On Sunday, the 23rd of March, 1941, the *Visenda* was at sea about one hundred and fifty miles south-east of Iceland. The time was five minutes to eight in the morning watch and the little trawler was going flat out trying to overtake and identify a mystery merchantman, which was also steaming away at the full extent of her boiler power.

The signalman on the bridge of the *Visenda* who had

been flashing the merchantman on his 10-inch signalling lamp had at last managed to establish that the shyly retiring stranger was in fact the Belgian s.s. *Ville de Liege* when some four miles distant the sinister shape of a U-boat heaved itself out of the grey depths a bare rifle shot away from the hurrying Belgian. Winder at once sounded off action stations, and the *Visenda*'s signal lamp began blinking in urgent warning to the *Ville de Liege*. But the master of the merchantman had also spotted the menace which had unexpectedly bobbed up on his beam, and a sudden plume of inky smoke from her funnel testified to the renewed efforts of the black squad in the depths of her stokehold.

After a leisurely look round the submarine quietly sank beneath the waves again. Doubtless Kapitänleutnant Robert Schrott, commanding the 740-ton *U.551*, had decided he could ignore the ridiculous little trawler bouncing over the waves in the far distance and follow up the *Ville de Liege* to put a torpedo into her at his leisure.

But Lieutenant Winder and his trawlermen were about to prove to Admiral Doenitz that a British minor war vessel was just as efficient at its job as any of the more impressive-looking units of the Royal Navy. At ten minutes past eight, with Sunday morning breakfast forgotten, the *Visenda*'s asdic operator obtained his first contact with the submerged U-boat. Weather conditions were good for the time of year; there was a slight breeze blowing and a smooth sea undulated to a slow swell. Depth charges were set and, with all hands almost visibly quivering with anticipation like terriers approaching a promising rat hole, the trawler finally reached the position of the lurking U-boat.

As she steamed over the spot the *Visenda* let go her first pattern of depth charges. These were set to explode at depths of 250 feet, 350 feet and 500 feet respectively. If the submarine were suspended within that particular body of water when they exploded her crew would fervently wish themselves elsewhere. A moment later there sounded from the depths the tremendous thudding of the bursting explosives.

For five minutes – six minutes – eight minutes the trawler

steamed slowly ahead. Then, floating silently to the surface, came a single large air bubble. The *Visenda* swung round toward this odd marker and another pattern of depth charges was ordered to be made ready. But, not unnaturally, the depth-charge crew had become excited and over-anxious and they made mistakes in the settings, mistakes which squandered valuable moments of time in rectifying. When at last the charges were ready contact with the U-boat had been lost.

For fifteen minutes the trawler cruised around, her asdic beam combing the chilly depths like a blind man groping for an eel in a vast tank of water, for the sea in these northern latitudes is more than a thousand fathoms deep. The minutes continued to tick by with the monotonous tinny pinging of the asdic seeming to mock the tensely waiting trawlermen. Then suddenly came the echo of a contact. The tenuous thread of a mechanically projected supersonic impulse had again linked the stubby little ex-fishing trawler with the long sleek hull of *U.551*, a thread that Kapitän-leutnant Schrott sought irritably to break. If he could put sufficient distance between the two vessels he could surface and with his guns destroy this under-sized nuisance.

At 9 a.m., when buglers on board British warships in harbour would be sounding the call to summon ships' companies to Divisions and Prayers, another pattern of death sailed overside from the stern of the trawler *Visenda* fighting a duel of wits somewhere in the North Atlantic. This time Winder had ordered shallower settings, for the quality of the asdic echoes told him that the U-boat had not dived deep but was turning and twisting below them as it sought to throw off the pursuer.

Fanned out in diamond-shaped formation the canisters of high explosive detonated at depths of one hundred and fifty feet down to three hundred and fifty feet, the intense pressure waves thus set up reaching out like a giant hand to squeeze and crush the fragile hull plating of the U-boat. A few minutes later Winder ordered another carefully set pattern of depth charges to be fired. But now, maddeningly, the port thrower jammed; then one of the charges on the the rails stuck, and the *Visenda* steamed impotently over the spot where, her asdic indicated, the foe was probably suspended between surface and sea bed. Then again the thread snapped and she lost contact.

Ideally, success in U-boat killing by depth-charge attack requires at least two high-speed vessels nimble on the turn, one to hold the submarine in her asdic beam while her consort runs in and bombs, then for the process to be reversed, and finally for both to criss-cross the position in a final drenching. But on this March Sunday in the grey wastes of the North Atlantic one lone trawler had to rely on her own efforts and clawed determinedly at her unseen and slippery quarry like a puppy trying to unearth an elusive bone. Up, down and across a chosen area she steamed for twenty weary minutes. Then, blessedly, echoes replaced the steady pinging.

Closely following the asdic recorder trace, which indicates as a series of indelible marks on sensitised paper the movements of a submerged vessel in relation to the tracking craft above, the trawler began again to close in on her opponent. But a few more minutes of life were still to be granted to Schrott and his men, for without warning the *Visenda*'s asdic recorder pen jammed. Once more the trawler blundered blindfolded while the sweating operator worked to clear the fouled mechanism.

At twenty-five minutes to ten the *Visenda* established the final link with her enemy which would ensure that *U.551* would never destroy another innocent merchantman. The new contact detected the submarine manoeuvring close astern of the trawler. As swiftly as her helm would answer the *Visenda* wheeled in a one hundred-and-eighty degree turn and steamed in for the kill. A few minutes later she fired her third pattern of depth charges. Sinking to 250 feet, 350 feet and 500 feet, the pattern finally exploded, and above them the surface of the sea boiled in titanic convulsion.

Inside U.551 the crew were sprawled in semi-darkness, for most of the light bulbs had been shattered by the concussion of the *Visenda*'s earlier charges; seawater was spouting in from half a dozen different leaks in the weakened pressure hull; the air was so suffocatingly thick with dust and fumes that their brains reeled. Then came the third stunning pattern of explosions, and the steel walls about them heaved violently, then split open to admit a solid weight of water, smashing, engulfing, bearing them inexorably down to eternal darkness.

For seven minutes by Winder's watch after he had made the third attack the lieutenant and his men scanned the sea all around. Then from the shattered hull of *U.551* far below on the icy blackness of the sea bed, and unresponsive now to the trawlers asdic, there began to ascend a slow procession of air bubbles. One by one they floated to the surface, glistened momentarily in the daylight, then softly and soundlessly disintegrated.

But still the *Visenda* lay stopped, her asdic rhythmically pinging and her crew at their action stations. Winder was waiting for evidence, solid irrefutable evidence that a U-boat had been destroyed. For no longer were what had at one time been regarded as the normal traces of a U-boat kill considered sufficient for the keen-eyed committee of experts at the Admiralty. The Nazis were wily birds. They knew that a few air bubbles, a couple of gouts of diesel oil and perhaps a sailor's cap and some bits of wood released from a torpedo tube could fool the unwary into the belief that a depth-charge attack had been successful. Stronger proof was now required.

But there was no one alive in *U.551* to put the watchful *Visenda* off the track. As she lay gently heaving in the swell the evidence Winder sought began to appear. After an hour the sea around the trawler was covered with the involuntary offerings of the torn and twisted hull lying fathoms beneath. The *Visenda* lowered her boat and began to salve the wreckage.

When the crew's grisly catch was laid out on deck it was thoroughly inspected and carefully listed. There was a splintered plywood door with Gothic German characters painted on it; three mattresses; a sheepskin watchcoat; some cushions; a book; a number of blankets; clothing, pants, vests, socks, bodybelts, uniform collars, gloves, handkerchiefs, knitted balaclava helmets, and – even more macabre but more revealing than the rest – a human heart and some bloody portions of a man's lungs. Later when the *Visenda* reached base naval doctors would testify from their examination of the bottled viscera that the men from whom it had been torn had died as a result of the shattering blows administered by the trawler's depth charges.

When, four hours afterwards, the *Visenda* finally sailed for Kirkwall vast oil patches slicked the sea in position 62 degrees, 37 minutes North Latitude, 16 degrees 47 minutes West Longitude; while from the depths below huge air bubbles were still rising and bursting, gently, soundlessly.

## CHAPTER VII

## 'WE WERE BIGGER THAN YOU . . . '

THROUGHOUT the early months of 1941 the Libyan campaign swayed back and forth, and April found the British Army of the Nile forced to retreat to the Egyptian border. But they still held Tobruk, which remained under siege for 242 days.

A large number of trawlers, both minesweepers and anti-submarine vessels, had by now joined the Mediterranean Fleet. Among them were three Norwegian-manned whalers which formed the 168th Norwegian Minesweeping Group; they were the *Noble Nora, Transvaalia* and *Egeland*, which had been sailed round from Durban, their peacetime operating port. Three more 300-ton whalecatchers manned by S.A.N.F. personnel, the *Southern Maid, Southern Isle* and *Southern Sea,* also joined up with the Mediterranean section of the Lilliput Fleet, forming the 22nd South African A/S Group. During the Tobruk siege the trawlers, whalers, water carriers, and even sailing schooners which comprised a large part of the Inshore Squadron supplied the besieged garrison with 72 tanks, 92 guns, 33,946 tons of stores and 108 sheep. They also landed a total of 34,113 troops and embarked 32,667, evacuated 7,516 wounded and more than 7,000 Axis prisoners.

But persistent enemy minelaying and the massive daily air attacks took severe toll of the little ships. The minesweeping trawler *Stoke City* was a casualty, and the A/S trawler *Sindonis.* The whaler *Southern Isle* and the sloop *Flamingo* on one occasion together fought off no fewer than sixty dive-bombers, bringing down two Junkers apiece.

Across the water from Africa, Malta was for a time completely mined in, with almost all the minesweepers stationed in the beleaguered island sunk by bombing. But the little ships that survived carried on undismayed. There was for example the 4th A/S-M/S Group. With the drifters *Lady Margaret* and *Ploughboy,* this Group comprised at the time the trawlers *Beryl, Coral* and *Jade.* The *Moonstone* which had originally formed one of the unit had, as we have seen, been transferred earlier on to work from Alexandria. Of the three 'Gem' class trawlers remaining in the George Cross island the *Beryl* was eventually to be dubbed by the admiring population 'the flagship of Malta'. For she alone of the Group served throughout the entire siege and survived the long-drawn-out blitzes.

The *Beryl,* at one time the Hull trawler *Lady Adelaide* owned by Jutland Amalgamated Trawlers Ltd, had been built in 1934 and purchased by the Navy in the following year. After her transformation into a minor warship her displacement had been increased to 615 tons, she was equipped with asdic and minesweeping gear, armed with a 4-inch gun and several smaller weapons and could steam at twelve knots.

Like other 'Gems' acquired from the fishing industry before the war the *Beryl* was not manned by a Patrol Service crew, but by general servicemen of the Royal Navy, and in 1941 she was commanded by Boatswain Victor Rhind. Her first lieutenant was Sub-Lieutenant G. J. Allen, R.N.V.R., who hailed from Cricklewood.

Scarred by bomb fragments, bullets and shell splinters, the *Beryl* carried out the most hazardous rescue work on bombed and torpedoed ships struggling to get through to Malta. She dodged bombs, beat off air attacks and frustrated E-boats; she carried out anti-submarine patrols and helped to sweep up the hundreds of mines strewn by the enemy around the island. One of her most nerve-racking tasks was to wait at a buoy outside the harbour after dark to meet and lead in through the war channel the fast minelayer which periodically made a lone dash to convey vitally needed stores and supplies to Malta.

The *Jade,* too, distinguished herself before she was finally overwhelmed by a hail of bombs in 1942, and not least in her lone battle with E-boats off Cape Passero in Sicily.

Purchased in 1939, the *Jade* had started her fishing career in 1933 as one of the ten 'ladies' owned by Jutland Amalgamated Trawlers Ltd., of Hull, for she had originally been christened *Lady Lilian*. Most of her crew came from the Chatham Port Division, and she was commanded by Boatswain William Fellowes, R.N. He had as his first lieutenant Midshipman J. C. Creasy of the R.N.R., while on board for a period of training was another young R.N.R. officer, Sub-Lieutenant J. A. Jones.

It is a measure of the valour characteristic of all the tiny units of the Lilliput Fleet that in carrying out a sweep in search of a missing Hurricane pilot from Malta the captain of the *Jade* did not hesitate to pursue his search almost to within shouting distance of the Sicilian coast. By the cold white light of the moon in the early dawn of a June morning the *Jade* discovered, not the missing airman in his rubber dinghy she was seeking, but two powerful patrolling E-boats.

Trawler and enemy craft challenged together, but the trawler was first off the mark with her 4-inch. Tactically she was in the worst position since her stubby hull was silhouetted to seaward against the moon, while the E-boats had as their background the shadowy coastline of Sicily. The first burst of enemy fire mortally wounded the *Jade*'s youthful First Lieutenant, but with her third round of 4-inch the fighting trawler scored a direct hit on the stern of the larger of the two E-boats, a craft more than a hundred feet long, which jerked her bodily upwards out of the water. Thereafter this boat took little further interest in events. Until that happened Boatswain Fellowes had duelled skilfully with his swifter opponents, hauling the trawler round on her tail to comb the tracks of the torpedoes they loosed at him in their darting thrusts, yet maintaining the best field of fire for his heaviest weapon. For half an hour the battle raged at no more than four hundred yards range. But after two rounds from the *Jade*'s 4-inch had near-missed the remaining E-boat which continued the combat after its consort had been hit, the enemy broke off and retired. At her maximum speed of nine and a half knots the victorious trawler returned to Malta.

Midshipman Creasy died on the way back to harbour, but

his death was subsequently avenged by the R.A.F. For, a few days later, a flotilla of E-boats escorted by Macchi 200s made a determined attack on Malta's Grand Harbour. Hurricanes of No. 185 Squadron swooped on this combined sea and air assault and destroyed four of the E-boats; the remainder fled. During the action a Hurricane piloted by Pilot Officer Winton had raked one of the E-boats with machine-gun fire, but his own aircraft had been damaged and he was forced to bale out. He swam to the E-boat he had attacked and climbed aboard, pistol in hand. But on the decks lay only dead men, victims of his own marksmanship. Determined to salve his capture he went below and tried to start up the engines. But the Navy had been keeping a close eye on affairs. Out from Malta steamed the trawler *Jade*, which came along side the damaged E-boat, put a line aboard, and towed the enemy vessel and its R.A.F. captor into habour.

*     *     *

While the *Beryl* and *Jade* and their consorts in the George Cross island and the hard-pressed ships of the Inshore Squadron were earning undying glory in their own embattled areas, elsewhere in the Mediterranean other units of the Lilliput Fleet were also in the forefront of unpleasant events. For, closely following on the evacuation of our troops from Greece the nearby island of Crete was threatened with invasion by the Nazis. Allocated to the Naval Officer in Charge at Suda Bay for patrol duties were seven little ships, five of them belonging to the Patrol Service. They were the *Moonstone, Salvia, Syvern, Kos 21* and *Kos 23* and the tiny 103-ton ex-Lowestoft trawler *Lanner*, the latter commanded by Skipper William Stewart of the R.N.R., with a Maltese crew. The seventh was the sloop *Derby*, later relieved by the sloop *Widnes*.

Their main task was to guard the entrance to Suda Bay by day and night. But when not actually on patrol these little ships were kept busy on other important jobs. They escorted lighters carrying stores and guns, they carried out ferry duties in the harbour, supplied water for fire-fighting in bombed merchantmen, and steam for working the winches of disabled ships. All this under day-long bombing and machine-gunning as the Germans softened up the island prior to assault.

So fierce and concentrated did the air attacks on the little ships become that to conserve losses the N.O.I.C.' ordered their crews to lie up in caves during the day and patrol their beat only at night. A brief account of the experiences of the whaler *Syvern* will give an idea of the nerve-shattering conditions endured by those units of the Lilliput Fleet which served so gallantly in Crete.

H.M.S. *Syvern* was a whalecatcher of 300 tons, built in 1937 by Framnaes Mek Verks of Sandefjord, in Norway, and she had been Norwegian owned. She was a sturdily built little craft, 125 feet long with a beam of 25 feet, and her engines were oil-fuel powered. As her main armament she had a seventy-five millimetre gun mounted in place of her peacetime whale gun, and a number of machine guns. In command was Lieut.-Commander R. E. Clarke, R.N.R., who was also Senior Officer of the 16th A/S Group (Whalers).

On April 23rd the *Syvern*, steadfastly patrolling her hazardous beat at the harbour entrance, underwent a shattering attack by a concentration of Ju. 87s. Again and again the dive-bombers snarled down on the twisting, turning whaler, spraying her with bullets and cannon-shells as, miraculously, she managed to dodge the bombs hurled at her. When the baffled Stukas finally zoomed away the bullet-scarred vessel limped back to her cave berth with many of her crew dead or wounded, among the latter Commander Clarke with a bullet in the stomach. Due to this wound he was later forced to hand over his command to Lieutenant A. R. Tilston, R.N.R.

A few days afterwards the little *Syvern* was again singled out as the target of several squadrons of Ju.88s. From a height of only 700 feet the Nazis tore in to try to blast the defiant little ship out of the water. But their fiercely concentrated assault brought about only the self destruction of one of their own pilots. As the Junkers dived on her with blazing guns, an enemy bullet smashed into the whaler's 75 mm. ammunition locker. One of the shells promptly burst, showering the dive-bomber with flying fragments. The pilot lost control of his machine, which scythed through the *Syvern*'s foremast, crashed into the sea and disintegrated. Crawling in to land her dead and wounded, the whaler, which presented a terrible sight with her bridge and upperworks a shambles, was again murderously attacked by a number of Ju. 87s. The casualties in her crew, which amounted to more than fifty per cent, were later made up with men from the *Widnes* and *Kos 23*, both of which had been beached after being badly damaged by bombs.

On May 26th orders were received for the final military evacuation of Crete. The little ships which had survived were instructed to make for Alexandria if they could; otherwise they were to be destroyed and the crews to make their way on foot to Sphakia from whence they might hope to be evacuated. In company with the *Kos 22*, which had earlier relieved the *Moonstone*, the gallant little *Syvern* set off at dawn on the 27th. During daylight both ships lay up close inshore. But at dusk they were discovered by prowling dive-bombers who joyfully swooped to the attack. For seventy-five minutes the vessels fought back, but finally they were overwhelmed. First the *Kos 22* was hit and set ablaze, then the *Syvern*. An hour later, with her ensign still flying, the whaler blew up. In good order her survivors marched overland to Sphakia.

\* \* \*

At home minelaying by the Luftwaffe continued on an intensive scale. In a week 140 German bombers strewed the Humber alone with more than 200 mines. Casualties to the little ships combating the menace were severe. Nevertheless the Admiralty were able to announce that:

'In spite of heavy and continual minelaying by the enemy our ports and harbours are being kept open. This great success is due to the sustained gallantry and devotion to duty of the officers and men of our minesweepers.'

And in waters outside these islands the trawler *Lady Shirley* added lustre to the daily deeds of the Lilliput Fleet.

\* \* \*

If an astrologer had told Arthur Callaway on the day he joined the Royal Australian Naval Volunteer Reserve at Rushcutter Naval Depot in Sydney that by his action he had ensured that a German named Wilhelm Kleinschmidt would never marry the girl of his choice he would have hooted with laughter.

'Wilhelm who?' he might have asked. 'You're way off track, cobber. I've never even heard of him.'

Yet the stars were right. For although the two men remained unaware of each other's existence and never met face to face, their encounter with its fateful consequences was indeed destined to take place due to Callaway's action, under circumstances of which at that time neither he nor Kleinschmidt ever dreamed.

A keen amateur yachtsman, like so many of his countrymen, Callaway was more than half a sailor when he joined the Reserve and soon qualified for promotion. Early in 1939 he took a course in submarine detection since there was a growing need for specialists in that branch of the naval service. In June he jubilantly shipped the extra half stripe of a lieutenant-commander, with the letters 'A/S' appearing after his name in the Navy List. Three months later Britain and the Commonwealth were at war with Nazi Germany.

One of the most urgent requirements of the Royal Navy in those early days of the war was for officers with the A/S specialist quailification to serve afloat in destroyers and other escort ships needed to shepherd our convoys. The Dominion Navies and their Reserves were requested by the Admiralty to send all available A/S-trained officers to this country. Among those from Australia, after he had undergone a short refresher course at Rushcutter, came Lieutenant-Commander Callaway.

Soon after his arrival in England he was appointed to a command of his own. With him as first lieutenant went another Australian Naval Volunteer Reservist like himself, Lieutenant Ian Boucaut, also an A/S specialist.

At first sight of her Callaway was by no means enamoured of his new ship. She was not the dashing destroyer or brand-new corvette he had hoped for: merely a stubby little ex-fishing vessel. She was in fact H.M. Trawler *Lady Shirley*, in her own way also a volunteer for service with the Navy. She was young in years, having been built and launched as recently as 1937 by Cook, Welton and Gemmell for Jutland Amalgamated Trawlers of Hull. Lloyds Register gave her peacetime tonnage as 472 gross, she had a cruiser stern, a beam of 27 feet and measured 163 feet overall.

To transform her into a warship she had been given a 4-inch gun mounted on the forecastle, a brace of .5-inch machine-guns and a couple of Hotchkiss. Her anti-submarine equipment comprised an asdic set, and the customary depth-charge rails and throwers aft. Except for Signalman Warbrick, a general service man, her crew hailed from the Patrol Service Central Depot and were all trawlermen. Somewhat unusually, her coxswain, William Mackrill, with five years' peacetime service in the R.N.R. Patrol Service to his credit, held the important non-substantive rate of Higher Submarine Detector. He was thus probably the busiest man on board, for the coxswain of a Patrol Service vessel combined the duties of the Chief Boatswain's Mate, Master-at-Arms, Captain of the Hold and Supply Petty Officer. Mackrill was also a very good asdic rating, both in operating and maintenance.

By September, 1941, the requirements of higher strategy, as directed through the medium of the Operations Division at the Admiralty, had allocated the trawler *Lady Shirley* as a unit of the 31st A/S Group attached to the North Atlantic Command with her base at Gibraltar. Her operational beat for patrol and escort duties lay between Gibraltar and the Canary Islands. The area was a very important one, for with the Azores to the west it formed a sea gateway through which funnelled all our convoys to and from the Cape and beyond. The Germans were well aware of its importance and this sector of the North Atlantic became a happy hunting ground for U-boats. To it in due course came *U.111*.

Built at the Deschmag Yard in Bremen in 1940 and commissioned at Kiel just before the end of that year, *U.111* was a 740-ton submarine of the class known at Type IX.A. She was commanded by thirty-four-year-old Kapitänleutnant

Wilhelm Kleinschmidt, a native of Oldenburg in Schleswig-Holstein, who, with unconscious irony, had chosen for his boat's distinguishing symbol a black heart. As was customary in the Nazi U-boat fleet this symbol was painted on the vessel's conning-tower.

Kleinschmidt was somewhat over the age for the normal run of U-boat commanders, but he was, an experienced seaman who could boast seven years' service in the merchant marine, duly recognised when he joined Hitler's Navy by the grant of two years' seniority over the rest of his class. A torpedo specialist, he had served in E-boats, in the cruiser *Konigsberg* until she was sunk in Norway by dive-bombers of the British Fleet Air Arm, and subsequently as torpedo officer of the cruiser *Nurnberg*. He volunteered for the U-boat service in 1940.

On his first trip in command of *U.111* Kleinschmidt had sunk 20,000 tons of Allied shipping. His second tour of operations had taken him as far as the South Atlantic, but he had netted only two ships for his trouble, one Dutch and one British. This lack of success was irritating for, sailing with him on this cruise to gain experience prior to taking over command of a U-boat of his own, was an officer senior to himself, Commander Hans Joachim Heinecke. Heinecke was the same age as Kleinschmidt but had joined the Navy after him and qualified as a gunnery specialist. He was also an old shipmate for he, too, had been serving in the cruiser *Konigsberg* when she was sunk.

Towards the end of September *U.111* was on her way back to La Rochelle, her base in the Bay of Biscay. Kleinschmidt was looking forward to their return even more than his crew, for he was engaged to be married and the nuptials were due to take place during his forthcoming leave. Heading northwards towards the Canary Islands he was somewhat annoyed to receive a signal from U-boat Headquarters ordering him to rendezvous with *U.68* just south of the islands and transfer to her his unexpended torpedoes.

Kleinschmidt decided to risk not carrying out this order to the absolute letter. After all, on the trip from the Canaries to La Rochelle he hoped to be presented with the opportunity to add to his rather meagre total of enemy

7                    97

tonnage sunk, and it would be infuriating to encounter a perfect target with no torpedoes in the tubes. Avoiding collision by a hairsbreath with the patrolling British submarine *Clyde*, which unexpectedly popped up near him, he kept the appointment with *U.68* and duly transferred to her some of his remaining torpedoes. When the two submarines finally cast off from each other *U.111* resumed her voyage to La Rochelle.

While this U-boat activity was going on the trawler *Lady Shirley* had accompanied a consort, the *Erin* of the 7th A/S Group, as anti-submarine screen for the ocean boarding vessel *Maron* on a voyage from Gibraltar to the Canary Islands. On September 29th the *Lady Shirley* was ordered by the senior naval officer in the *Maron* to rendezvous with the Free French sloop *Commandant Dubac*, which was towing the s.s. *Silverbelle* to Las Palmas, and lend a hand. The trawler duly reached the rendezvous some 300 miles west-south-west of Teneriffe on October 1st and commenced a regular sweep to east and west of the position in search of the sloop and her charge.

At twenty minutes to nine on the morning of Saturday, October 4th, the lookout in the crow's nest of the *Lady Shirley* reported an object away on the starboard bow. Lieutenant Boucaut, the officer of the watch, could see nothing of this from his little compass platform above the wheelhouse. Thinking that the object might be either the *Commandant Dubac* or the *Silverbelle,* he climbed up to the crow's nest to have a look for himself. There was certainly something low down on the horizon and it might well be a merchant ship's funnel refracted from beyond the horizon, he thought. He dropped down again to the bridge and through the communicating voicepipe called the captain.

Callaway was soon up there beside him carefully studying through his binoculars the object Boucaut had indicated.

'You may be right,' he told the first lieutenant finally, 'but that could be a submarine's conning-tower. We'll go and have a look.'

The *Lady Shirley*, then on the westerly leg of her search course, swung her bluff bows round to the northward and increased speed. In his cabinet the asdic operator started the recorder motor. Only the day before this vital piece of equipment had developed a defect, but by working flat out in his own time Coxswain Mackrill had managed to repair it.

Soon after the trawler's alteration of course the mysterious object disappeared, but the *Lady Shirley* held on her way, asdic beam busily probing the depths around her. Then at four minutes past ten the operator excitedly reported a contact off their port bow and distant less than a mile. Callaway promptly pressed the alarm button for Action Stations and took over operation of the asdic set himself.

Having swiftly overcome his intial disappointment at finding himself merely the captain of a little trawler, Callaway had set to work to turn his ship into a smart and efficient anti-submarine unit. He had infected his crew with his own enthusiasm and, although to the casual onlooker in harbour the trawlermen appeared to run their ship in free and easy fashion, they were in fact a well-trained team.

With guns' crews at their weapons, and depth charges under the supervision of Boucaut, the *Lady Shirley* worked up to her top speed and began overhauling the contact. Aware of the approach of a pursuer the unseen target was jinking beneath the surface, veering first to port and then to starboard. But she could not shake off the relentlessly stabbing finger of the trawler's asdic beam.

At last the straining vessel reached a favourable firing position. As she passed over the submarine a pattern of four depth charges from throwers and rails sank overside in her foaming wake. Hardly had they exploded, it seemed to Lieutenant Boucaut gazing astern, than a periscope bobbed up barely six hundred yards away from the trawler's port quarter. Immediately he saw it Callaway ordered 'Hard aport! Stand by to ram! All guns' crews open fire as soon as you bear.'

Forward, the loaded 4-inch under the watchful eye of Temporary Sub-Lieutenant Frederick French, R.N.R., the *Lady Shirley*'s navigating officer, was trained round to the extreme after bearing. But even at its fullest limits the weapon was temporarily blanked off from the target until the trawler should come round and bring the surfacing enemy on to her beam.

Gushing seawater from her vents as she rose the *U.111*'s conning-tower and deck casing were now fully visible to the eager trawlermen. A stream of tracer from the *Lady Shirley*'s Hotchkiss guns promptly leapt out to span the intervening five hundred yards of water between the trawler and the U-boat, the bullets bouncing and ricocheting off the greasy steel-plating. The submarine's conning-tower hatch clanged open, Germans swarmed out, scrambled down to the casing and began to make for their foremost gun. But the trawlermen mowed them down before they could attain their objective and those still unhit dashed back for cover.

The *Lady Shirley* was still swinging under helm when there came a crash from the forecastle as the 4-inch opened fire. But now the U-boatmen in the conning-tower began to reply with their heavy machine-guns. Almost at once Seaman Leslie Pizzey, the trawler's 4-inch gunlayer, was hit in the stomach by an explosive bullet and died instantly. Sub-Lieutenant French promptly slid into his place and the gun continued to fire.

Now the little trawler and her big opponent began to slog it out practically toe to toe, for the range was nearly point blank. The German fire was accurate and sustained. Signal-man Warbrick, on the bridge with Lieutenant-Commander Callawy, was the next Biritish casualty, with a bullet smashed thigh bone. Seaman William Windsor and Sidney Halcrow, manning the Hotchkiss guns, were both hit, Halcrow being badly wounded, but both continued to fire their weapons. The two seamen on the point-fives, Kenneth Hibbs and George Bussey, maintained their fire imperturbably. Forward, the *Lady Shirley*'s 4-inch banged away, with French using semi-armour-piercing projectiles with the object of puncturing the submarine's vulnerable pressure hull. For several minutes when the action was at its height Callaway's overall view of the battle was obscured when an enemy bullet ruptured a main steam pipe on the trawler's well-deck, and a cloud of white vapour enveloped the *Lady Shirley*, until one of the engine-room staff discovered and shut off the source. Another incendiary bullet from the U-boat started a small fire in the trawler's provision room; her bridge windows were shattered, the deck planking and wheelhouse scored and splintered, and her lifeboat holed in several places.

But *U.111* was suffering more severely than her small opponent. The fourth, fifth and sixth rounds from the *Lady Shirley*'s 4-inch scored direct hits on the U-boat and the next two, so far as Callaway could estimate, were either hits or near misses. Sub-Lieutenant French then switched ammunition and began using shrapnel with the object of driving the enemy gunners below decks. But after only two more rounds of 4-inch had been fired the Nazis threw up their hands and surrendered. By then the submarine was losing way rapidly and her stern was dipping under water. Callaway ordered his men to cease fire and glanced quickly at his watch. The whole action had taken a quarter of an hour.

Four minutes later *U.111* sank stern first. Unknown to Lieutenant-Commander Callaway the corpse of the man he had been fated to kill lay sprawled across the entrance to the submarine's control room. Waiting with the rest of the crew to plunge into the sea as their vessel sank beneath them was Kleinschmidt's shipmate, Commander Hans Joachim Heinecke. But he had done his best for his dead comrade; he had helped to open the vents which would ensure that the U-boat went to the bottom.

One by one the swimming Germans were hauled on board the victorious trawler and placed under armed guard. All told, they totalled forty-five, far outnumbering the crew of the *Lady Shirley*. Seven had been killed and five of the survivors were wounded. The latter were given first aid by Lieutenant Boucaut, for ships of the Lilliput Fleet carried neither doctor nor sick-berth rating. One man, Hans Ruskens, had somehow made the journey from the sinking U-boat with his legs shattered by British shellfire. Boucaut applied a tourniquet and did his best to ease the man's agony. But Ruskens died a few hours later and was given a sailor's burial next day.

Squatting sullenly on deck before being led away to be imprisoned in the trawler's wardroom, the only compartment roomy enough to hold all the captured Germans, Gerhard Hartig, Boatswain's Mate of *U.111* counted the twenty-eight officers and men of the *Lady Shirley* with mounting disgust. The submarine's complement had been almost double that number. Later when he and his shipmates were let out two at a time for a daily airing on deck he could not contain his chagrin.

'We were bigger than you,' he complained to the trawlerman guard. 'You could not see us but we could see you – yet you won!'

The crew of the *Lady Shirley* never knew that Boatswain's Mate Hartig, a good Nazi, did more than merely whine about the defeat of *U.111*. He actively plotted a *coup d'état*. During the trawler's five-day voyage to Gibraltar Hartig worked on his fellow prisoners, trying to persuade them to fall in with his plan, which was simple. Together they would break out of the flimsy wardroom and overpower the sentry, storm the trawlermen's quarters, capture the ship and sail her to Germany. How they were to obtain fuel for the journey Hartig did not bother to inquire. For when she encountered *U.111* the *Lady Shirley* had coal for barely seven days' steaming left in her bunkers. In the event Hartig's plotting came to nought. His shipmates had had enough of Hitler's war, and they told him to go and boil his head.

During the passage to Gibraltar Callaway learned from Heinecke of the action taken on board the U-boat when her captain sighted the trawler.

'Because you are coal-burning we thought you were a much bigger merchant ship,' said Heinecke. 'We were just getting into position to torpedo you when to our amazement you steamed straight at us and started dropping depth charges. The speed at which you attacked was incredible.'

When the trawler's depth charges began exploding Kleinschmidt, with his boat at periscope depth, lost his head completely. First he had ordered the submarine to surface, then to dive. But before his bewildered crew could obey his last order the submarine had involuntarily surfaced, to be met by a hail of accurate fire from the *Lady Shirley*'s gunners.

Kleinschmidt had led the way out of the conning-tower hatch, followed by his first lieutenant, a petty officer and the crew of the foremost gun. When Kleinschmidt had been killed Heinecke had been aft in the U-boat's engine room, thick with swirling smoke and choking diesel fumes, helping the engineer officer try to repair the damaged motors. When the crew surrendered the two officers opened the vents and groped their way back on deck.

Around midnight on October 8th, as the *Lady Shirley* neared Gibraltar, she was met by the British destroyer *Lance*. The latter sent over her doctor to tend the British and German wounded, and remained in company as escort.

Just before nine o'clock next morning the little trawler entered harbour to be greeted by cheers from the crews of assembled warships. Two early arrivals to congratulate Callaway and his men after she had secured alongside were the Commander of their A/S Group and the Vice-Admiral, Gibraltar. And they were due to be still further honoured for, on the 10th October, the trawler's ship's company fell in somewhat self-consciously on their bullet-splintered well-deck to hear read a special signal of congratulation. It was a personal message from the Prime Minister.

Lieutenant-Commander Callaway was awarded an immediate D.S.O. 'for daring and skill in a brilliant action against a U-boat in which the enemy was sunk and surrendered to H.M. Trawler *Lady Shirley*.' Lieutenant Boucaut and Sub-Lieutenant French were both awarded the D.S.C. Seaman Halcrow who, in the words of the citation 'was so badly wounded that he was ordered to go below but stood to his gun until the action was over, when he fainted,' received the Conspicuous Gallantry Medal. Six others of the crew were awarded the D.S.M., and a further five received Mentions in Despatches.

It is sad to have to record that the hard-fighting *Lady Shirley* and her gallant crew were soon to form the subject of a tragic communiqué. Three months after their battle with *U.111* the Admiralty regretted that 'H.M. Trawler *Lady Shirley* (Lieut.-Commander A. H. Callaway, D.S.O., R.A.N.V.R.) is overdue and must be considered lost.' Captured German documents at the end of the war revealed her fate.

The Nazis had smarted under the stigma of a second U-boat surrender, and to a miserable little trawler (the first had taken place in August, 1941, when *U.570* surrendered to an aircraft of R.A.F. Coastal Command in mid-Atlantic after having been depth charged). A few hours before dawn on December 11th, 1941, the captain of *U.374* lined up his periscope on a certain minor British war vessel patrolling in the Strait of Gibraltar. When the vengeful torpedo struck, H.M. Trawler *Lady Shirley*, late of Hull, and her entire company were blown to fragments.

A month later *U.374* was herself sunk by the British submarine *Unbeaten*.

## CHAPTER VIII

## MEN AND SHIPS

By 1941 there was scarcely a theatre of war in which ships of the Lilliput Fleet were not actively engaged. Sweltering in the heat of Karachi early in July of that year was the little ex-Milford Haven trawler *Arthur Cavanagh*. 277 tons gross, 125 feet long and 23 feet in the beam, the *Arthur Cavanagh* had been built at Paisley in 1918 and taken over by the Navy on August 30th, 1939.

By May, 1940, she was serving in the Mediterranean as a unit of the 91st Minesweeping Group along with the trawlers *Muroto, Raglan Castle* and *Milford Countess* with whom often in peacetime she had fished the distant-water grounds. She had been kept busy since her arrival from Britain minesweeping around Tobruk, Port Said and the Suez Canal area. Now she had been chosen to take part in an operation in more distant waters.

Anchored off Bandar Shahpur at the head of the Persian Gulf where they had cocked a snook at the British Navy since the beginning of the war lay a number of Axis merchantmen. Five of these were German ships, the *Marienfels, Sturmfels, Hohenfels, Wildenfels* and *Wiessenfels;* and three Italian, the *Caboto, Bronte* and *Barbara*, the two latter being tankers. It was now decided, as part of a larger operation, to go in and capture these vessels, and if the Iranian Navy (two gunboats) attempted to interfere, to put it out of action.

Accordingly one blazing hot August day a very odd-looking force indeed sailed up the Persian Gulf heading for Bandar Shahpur. Headquarters vessel and troopship for the expedition was the Armed Merchant Cruiser *Kanimbla*, preceded by two tugs belonging to the Anglo-Iranian Oil

Company. Astern of the armed merchant cruiser came the Royal Indian Navy sloop *Lawrence*, the corvette H.M.S. *Snapdragon*, the ex-China river gunboat *Cockchafer*, and the *Arthur Cavanagh*. Reconnoitring ahead of the flotilla was a dhow manned by British sailors disguised as Arabs and a Royal Air Force picket boat.

Aboard the *Kanimbla* were troops whose task was to capture the town; they comprised three hundred Baluchis and a detachment of Ghurkas. The work of cutting out the Axis merchantmen was to be accomplished by parties of blue-jackets, most of whom belonged to the Royal Australian Navy, carried in the warships. While the five German vessels and one of the Italians were being dealt with by the bigger ships of the flotilla the little Milford Haven trawler, carrying a boarding party of twelve brawny sailors and two officers, would tackle the two Italian tankers.

D-Day was August 25th and H-hour 4 a.m. As the motley collection of ships steamed towards Bandar Shahpur in the darkness of the tropic night the Baluchis aboard the *Kanimbla* chanted war songs as they cleaned and oiled their rifles, carefully polishing each bullet and offering up a prayer for its safe lodgment in an enemy. Nearby the Ghurkas sharpened their kukris to razor keenness, and the blue-jacket in khaki rig overhauled their tommy guns and grenades, their scaling ladders and grapnels. Skipper Tom Kirby in the *Arthur Cavanagh* checked over his orders. First he was to go alongside the tanker *Bronte* lying in the Khor Musa Inlet, and when she had been captured by his Australian boarding-party move on to the *Barbara* and repeat the process. Kirby and his men were well pleased to be in on this little jaunt; it made a change, they felt from the monotony of minesweeping.

The German ships were anchored in the stream nearest the entrance to the inlet, the *Marienfels* by herself, then the *Sturmfels* alongside the *Hohenfels*, and the *Wildenfels* close by the *Wiessenfels*. The three Italians were moored in a single line nearest the town. Between the two groups of merchantmen lay the Iranian gunboats *Karkas* and *Chabraz*.

The *Marienfels* was the first to be captured, but the unexpected appearance of the naval boarding-party on her deck was the signal for the outbreak of trouble elsewhere. The *Wiessenfels* promptly burst into flames, and a machine-gun began chattering on board the *Sturmfels* as soon as the *Snapdragon* bumped alongside her. With the *Kanimbla* looming menacingly over them the Iranian gunboats, how-ever, lost no time in surrendering both themselves and the town.

Ignoring the clamour going on around, the *Arthur Cavanagh* steamed steadily past the line of attacked merchantmen and headed towards the *Bronte*, still with her consorts lying dark and quiet. But the noise and glare of fires from down-stream had alerted the Italians for, as the trawler nosed in to her quarry, flames broke out on board the *Bronte*. Kirby had his hoses ready rigged for just such an eventuality, and the boarding-party stood poised with their grapnels and scaling ladders. This was just as well for, while the trawlermen were busy spraying the fire-wreathed deck of the merchantman, the brawny Australian bluejackets dealt capably if urgently with the Italian members of the tanker's crew who with drawn guns were unwise enough to try to rush the *Arthur Cavanagh*.

Leaving half the boarding-party in the *Bronte,* upon which the *Kanimbla* was now also directing hoses, the trawler presently cast off and made for the *Barbara*, last ship in the line. But she too had flames spurting up from deck and hatchways, for all the enemy ships, it was afterwards dis-covered, had long been prepared for destruction at short notice by scuttling and burning. Kerosene, oil and tar had been liberally scattered about ready for instant ignition.

But despite their efforts at self-immolation all the enemy vessels except one, the *Wiessenfels*, were saved intact. The boarding-parties were able to nip off the fuses and the fires which had already been started were extinguished by the efforts of the *Arthur Cavanagh* and her sisters. One task the trawlermen were called upon to undertake in a hurry was to shovel grain from the holds of the *Sturmfels* to pre-vent her from capsizing.

Thus 'Operation Bishop', important offshoot of 'Opera-tion Countenance', an overall measure designed to forestall Nazi infiltration into Iran, was a complete success; and a few days later the Shah abdicated.

For his part in the operation Skipper Kirby received a well-merited M.B.E.

* * *

In August, 1941, convoys to Russia were begun. Twelve anti-submarine trawlers were at first attached to the Iceland Command to support the ocean escorts for the much-tried merchantmen who were to run the frightful gauntlet to Murmansk. They were the ex-Hull trawlers *Ayrshire*, *Cape Palliser*, *Lady Madeleine*, *Lord Austin*, *Lord Middleton*, *St Elstan* and *St Kenan*; and the ex-Grimsby trawlers *Vizalma*, *Northern Pride*, *Northern Spray*, *Northern Wave* and *Northern Gem*. None was larger than 570 tons gross.

Although their maximum speed was but ten knots and, due to their gruelling naval service this could only be attained by dint of mustering all spare hands to help in the stokehold, they were comparatively lightly armed and could carry only a strictly limited outfit of high-explosive ammunition, these little ships rendered gallant service on this most hazardous of operations both as escorts and rescue vessels.

Considerations of space preclude mention of the exploits of more than two of them, both of which have previously figured in episodes related in these pages. But if the ships are the same their captains and crews are new.

On June 27th, 1942, a convoy of thirty-seven merchantmen left Hvalfjord in Iceland, for Archangel. Their original destination had been Murmansk but this was changed due to severe bombing of the latter port. Most of the ships in the convoy were British but some were American. Two days out when they had reached a point south-west of Jan Mayen Island the convoy and its shepherding warships were joined by the ocean escort. Four trawlers were included, the *Ayrshire*, *Northern Gem*, *Lord Austin* and *Lord Middleton*. The convoy they guarded, which was to suffer the worst losses of all the Russia convoys, was the ill-fated P.Q.17.

Attacks by the enemy began on July 2nd after a shadowing Focke-Wulf had made its appearance the day before.

But on the 4th the Nazi assault began in earnest, heralded by the sinking of one merchantman by a single aircraft. At nine o'clock that same evening after a series of fierce attacks by torpedo-bombers came an urgent signal from the Admiralty ordering the destroyers of the escort to leave their charges and rejoin the cruiser screen, and for the ships of the convoy to scatter. Heavy German surface forces, which included the *Tirpitz*, were reported to be in the vicinity. Now began the agony of P.Q.17 for, although the German battle fleet had in fact turned back, U-boats and aircraft were to account for twenty-three of the luckless merchant ships. One had returned to port with ice damage at the outset of the voyage. Four of the thirteen which eventually reached Russia were saved by the efforts of the trawler *Ayrshire*.

Since that grim day in 1940 when, under the command of Sub-Lieutenant Dixon, the *Ayrshire* had fought her gallant lone battle off the Orkneys after her consort had been bombed and sunk the trawler had been recommissioned with a fresh crew from the Patrol Service Central Depot, and new officers had been appointed to her. The captain was now Temporary Lieutenant Leo Gradwell, R.N.V.R., her First Lieutenant, Temporary Lieutenant R. W. Elsden, R.N.V.R., and the third watchkeeping officer Temporary Sub-Lieutenant R. Whyte, R.N.V.R.

In civil life Gradwell was a barrister, his First Lieutenant a solicitor, and Whyte a medical student. For now that the flow of fishermen and other professional seamen subject to call up had almost ceased the personnel of the Royal Naval Patrol Service was rapidly changing. Its ranks, both of officers and ratings, were soon to include men from every walk of life. Like them, Gradwell and his crew were to reveal in full measure that aptitude for sea life which is the heritage of every Briton.

When the fateful order for the convoy to scatter was received the ships were north of Bear Island and well inside the Arctic Circle. The warships remaining after the escort destroyers departed took the various undamaged merchantmen under their respective wings and steamed away in different directions at their best speed. Gradwell in the *Ayr-*

*shire* considered that the safest area for which he could make was northward to the ice barrier, which at that time of the year undulates between Latitudes 76 and 77 North, and make his way to Russia along its edge.

By signal lamp he instructed the two merchant ships nearest to him to follow, and turned northwards. The vessels were the *Troubadour* of Panamanian registry and the American *Ironclad*. During the recent air and U-boat attacks the *Troubadour* had been struck by a torpedo. Fortunately it failed to explode and passed under the ship after hitting her and then surfaced. In the early hours of the following morning the *Ayrshire* sighted another escaping merchantman and she, too, joined up with the little convoy. She was also American, the *Silver Sword*.

At six o'clock that evening the *Ayrshire* boldly led her flock some twenty miles into the drifting ice. There Gradwell called the three masters on board for a conference. He told them he proposed to remain in the ice until the immediate danger of attack was past, and instructed them to have the sides and upper works of their vessels painted white to aid her concealment. This they did. All next day the trawler and her charges lay quietly inside the ice floes, crews alert at their guns in case a snooping aircraft should come around. But next day a southerly wind sprang up which threatened to pack the ice around their hulls. Now they were forced to move to avoid being locked in.

Although he possessed only a small-scale chart of the area Gradwell confidently led the ships back to the open sea, turned east and began to creep cautiously along the edge of the ice barrier. Then towards late afternoon the following day they heard the sound of aircraft engines. A Focke-Wulf Condor was searching the wreckage-littered waters of the Barents Sea, newly the graveyard of twenty-three fine ships, for remnants of the convoy still unharmed upon which to home the greedy U-boats. But a providential patch of fog came down to cloak the trawler and her flock from the roving eye of the snooper. At two o'clock on the morning of July 9th they sighted land; it was Novaya Zemlya.

Thankfully they steamed into a fjord and their anchors rattled down. But they were still five hundred miles from

110

safety. Reduced by now to the last shovelful of dust in her bunker, the *Ayrshire* took coal and water aboard from the *Troubadour*. While these replenishments were being effected Gradwell held another council of war in his cabin with the merchant-ship masters. Despite the terrific strain of the last few days he was as cheerful and confident as ever.

'Well, gentlemen,' he said, 'as soon as I've fuelled we'll go round to the Matochkin Strait where we are less likely to be spotted from the air. Later I intend to make for Archangel.'

Entering the winding Matochkin Strait, some miles to the southward, the *Ironclad* ran herself aground. Patiently Gradwell nosed the *Ayrshire* close in to the stranded merchantman, risking damage to the trawler's asdic dome in the process, put a line aboard and tugged the American ship off. Then the flotilla continued for about nine miles up the Strait and anchored. On shore nearby a wireless station reared its spider-web masts. Uncertain whether Germans or Russians were in possession Gradwell sent ashore an armed party of sailors under charge of Elsden to check up. But the First Lieutenant returned in due course with the reassuring news that the station was still in Russian hands and the information that a better anchorage would be found higher up the Strait.

Pausing to pick up three lifeboats containing survivors from one of the ships sunk in the convoy Gradwell duly moved his flock, discovering en route another escaper from the ill-fated P.Q.17, the American ship *Benjamin Harrison*.

On the 13th a Russian flying boat on routine patrol landed near the ships, and Gradwell sent a message by the pilot to the Senior British Naval Officer at Archangel, telling what had happened. Next day, however, as the weather became thick and hazy the intrepid trawler captain decided to take advantage of the poor visibility to make a final dash for safety. Accordingly the *Ayrshire* and her charges weighed anchor and set off for the open sea.

But before they had gone very far the *Troubadour*, losing sight of her consorts in the mist, steamed up a blind channel and went aground. Back came the *Ayrshire* in search bringing with her a Russian trawler they encountered in the Strait. Together the two small ships lugged the merchantman off into deep water. Only then did Gradwell learn with difficulty from the Russian skipper, for the man could speak no English, that British warships were coming to their aid. A week later they were found by three scouting corvettes and escorted into Archangel.

Later in the year the *Northern Gem* was accompanying Convoy JW.51B. from Loch Ewe to the Kola Inlet. Her consort in the escort force, which comprised six destroyers, two corvettes and a fleet minesweeper to guard fourteen merchant ships, was the trawler *Vizalma*. Commanding the *Northern Gem* was Skipper Lieutenant William Mullender, R.D., R.N.R., while the captain of the *Vizalma* was Temporary Lieutenant John Anglebeck, R.N.V.R.

On the morning of New Year's Eve convoy and escort were battling through heavy seas whipped up by a northwesterly gale on the previous day. The weather was bitterly cold with sixteen degrees of frost and all the ships were heavily iced up. Due to the gale convoy and escort had become partially scattered. The destroyer *Oribi* had developed a defect in her gyro compass and lost touch; the *Vizalma*, stationed astern of the convoy, had fallen behind with two of the merchantmen who had been compelled to heave to due to steering breakdowns. In any event heavy seas crashing aboard had flooded the *Vizalma*'s magazine to a depth of three feet so that she could scarcely make headway. Plugging along at nine knots the *Northern Gem* had managed to keep up with the main body. Unknown to Captain Sherbrooke commanding the escort in the destroyer *Onslow* the heavy German cruisers *Admiral Hipper* and *Lutzow* with six destroyers were heading for the convoy. Away to the northward was a small British cruiser screening force.

As soon as the approach of the German ships had been reported by the *Obedient*, one of the flank destroyers, the other ships of the escort were ordered to make smoke to conceal the convoy, and concentrate on their leader to intercept the enemy. But before Captain Sherbrooke could launch his thrust the *Hipper*, coming up at high speed, opened fire on the destroyer *Achates* and badly mauled her. Then the big German cruiser shifted her fire to the *Onslow*, scoring four direct hits and wounding Captain Sherbrooke severely. But although nearly blinded the latter gallantly continued to direct the movements of his destroyers. Meanwhile the *Northern Gem* and the corvettes stood by the convoy ready to interpose their frail hulls between the enemy warships and the plodding merchantmen.

In the eerie half light of that December day the British destroyers fought an epic battle, darting in and out of their own smoke screens to harry their big assailants. The crippled *Achates*, now helping to cover the convoy, again came under heavy fire, this time from the *Lutzow*, which killed her captain and reduced her to a shambles. Soon afterwards she asked the *Northern Gem* to stand by her and half an hour later she sank. Regardless of the danger from the destroyer's depth charges which were exploding almost under her stern the trawler boldly closed in and picked up her survivors.

But aid for the convoy and its hard-pressed escorts was on the way in the shape of the cruisers *Sheffield* and *Jamacia*. When they appeared the enemy retired at high speed, leaving one of their own destroyers sinking.

On board the little *Northern Gem* her cramped messdeck and ward-room was chock-a-block with survivors while Ordinary Seamen Eric Mawer of her ship's company did his best for the badly wounded among them with the trawler's slender first-aid kit. A cashier in civil life, Mawer was married to a State Registered Nurse and his best friend was a doctor. Thus he had acquired a smattering of medical lore which he put to good use, for during her active service with the Navy his ship fished out of the sea over a thousand survivors from British and Allied ships. But with more than eighty casualties to care for all at once he needed expert help. With Skipper Lieutenant Mullender himself at the wheel the crazily gyrating trawler was cleverly edged alongside the destroyer *Obedient* who transferred her doctor to the little ship. Then while Convoy JW.51B resumed its interrupted voyage to Kola Inlet the naval surgeon performed no less than nine major operations in the bucking wardroom of the *Northern Gem*. Ordinary Seamen Mawer, cashier turned trawlerman, was his skilful assistant.

8                           *     *     *

Farther south another exploit by a unit of the Lilliput Fleet brought a welcome ray of light to the gloomy situation which had developed in the eastern Mediterranean. With the 8th Army forced back to the Alamein Line Rommel's threat to Alexandria had compelled a hurried dispersal of the British warships based on that port. Some had retired to the Red Sea, others to Haifa.

Patrolling off the swept channel at the latter port was the anti-submarine trawler *Islay*. Commanded by Skipper Lieutenant John Ross, R.N.R., the *Islay* was an Admiralty-designed vessel, one of the 'Isles' class, of which more than a hundred were built for the Patrol Service during the war. Among the first dozen to be launched in 1941, the *Islay* displaced some 560 tons, and she was 164 feet long with a 27-foot beam; she carried a complement of thirty-three officers and men, could steam at fifteen knots and was able to range over three thousand miles of ocean without refuelling.

In build she was more compact than the average fishing trawler of comparable tonnage, with a larger bridge and an additional gun sponson on the forward well-deck. The 'Isles' were designed to mount a 4-inch gun on the forecastle as their main armament, but at the time she was about to distinguish herself against the Italian Navy the *Islay* mounted only a 12-pounder forward, and twin point-fives aft.

On August 10th, 1942, an unseen threat was approaching Haifa. For, four days previously, the Italian submarine *Scire* had sailed from the island of Leros carrying a cargo of trouble for the British warships anchored in Haifa harbour. Launched in 1938, the *Scire* was an 850-ton vessel, 197 feet overall, with a surface speed of fourteen knots. Her original armament had included a 3.9-inch gun mounted forward of the conning tower. But soon after Italy's entry into the war the *Scire*'s big gun had been removed and three long steel cylinders fitted to her casing instead, one for'ard of the conning-tower and two aft. They were watertight cases for the stowage of two-man torpedoes.

Under the command of Count Valerio Borghese, the *Scire* and her human torpedoes had managed to sink or damage fourteen Allied ships anchored in Gibraltar Bay. Subsequently she had successfully taken part in attacks against

Malta and Alexandria. Aware of the dispersal of British warships caused by the Axis threat to Egypt, the Italians planned an attack on those which had been moved to Haifa to be carried out by frogmen using limpet charges. The swimmers would operate from the *Scire*, who accordingly embarked for the purpose at La Spezia eight frogmen and their equipment, a senior technical officer and a doctor. The *Scire*'s hull was painted pale green and as camouflage she had daubed along her sides, ironically enough, the silhouette of a trawler. In command was an experienced submariner, Lieutenant-Commander Bruno Zelich.

At about two o'clock on the afternoon of the 10th the asdic operator on board the *Islay* reported a submarine contact. At once Ross went into action, and a few minutes later his first pattern of depth charges was on its way. But in his enthusiasm the trawler captain ran out too far on his attack and contact was lost. Hastily he commenced a search and shortly afterwards, to his relief, the empty pinging of the asdic was replaced by unmistakable submarine echoes. It was clear from their nature that the vessel was now lying stopped. It might be, thought Ross, that his first pattern had damaged the U-boat. Down went a six-charge pattern to add to her troubles.

Opening the range to four hundred yards while the depth charges were convulsing the ocean in his wake Ross swung his vessel round in time to witness a heartening sight. Bouncing to the surface as if kicked from beneath came the streaming green hull of a submarine. Spouting water from the vents of her ballast tanks as she porpoised it seemed that the U-boat commander was having difficulty in maintaining his craft on the surface. For almost at once the camouflage-daubed hull began to founder by the stern.

The *Islay*'s point-fives opened up their ear-splitting racket, to be followed almost immediately by the sharp bark of her 12-pounder. For just as long as it took the excited trawler gunners to load and fire seventeen rounds from the 12-pounder the submarine continued its crazy flounderings. Through his glasses Ross had time to note the absence of a gun on her fore-casing and the curious-looking cylinders strapped to the deck. Twelve direct hits were scored on the

*Scire*'s hull, while inside the frantic Zelich fought to regain control. Then she began to slip back swiftly, seeming to hang suspended by her vertically pointed nose like a dying shark at the last before finally plunging down to the sea bed.

There was little doubt in Ross's mind that the submarine was mortally stricken. Nevertheless war is war and the total destruction of the enemy must be ensured. The *Islay* steamed purposefully over to the spot from whence concentric wavelets were still spreading to administer the *coup de grâce*. Six more depth charges sank into the pale depths and again the sea heaved in violent tumult. When the trawler finally turned and headed for harbour an hour later a vast oil patch covered the area. From its centre bubbles were slowly rising, each as it burst releasing a tiny cloud of fetid green gas.

Four days later the bodies of two Italian sailors were washed ashore in Haifa, and buried with full naval honours. In Rome a gold medal for gallantry was pinned to the flag of the submarine *Scire*, a crack unit of the Fascist underwater fighters, whose Nemesis had been a little British trawler.

\*    \*    \*

But there were many grim days ahead. Japanese submarines were roaming the Indian Ocean. In addition to at least five well-armed surface raiders the Germans had some two hundred and fifty U-boats operating at sea. By the end of 1941 they were becoming active off the east coast of the United States, sinking American tankers by gunfire and torpedoes. Since the U.S. Navy was deficient in anti-submarine vessels the British Admiralty offered the loan of twenty-four A/S-fitted trawlers to patrol in the threatened area. The offer was gratefully accepted and in March, 1942, British fishing trawlers-turned-warships came under American command.

These 'rugged little coal-burners', as the Americans called them, none grossing less than 500 tons, were some of the cream of the peacetime Hull and Grimsby fishing fleets. From the former port came the *Arctic Explorer, Kingston Ceylonite, Lady Elsa, Lady Rosemary, Pentland Firth, St Cathan, St Loman, St Zeno* and the *Stella Polaris*; from the latter the *Bedfordshire, Coventry City, Hertfordshire, Le Tigre, Northern Chief, Northern Dawn, Northern Duke, Northern Isles, Northern Princess, Norwich City* and *Wellard*; the *Senateur Duhamel*, a 900-ton giant of French registry which had been brought over to Britain after the fall of France, *Cape Warwick*, and the *Wastwater* and *Buttermere*, two vessels of the new Admiralty-designed 'Lakes' class. Four of the trawlers were stationed off New York, in the Hampton Roads, eight at Charlestown and six at Boston.

Five were sunk during their service in American waters; the *St Cathan, Senateur Duhamel* and the *Pentland Firth* due to collisions, the *Kingston Ceylonite* by mine, and the *Bedfordshire* torpedoed by a U-boat. One trawler, the *Northern Princess*, was lost in the Atlantic from an unknown cause. To balance these casualties, however, the *Le Tigre*, living up to her name, sank the *U.215*. By October eighteen of them were on their way back east for, due to a spurt of U-boat activity in South African waters, the Admiralty had to request their return to strengthen our convoy escorts in the South Atlantic.

At home the ships of the Lilliput Fleet were busier than ever. German minelaying continued unabated. One in three of the Luftwaffe bombers raiding Britain nightly carried mines to shed in our ports and harbours instead of the normal bomb load. E-boats were now added to the daily hazards faced by our minesweepers and convoy escorts. In fact, due to their attacks the east coast convoy run now became notorious as 'E-boat Alley'.

Although it would be invidious to single out any particular trawler unit for special mention the record of the 19th A/S Group based at Harwich provides a fair illustration of the daily activities of an escort trawler group in E-boat Alley. Shepherding convoys back and forth between the Thames Estuary and Methil, in Fifeshire, the Group comprised the trawlers *Greenfly, Kingston Olivine, Lord Plender* and *Lady Philomena*. Each ship of the Group individually steamed a distance equivalent to four times round the globe; collectively they towed to safety some eighty thousand tons of bomb- and mine-damaged warships and merchantmen; saved more than a thousand survivors and escorted a total of well over seven hundred convoys. In their numerous battles with the enemy they logged an impressive record of aircraft shot down or damaged and E-boat attacks repelled.

The little ships of the escort groups regarded it as a point of honour to bring every member of their flocks safely into port no matter how badly damaged some of them might be with consequent justification for abandonment, and regardless of the dangers and difficulties involved. Although neither built nor fitted for salvage work they cheerfully faced daunting odds when endeavouring to drag crippled ships into harbour.

On the evening of March 17th, 1942, coastal convoy FN.57 was steaming north past Aldeburgh from its assembly point off Southend, bound for Methil. Suddenly the steamship *Cressdene*, a 4,000-ton freighter, heaved upwards with a mighty shudder as a mine exploded immediately beneath her hull. Her midships structure collasped like a pack of cards, deck beams and hatches gave way and tumbled into the holds, the port lifeboat was shattered to matchwood, and the compasses were destroyed. Way fell off the stricken ship and she lay wallowing helplessly while the rest of the convoy steamed on.

Shaded signal lamps winked urgently for a few minutes, then a small naval trawler slid alongside the broken *Cressdene*. On her bows were the white-painted letters 'K.O.' The *Kingston Olivine* – known inevitably to her crew and those of her sisters and the base staff as 'the Knock-Out ship,' but also more proudly by the title she had justly earned as 'the E-boat Alley Ambulance' – was on the job.

Built in 1930 for the Kingston Steam Trawler Company of Hull, the *Kingston Olivine* was of some 370 tons gross, measuring 150 feet overall with a beam of 24 feet. She was armed with a 4-inch gun with which her gunners had, somewhat suprisingly, managed to knock down more than one prowling Junkers 88, a .5-inch machine-gun, and a Holman projector – the latter weapon being a kind of steam-driven mortar for hurling grenades at divebombers; in addition she carried depth charges.

In command was Lieutenant Trevor Lewis of the Royal Australian Naval Volunteer Reserve, with another young

Australian Volunteer Reservist, Sub-Lieutenant Patrick Mc-Cormick, as his Number One. Her crew of twenty-six hailed from the Patrol Service Central Depot at Lowestoft, and included two former Yorkshire miners and an ex-Glasgow city policeman.

At the time that the *Cressdene* struck the mine the weather was foggy and heavy rain was falling. Just the night, in fact, for lurking E-boats to arrive and finish off the crippled freighter and her lone helper, for convoy and escort had to press on and leave them. The shocked and injured crew of the *Cressdene* clambered thankfully down into the trawler's boat but Captain Jones, her master, was reluctant to abandon his ship while she was still afloat and there was a chance of saving her. With McCormick and his Second Officer he made a swift assessment of the damage. There was hope, he thought, that she would hold together for a tow.

In the pitch darkness lines were passed from the trawler to the *Cressdene*, and presently the slow and dangerous journey commenced. At something less than three knots the *Kingston Olivine* hauled the broken ship towards the distant land. But as the freighter had taken a heavy list to port and was slowly going down by the head she was painfully difficult to steer. Meanwhile Sub-Lieutenant McCormick and Second Officer Jones groped about in the darkness and swirling water of the flooded holds trying to plug some of the leaks. In the *Kingston Olivine* lookouts and guns' crews peered anxiously into the darkness, for had a U-boat or enemy surface craft appeared the trawler would have been overwhelmed before she could cast off the freighter.

Once the tow rope parted under the strain of a sudden vicious yaw by the *Cressdene*, but Lewis imperturbably passed another and the slow, heartbreaking journey was resumed. Salvage tugs were on their way and Captain Jones was desperately hoping they would arrive in time. But to Lieutenant Lewis, closely watching the labouring *Cressdene* from the bridge, it was a hope doomed to disappointment for the freighter's bows were steadily sinking lower and lower in the water.

Finally, fearing that she might go at any moment, he

eased the tow and came alongside to try to persuade Jones to board the trawler. While they were arguing the salvage tugs appeared, but they were too late. An ominous rending crash from the bowels of the *Cressdene* announced that an overstrained bulkhead had finally given way. A moment later she began her last dive. As the trawler backed away, Captain Jones, last to leave his ship in accordance with tradition, took a flying leap on to her deck, and knocked himself unconscious.

Bad weather was also added to the hazards of the war at sea faced by the little ships.

On December 4th 1941, the steamship *Sauternes*, carrying a cargo of supplies for the small British garrison in the Faeroe Islands, which included such seasonal additions as Christmas trees and rum, rendezvoused with her escort off Auskerry Light in the Orkneys. This was the A/S trawler *Kerrera* commanded by Skipper Lieutenant Richard Utting, R.N.R., a verteran trawlerman of wide experience.

Newly accepted into the Navy at that date the *Kerrera* was one of the Admiralty 'Isles' class trawlers, and belonged to the 8th A/S-M/S Trawler Group based at Scapa. Like the *Islay* she was a 560-tonner and similarly armed and equipped.

When the little convoy rounded Dennis Head at the tip of the Orkneys and shaped course for the Faeroes a south-westerly gale was blowing. During the passage up from Leith the merchantman had already run into bad weather and somehow developed a persistent list to starboard. Due to this and her deck cargo she was rolling heavily and could make only slow headway.

Early on December 6th land was sighted and the trawler and her charge went close in to await daylight when they could see to check their whereabouts. But when dawn came it brought a typical Faeroese sea mist which blotted out all landmarks. Groping along the coast through this unpleasant blanket Utting eventually managed to identify their land-fall as the tiny island of Fuglo, which is the northernmost of the group. It was then too late to make Thorshavn before dark, and Utting asked permission of the Naval Officer in Charge to anchor for the night off Fuglo. This was approved, especially as warning had been received that a south-westerly gale was imminent and the island would therefore provide the ships with a safe lee.

But although Utting had never been to the Faeroes before he could smell bad weather, and he did not like the look of the barometer which had dropped abruptly to a low level. Furthermore, the wind, which was now freshening, was in fact blowing from the northward. Instead of being sheltered their anchorage would be exposed to the full force of the gale if it should develop.

In a fantastically short space of time Utting's fears were realised for a northerly blizzard came howling down on them, curtaining the ships in fierce squalls of snow and sleet. But by then the trawler skipper had got under way and was piloting his charge to the open sea where they could ride out the gale. As he passed ahead of the *Sauternes*, then still hauling in her anchor cable, he shone a bright light from his stern as a guide for her to follow. Visibility was then down to fifty yards.

Later on the British Vice-Consul at Thorshavn declared that never before during his long service in the islands had they experienced such a hurricane. Ashore the islanders were terrified lest at any moment the roofs of their houses should be bodily torn off and blown out to sea. Gusts of one hundred and twenty-five miles an hour were recorded.

During that awful night the little *Kerrera* battled with wind and sea in a desperate struggle to keep afloat. At one time a colossal comber broke over the bows and clawed high up the mast and bridge structure, cracking the tough metal shields and shattering the thick plate glass of the bridge windows. Seas flooded in everywhere, putting the wireless and the dynamo out of action. Sea water to a depth of three feet swirled about the crew's messdeck where all but six of the men were huddled, too miserably ill to move.

Utting, who had been on the bridge for twenty-four hours without respite, had little idea of their position since he held no proper chart of the area and had only a hand-torch for illumination. Later, calculations showed that in twenty-nine hours the *Kerrera* made only forty-three miles.

It was the most severe battering he had ever taken in twenty-two years at sea.

Around noon on the 7th the gale began slowly to moderate, and late that evening Utting was able at last to turn the trawler and run for Thorshavn, where she arrived at noon the next day. Much of her superstructure had been torn away or smashed by the fury of the seas and her decks were badly sprung, while the mental and physical strain Utting and his men had undergone was etched in deep lines of fatigue on their drawn features.

As for the ill-fated *Sauternes*, she had been driven aground before she could get clear of Fuglo and smashed to pieces, all her crew being drowned. Utting felt the loss of his charge keenly, but his first duty had been to his own ship: no man could have done more. And the abnormally severe winters of the war years brought about many such tragedies.

## CHAPTER IX

## THE ROARING TIGER

IN the latter half of 1942 the war news broke into a blaze of banner headlines. In October the roar of a thousand British guns in the Western Desert heralded the great battle of El Alamein which was to end in the rout of Axis hopes in Africa. Then, a few days later, another momentous piece of news shouldered the jubilant accounts of the Eighth Army's rapid advance off the front pages. British and American forces had landed in North Africa. At long last, it seemed, the tide of war in the west was about to turn in favour of the Allies.

In the van of the great armada from which troops of the First Army had poured ashore at Oran, Casablanca and Algiers went the minesweepers of the Lilliput Fleet. But fortunately there were no mines for them to clear. Following in the wake of the landing ships came anti-submarine trawlers to strengthen the patrols around the port approaches. In anticipation of a rich harvest of sinkings among the Allied transports and supply ships the Italian High Command hastily despatched submarines to lie in wait along the convoy routes.

On November 10th, two days after the landings, the A/S trawler *Lord Nuffield* of the Gibraltar Trawler Force was steaming from Oran to Algiers to take up anti-submarine and escort duties at the latter port. The trawlermen were on their toes, for Axis reactions to the Allied assault were expected to be manifested in a number of unpleasant ways. The Italian battle fleet might even make a sortie to attack our transports and their support craft. Enemy submarines would certainly be lurking about. For her two-hundred-mile voyage the little White Ensign trawler would have to fend for herself.

The *Lord Nuffield* had been built in 1937 by Cochrane's of Selby for her pre-war owners, the Pickering and Haldane Steam Trawler Company Ltd., of Hull. She displaced some 466 tons, measured 160 feet overall and had a beam of 26 feet. She was a welded ship, with a cruiser stern and raked bow, and boasted a top speed of twelve knots. The Navy had armed her with a 4-inch gun on a pedestal mounting on her forecastle when it took her over, had added an Oerlikon aft and machine-guns in specially built sponsons at either side of her lower bridge. On her narow after-deck she was fitted with depth-charge rails and throwers. Her captain was Skipper Lieutenant David Mair, and experienced veteran both of the fishing industry and the R.N.R. Patrol Service. He had been trained as an anti-submarine specialist.

At about twenty minutes past ten on that bright November morning, when the *Lord Nuffield* was about fifty miles from Algiers, her asdic operator suddenly stiffened like a pointer. In his earphones there had sounded the unmistakable echo of a close underwater contact, and the asdic recorder pen began swinging, tracing the mark of the echo on its slowly moving roll of sensitised paper.

The bearing of the contact was fine on the trawler's port bow, almost a mile ahead and moving slowly away. With concentrated attention the operator noted the changing range and bearing at the unseen finger of the asdic stabbed the sea ahead of the trawler. Simultaneously with the report of the contact Skipper Lieutenant Mair sounded the alarm bells and the trawlermen dropped what they were doing and raced to their action stations. Depth charges were made ready on rails and throwers.

Now, one attack on an enemy submarine may seem to be very much like another, each made according to a regulation routine of approach, of depth-charge settings and patterns. Yet each is different; each is an individual affair conducted according to circumstances and the personalities of the protagonists engaged. Of little use for the surface ship merely to drench a suspected area with depth charges in the hope of blindly destroying the enemy by sheer weight of explosive. U-boats were tough, amazingly so, and hard to destroy, as will later be seen. One German submarine attacked in the Atlantic dived to eight hundred and twenty feet and, remaining at that colossal depth for two days, withstood no fewer than two hundred and fifty-two depth charges before finally being forced to the surface due to lack of air. And in a single ship duel between even so powerful a vessel as a destroyer and a U-boat some experts consider that the odds actually favour the latter. How much more, then, are those odds stacked against a slow-steaming, lightly armed trawler?

The crew of a small surface ship engaged in an unsupported attack on a submerged U-boat experience something of the apprehensive thrill of the lone hunter who stalks a fierce and dangerous animal. Every movement of the submarine, increase or decrease of speed, rise or dive, turn to port or starboard, must be skillfully anticipated by the would-be destroyer, and his depth charges placed with the precision of a matador delivering the *coup de grâce* to the bull. If and when finally forced to surface the U-boat must be instantly met and overwhelmed by a concentrated hail of accurate gunfire or the attacker may himself be overwhelmed, just as the savage animal brought to bay will turn and rend the over-confident hunter. It is a case of destroy or be destroyed.

Steaming at full speed the *Lord Nuffield* gradually overhauled her quarry. The clicking of the asdic set ceased as the trawler's hull began to pass over the contact. Mair was about to order the first pattern of depth charges to be fired when there came a shout from the deck below. He swung round at the interruption to see before his astonished eyes the dripping whaleback of a submarine rearing itself from the depths so close to the trawler's port quarter that the wakes of both vessels met and recoiled in a foaming maelstrom. Then, like a huge shark suddenly aware of imminent danger, the submarine swung her slender stern violently away from the trawler's blunt counter and at the same moment the U-boat began to crash dive. But even as the waves broke and surged over the submerging whaleback the trawler's depth charges plummeted through the air and splashed into the water.

Mair and his men scanned the sea astern keenly as the *Lord Nuffield* drew away under the steady thrust of her propeller. The submarine had now disappeared but, parallel with her gliding descent to the sea bed, the canisters of high explosive were also plunging downwards. Oblivious of the excitement on deck the trawler's asdic operator pressed his earphones tighter to his head as he sought to pinpoint again the tell-tale echo which would reveal the position of the submarine. Instead came the thunderous reverberation of the exploding depth charges, then silence. Either the target had moved out of range or the charges had done their deadly work efficiently.

But the asdic operator knew that such luck was too much to hope for. The swifter quarry had probably managed to elude the slower-moving hunter, close though their recent brush had been. Then again the echoes returned. But they were faint and growing fainter, until presently they were lost altogether. The submarine had glided away. Doubtless she was twisting and turning far below in the depths, hydrophones alert for the propeller noises which would indicate to her crew that their small pursuer was still trailing them.

On the bridge of the *Lord Nuffield* Skipper Lieutenant Mair consulted briefly with his First Lieutenant, both men poring over the chart spread out on the table of the small hooded bridge shelter. 'We'll do a square search,' decided Mair, and the trawler began turning to start a relentless combing of the marked-off area in which the enemy submarine would probably still be moving.

Up and down the patch of sunlit sea she ploughed, the Chief Engineman below keeping his hand hovering close to the throttle ready to give the necessary burst of speed to bring the trawler over the top of her enemy when the asdic should detect her presence. Then it happened. The echoes were recaptured and they were loud and clear. The lurking U-boat was little more than half a mile away from them. With her engines throbbing at full power the *Lord Nuffield* steamed towards the new contact.

At some spot nine hundred yards ahead of the speeding

trawler and twenty degrees off her port bow the rhythm of the waves was suddenly interrupted. A slim cylindrical object began to slice through the water, to be followed by the line of a taut wire stay from which spray fled in diamond-flashing cascades. Then came a submarine's conning-tower and finally her long slim hull, greenish spume streaming as she attained surface trim. White-clad figures climbed swiftly down to the dripping casing and ran to the guns mounted for'ard and aft.

But the trawlermen had the submarine in their sights. No need for range and deflection settings for the target was almost point-blank. With a crash the first 4-inch shell sped on its way. Another followed, and another, and this time the result was a direct hit. Those of the enemy crew who were shinning down the after-ladder of the conning-tower when it struck were blown to shreds. Shells from the submarine's foremost gun now came whining over the trawler, but the speed of the little surface ship's attack had jittered the enemy gunners so that their aim was wild. Two more rounds of semi-armour-piercing shell from the *Lord Nuffield*'s 4-inch scored direct hits forward and aft the submarine's conning-tower. Then, on orders from Mair, the trawler gunners began firing shrapnel to scatter the U-boatmen. Her entire armament was now in action, the Oerlikon barking rhythmically, and streams of tracer from the chattering machine-guns hosepiping the full sweep of the submarine's deck.

Abruptly confusion and panic seized the enemy gunners. The ammunition handlers dived for their hatch, the gun's crew scrambled for the shelter of the conning-tower. Through his binoculars Mair stared in amazement as a trimly clad officer ran along the submarine's casing to the deserted weapon and began to load and fire it at the trawler. But the officer's aim was as execrable as that of his men, and presently he, too, vanished when he found himself unsupported by his craven crew. Suddenly the submarine sprouted sailors all frantically waving their arms in token of surrender and Mair ordered his men to cease firing.

As the trawler closed in he could see that the submarine was sinking fast. Even as he lowered his binoculars she

127

began sliding swiftly into the depths, the men on her bridge and casing hurling themselves into the sea. Then she vanished, leaving only a vast swirl on the surface dotted with the heads of her swimming crew.

That evening when the trawler *Lord Nuffield* steamed into Algiers harbour she carried below decks under guard fortynine dejected Italian submariners including their captain. Over and over again in incredulous tones the black-haired Fascist naval officer repeated the same words:

'Basta! But you looked so small in my periscope I thought you were just a tugboat. I ignored you!'

Skipper Lieutenant Mair smiled contentedly as he listened. The odds had been all on the side of the lamenting Italian. His vessel had been the *Emo*, a submarine of 1,260 tons, launched in June, 1938. Measuring 290 feet overall, she could boast a surface speed of seventeen knots and with her quick-firing 3.9-inch guns could have made rings round the little Hull trawler. As it was the *Lord Nuffield* had suffered but one man slightly wounded in return for depriving Mussolini's Navy of one fine modern submarine. Lieutentant Mair felt as pleased as if he had been returning to Hull in peacetime with a brimming catch in the fish-hold.

*  *  *

But if the war in the west now began to favour the Allies, in the east the situation remained sombre and threatening. Everywhere the Japanese had been victorious. They had overrun Malaya, the Dutch East Indies and Burma, and stood poised on the threshold of India. They had cleared the eastern seas of Allied warships in the battle of the Java Sea; their fleet had steamed west and their aircraft had bombed Colombo and Trincomalee, sinking two British cruisers, an aircraft carrier and some smaller warships. The remaining units of Britain's Eastern Fleet, a number of old and slow battleships, had been forced to retire to a base in East Africa. Except in the Pacific the Japanese Navy roamed almost unchallenged.

On the morning of November 11th, 1942, two ships were steaming across the southern Indian Ocean. The day was beautiful and sunny, the sea calm, its smooth glittering surface lightly streaked now and then by the brief skimming flights of flying fish. The vessels, their bows cleaving the blue-green water in line ahead formation at a steady ten knots, were vastly different in size and appearance. The leading craft was a small but sturdily built warship, the light-grey enamel on her hull daubed over with great curving sweeps of black camouflage paint, the result effectively concealing her true size and outline when seen from a distance. From the gaff at her stumpy mainmast flew the White Ensign. She was His Majesty's Indian Ship *Bengal*, and she rated in the Navy List as a fleet minesweeper.

Strickly speaking she was not a Patrol Service vessel. Yet she can be regarded as a unit of the Lilliput Fleet for she differed little from those of her sisters whose crews hailed from the Patrol Service Central Depot at Lowestoft, and her armament was certainly vastly inferior to theirs. Moreover, she ranked as only a very minor war vessel, and the story of her 'David and Goliath' action belongs with those of the other little ships manned from Britain and the Commonwealth who operated in global waters and fought with matchless courage against great odds.

The *Bengal* was a new ship and this was her maiden voyage. Her keel plate had been laid down in the shipyards at Cockatoo Island in Sydney, Australia, on December 3rd, 1941; she had been launched at the end of May of the following year and completed for service three months later, when her crew had joined from India. Little more than a large-sized trawler, the *Bengal* displaced 650 tons, she was 186 feet long and had a beam of 31 feet. She was armed with one 12-pounder gun mounted on her forecastle, and a single Bofors and two Oerlikon guns aft. Her engines were designed to develop two thousand four hundred horse power which could thrust her through the water at a top speed of 15 knots. She had four sisters, all built in Australia for the Royal Indian Navy, and each named like herself after a province of the great sub-continent: *Bombay, Madras, Punjab* and *Sind*. She carried a total complement of seventy, seven officers and sixty-three ratings, the latter all Indians. Her captain was Lieutenant-Commander William J. Wilson

9

of the Royal Indian Naval Reserve, a minesweeping specialist.

Astern of the minesweeper, her high bow knifing through
the creamy wake left by her tiny escort, steamed the motor
vessel *Ondina*. First of her class, built and launched just
before the outbreak of the Second World War, the *Ondina*
had been laid down as a petroleum carrier, and she displaced
some 6,200 tons. Her owners were the Dutch firm of N.V.
Petroleum Maats and her port of registry was The Hague.
But since the country of her registry had been overrun by the enemy the ship, although she still flew the Dutch
flag, was now being operated on behalf of Britain's
Ministry of War Transport as a valuable addition to the
Allied tanker fleet.

She was a smart-looking vessel, 425 feet long with a beam
of 54 feet and a cruiser stern. From a pedestal mounting on
her poop poked the snout of a 4-inch gun. She was commanded by Captain William Horsman of the Netherlands
Mercantile Marine, and she carried white Dutch officers
and a Chinese crew. Because of the weapon she mounted
on her poop deck she also numbered among her complement six D.E.M.S.[1] gunners. They were Able Seamen Bay-
liss, Boyce and Brooklyn of the Royal Navy; Able Seaman
Bert Hammond of the Royal Australian Naval Reserve,
and Bombardiers Nicoll and Ryan of the Marine Artillery.

The *Bengal* and her charge had left Fremantle in Western
Australia on November 5th bound for Colombo. But their
first port of call was to be Diego Garcia, a fuelling base in
the Chagos Archipelago, a group of islands which lie like a
handful of pebbles carelessly tossed by a giant hand into the
vast bosom of the Indian Ocean about half way between
Sumatra and Zanzibar. From Diego Garcia the ships would
then head northwards for Colombo where the *Bengal* was
due to join the 37th Minesweeping Flotilla of the British
Eastern Fleet.

The two captains were thoroughly aware of the risks their
long voyage entailed as they steamed steadily north-west-
wards on a course of 299 degrees on this bright sunny
November morning. But there was nothing to be gained

[1] Defensively Equipped Merchant Ships.

by worrying. There was a war on and they had jobs to do; Captain Horsman to deliver his ship where she was most needed; Wilson to protect his charge while she was in his care to the utmost extent of his power.

The distance from Fremantle to Diego Garcia is some two thousand five hundred miles. On November 11th the navigating officers of tanker and escort had just marked their positions on their charts as 19 degrees, 45 minutes South Latitude, 93 degrees, 40 minutes East Longitude, or just over halfway to their destination. If they had been aircraft instead of ships they might have said they had passed what pilots call the point of no return. The nearest land was the Cocos Islands, five hundred miles away to the north-east. All around to the south and west of their course lay nothing but the wide expanse of the Indian Ocean.

The ship's company of the *Bengal* in their white tropical rig and turbans were busy about their morning's work. For'ard on the forecastle the 12-pounder gun's crew under the supervision of Petty Officer Mohammed Ibrahim, the Quarters Rating, had been put through their paces after cleaning and oiling their weapon. There had not been much time for gun drills since commissioning, and Ibrahim would have preferred to have been handling a 4-inch instead of this pea-shooter. Doubtless, however, a heavier weapon would be installed when they arrived at their new base, for in the magazine below decks the *Bengal* carried a mere forty rounds of low-angle ammunition for consumption by her main armament, far short of what should be her normal outfit.

On the poop deck of the tanker the D.E.M.S. gunners who were keeping the forenoon watch sat or sprawled around their own 4-inch gun, their attitudes of ease deceptive, for they were ready to spring into instant action if required. They felt a trifle contemptuous of their escort. A little minesweeper with neither radar nor asdic, no armour and a couple of pop-guns. But why worry? There were plenty of blokes worse off than they were, commented Bert Hammond, the Australian. The *Ondina* was a bonzer soft number and life aboard was pretty comfortable, even if the officers were all square-heads and the crew a bunch of Chinks.

Beyond the distant horizon, as yet unseen and unknown, menace was approaching the little convoy as it plodded over the glassy surface of the sea.

At about 11.45 when the hands would normally be thinking about stowing away their brooms, scrubbers and paintwork cloths in anticipation of the pipe to secure from work for the forenoon, the masthead lookout in the *Bengal* suddenly hailed the bridge below. 'Red five, a ship!' he chanted importantly. The Officer of the Watch raised his glasses and focussed them on a distant smudge fine on the port bow. Yes, it was a ship, he decided. Couldn't make her out properly yet, though. He rang down for the captain. In a matter of seconds Lieutenant-Commander Wilson was standing beside him, his own binoculars levelled at the stranger. A long searching scrutiny, then his fingers sought the button of the alarm bells.

'Could be a Jap – probably is,' he said.

Normal mid-day lethargy vanished in a flash as the crew sped to action stations.

'Gun's crew ready and cleared away,' sang out Petty Officer Ibrahim smartly from his place at the 12-pounder.

The Bofors crew similarly reported, and the two steel-helmeted Oerlikon gunners braced inside their shoulder grips, leaned back and began testing the swing of their weapons.

The strange vessel was still about eight miles away but coming up fast. At a command from Wilson the *Bengal* began turning 90 degrees to starboard and, while the coxswain in the wheelhouse below was still spinning the spokes of the helm, a signal winked out from the warship's tiny bridge to the obediently following *Ondina*.

'Take station on my starboard beam,' it ordered.

Nine minutes from the time of the initial sighting report from the *Bengal*'s lookout the minesweeper had interposed her hull between her charge and the oncoming stranger, and was heading on a new course of 020 degrees to open the range between them. Wilson and his bridge staff were now convinced that the approaching ship was a Japanese raider. From the look of her she was a 10,000 tonner. In the minesweeper's wireless room the operator began to transmit an enemy sighting report, to be picked up among other listeners by the naval authorities in distant Fremantle.

'One enemy ship steering 110 degrees, unidentified.'

Ten minutes later another and more ominous stream of morse chattered into waiting headphones.

'Two enemy ships steering 310 degrees and 125 degrees, own speed seven knots, my position 295.'

The anxious listeners in London, Sydney, Kilindini, Fremantle and Colombo, who had thus been alerted, were powerless to help. At a tiny pinpoint in the vastness of the Indian Ocean, thousands of miles from any aid they could send, a small unit of the British Navy was about to face certain destruction.

Four minutes after she had altered course the *Bengal's* masthead lookout had reported to the bridge below that a second ship was in sight. Ten miles away and coming from almost the same direction as the first the newcomer was also steering at a fast rate towards the little convoy. The bridge staff, although still unable to identify the enemy vessels with any certainty, since neither flew an ensign, were nevertheless able to make a fairly accurate guess at their identity. In outline of hull superstructure, masts and derricks both were of typical Japanese construction and seemed to belong to the same class. Raider Number One they estimated to displace about 10,000 tons, and Raider Number Two slightly less. These estimates were not far off the mark, for the ships were in fact the *Hokoko Maru* of 10,493 tons, and the *Kyosumi Maru*, 8,631 tons. Both were armed with five 5-inch guns, were equipped with twin sets of above-water torpedo tubes, and they each carried two catapult aircraft. Together they were a match for at least any British cruiser.

When he had assessed the odds ranged against him Lieutenant-Commander Wilson made a swift decision. The first and most important consideration was the safety of the tanker. Before wirelessing his first enemy sighting report he had arranged an emergency rendezvous with the *Ondina*. Thus if, in order to elude observation, it should become necessary for the ships temporarily to part company they could meet again at the rendezvous when all danger was past to resume their voyage. There was now no hope of escape for the *Bengal*. But if the minesweeper could engage the attention of the Japanese the tanker might be able to get away. Accordingly he sent his last signal to Captain Horsman. 'Act independently.' The little *Bengal* then altered course, and at full speed made straight for the enemy.

As the three warships raced towards their mutual point of impact Wilson took careful note of his foes, and a stream of amplifying signals telling of the enemy's size, appearance and armament crackled through the ether from the *Bengal*'s wireless room. Studying the larger of the two raiders as the speeding vessel came nearer and nearer the *Bengal*'s gunnery officer breathlessly read off the ranges. It was vital that the enemy should come in close for otherwise the British ship would be not only outgunned but outranged. A brief glance over his port quarter confirmed to Wilson that the *Ondina* was making off as fast as she could in the general direction of Fremantle. But would the *Bengal* be able to hold both raiders for long enough?

At twelve minutes past noon Raider Number One opened fire on the cheeky little British ship speeding towards him. Five tall columns of greenish water stood up suddenly from the sea some four hundred yards ahead of the minesweeper, to become falling cascades of lacy foam shot through with iridescent rainbow colours.

'Range three thousand five hundred yards,' sang out the *Bengal*'s gunnery officer. The 12-pounder could now reach the enemy vessel. 'Stand by. Fire!'

Like sweating automatons Petty Officer Ibrahim, Able Seamen Mohammed Khan, Ismail Mohammed, Ragunath Sehae, Ismail Baba and Ordinary Seaman Bala Chandra continued to load and fire their gun, while the minesweeper weaved between the spouting shell bursts. Three minutes after her consort had fired her first salvo Raider Number Two had come within range and herself opened fire on the presumptuous little enemy flaunting her battle ensigns defiantly.

The the miracle happened. Split seconds after the sixth round from the *Bengal*'s 12-pounder had screamed away a terrific explosion rocked the big raider. Flames and smoke gushed from her after-superstructure and licked up to mast-head height. A direct hit either in her magazine or on the ready-use ammunition stowage above. A hoarse cheer went up from the *Bengal*'s watching crew, and the 12-pounder gunlayer executed a brief war dance of triumph.

But, steaming away in the distance, the *Ondina*'s gunners had also been taking part in the battle. Reluctant to leave his gallant little escort to fight it out alone the Dutch captain had ordered his own gun into action. At precisely the same moment as the sixth round from the *Bengal*'s 12-pounder left the gun muzzle the 4-inch gun on the poop of the *Ondina* cracked out its fifth round at eight thousand yards range.

Whether by some lucky chance both projectiles landed together on the target, or whether one of them was a harmless short or over will never now be known. The gunners of both minesweeper and tanker claimed the honour of this hit. The aim and intention were there, and it is right that both ships should share equally in the victory that resulted. But one shell, or even two, are not normally sufficient to sink a ship, and the hit or hits on Raider Number One which had caused the furious fire now raging at her stern had by no means put her out of action. Both enemy vessels, in fact, were now pouring a hail of shells in the direction of the weaving, twisting *Bengal*. A storm of flying shell fragments flailed the air all about her, and a red-hot lump of steel slammed through her thin plating forward, leaving a jagged hole just above the waterline.

But such an unequal battle could not continue indefinitely. The *Bengal* had begun the action with only forty rounds of 12-pounder ammunition in her magazine. When this was expended she would be at the mercy of her enemies, for short-range weapons would probably never be employed since the raiders had only to stand off and blast her out of the water. Wilson took another look at the tanker. She was about seven miles away now and going like a scalded cat. Both the Japanese were giving the little warship their undivided attention. But the amount of 12-pounder ammunition remaining as reported to him by the gunnery officer left him one alternative. Five rounds only were left.

These he would keep, break off action and lead the raiders as much of a dance as he could before they caught up with him.

'Cease firing,' he ordered. 'Make smoke!'

One by one the smoke floats were dropped over the side to pour out their acrid concealing clouds as the *Bengal* hauled round and began to head westwards at top speed. On board the *Ondina* a groan went up from Captain Horsman and those of his officers who had their binoculars trained on the fighting minesweeper as her outline was suddenly shrouded in an upthrusting column of smoke. The Japanese must have scored a direct hit on her, and now she was on fire and probably sinking. They marvelled that she had survived for so long.

The captain of Raider Number One, now considerably slowed down, must have come to a similar conclusion. for, although continuing to fire at his smaller antagonist with his starboard guns, he now brought his port battery into action against the luckless *Ondina*. Raider Number Two, intent upon finishing off the *Bengal*, continued to pursue the minesweeper firing salvo after salvo.

Glancing anxiously in the direction of the distant tanker, now herself under heavy fire, Wilson saw a shell burst just abaft her bridge which was followed by a quick gush of smoke. A few moments later the *Bengal* staggered under a direct hit on her stern which started a fire in an after-compartment. The minesweeper's damage-control party at once went into action with their hoses, and before very long the flames had been subdued.

The battle had now been raging for an hour and, as the *Bengal* continued to steam westwards at maximum speed, dodging and swerving to avoid the enemy shellfire, Wilson noted with grim amusement that Raider Number Two, their immediate pursuer, was hanging back well out of range of their 12-pounder. Raider Number One was now lying stopped, her crew evidently giving their whole attention to the blaze still raging in her afterpart.

A moment later Wilson knew without doubt that the blow they had dealt the *Hokoko Maru* was a mortal one, for even as he focused his binoculars in her direction, a vast

136

explosion shook the big raider. When the smoke and spray had finally cleared away there was no trace of the *Hokoko Maru*. The crew of the *Bengal* gaped unbelievingly at the spot where she had been.

The fire which had been started by the *Bengal*'s lucky hit had in all probability become completely uncontrollable, and the flames had finally reached her main magazine.

But there was no time for speculation as to what had happened. The second raider was still in vengeful pursuit of her small opponent, and for a full fifteen minutes the *Bengal* continued to dodge and twist under a wildly aimed hail of shells. At last, however, the sounds of firing died away and the columns of spray which had been flowering all round the straining vessel fell back into the sea and were not replaced. Peering cautiously through the smoke clouds still trailing round the stern of the minesweeper, her fabric throbbing under the fierce thrust of her engines, Wilson and his men scanned the sea astern in search of the Japanese ship. But the horizon was empty. The raider had vanished, and there was no sign of the *Ondina*.

The engine-room telegraphs jangled and the *Bengal* eased speed. The first lieutenant made a swift inspection of the ship to ascertain the extent of their damage, then hastened back to the bridge with his report. The wounds they had sustained were amazingly slight. The degaussing gear had largely been put out of action due to shellfire, as was most of the *Bengal*'s minesweeping equipment. In addition to the holes in her hull at bow and stern much of her side plating and superstructure had been gashed and scored by shrapnel and flying shell fragments. But most astonishing of all, there was not a single casualty among the ship's company! No one had even suffered a scratch!

Wrote Paymaster Lieutenant Roffe of the Royal Indian Naval Volunteer Reserve, who was on the bridge throughout the action and compiled the official narrative:

'Well over two hundred shells were fired at us, and considering that we received a direct hit and innumerable near misses it is incredible that no one was even slightly injured. Those who took part in this action will never cease to marvel at the result. To think that a small ship with only one

12-pounder gun should engage two raiders, both more than ten times her own size and each with about twenty times her gun power and so enable the tanker to escape, sink one raider and then get away herself is almost miraculous. The Royal Indian Navy should be justly proud of their little Bengal Tiger. She has had her tail twisted and has a few scars, but these will soon be healed and the Tiger will be roaring again.'

Although he was naturally jubilant at the outcome of the battle Lieutenant-Commander Wilson was wondering about the *Ondina*. Had she been able to escape, or had the enemy shell burst he had seen strike her superstructure been merely the precursor of many more, under the impact of which she had finally sunk? There was no means of telling. If he tried to raise her by wireless he might betray both their positions to the surviving enemy ship. If he went in search of her himself he might well encounter the raider again. With practically no ammunition left for the for'ard gun which comprised his main armament there would be no doubt this time of the outcome.

Before either of the two Japanese ships had approached to within range of their own guns he had signalled the tanker to turn and run for it, but had been disappointed to observe that the *Ondina* had not made anything like the drastic alteration of course he had expected. It was possible that she had left matters until too late. Nevertheless with scant hope of his own ship's survival he had steered the *Bengal* direct for the enemy. So well had the minesweeper managed to engage the attention of both the Japanese vessels that nearly an hour had elapsed before any Japanese gun was turned on the fleeing *Ondina*. Still worrying about the fate of the tanker, Wilson eventually decided that his main duty now lay in bringing his own ship safely to port. Accordingly he shaped course for Diego Garcia, arriving there on November 19th, and at Colombo itself four days later. It was here at last that the *Bengal*'s company learned of the fate of the *Ondina*. The story was of an action that matched their own in gallantry.

When the *Bengal* had steamed away towards the approaching raiders the *Ondina* had turned ninety degrees to starboard, thus bringing the enemy on her port quarter. Her gun was manned and, at the order from Captain Horsman, the tanker's 4-inch opened fire on Raider Number One. The second Japanese ship was keeping out of range to the southward.

As has been stated, the fifth round from the *Ondina* scored a possible direct hit on *Hokoko Maru* at the same moment as the shell from the *Bengal*'s 12-pounder smashed home. Soon after the explosion which followed, the big raider then opened fire on the *Ondina* with one of her guns. By now the tanker was steering eastwards, and both raiders were still closing as they hammered away at the fiercely firing minesweeper.

Still holding Raider Number One in their sights the tanker's gun crew scored five more hits in rapid succession on the enemy vessel. These, they claimed, landed on her bridge, superstructure and afterpart. A vast explosion then resulted which blew off the raider's stern. The Japanese ship ceased fire soon afterwards except for an occasional round from the foremost gun, and began to settle by the stern. Up to that time the only damage sustained by the tanker had been the loss of her topmast and wireless aerials.

When she observed that her consort was out of action the second raider then closed in to take a hand in the battle. But the *Bengal* continued to draw her fire. It was during the ensuing pursuit that the little minesweeper dropped the smoke floats which suddenly obscured her from sight in the *Ondina* and caused the tanker crew to conclude that the warship had been sunk.

Raider Number Two now turned her full attention to the *Ondina* and her 5-inch shells began crashing home. A direct hit wrecked the bridge, killing Captain Horsman and wounding others of the crew. Aft on the poop the 4-inch continued to bark defiance until the ammunition gave out. There seemed no point in inviting further punishment and a white flag was reluctantly run up in token of surrender. But as the Japanese raider ignored this and continued to fire on her helpless victim the order was given in the *Ondina* to abandon ship.

The undamaged boats were swung out, the wounded

lowered into them and, keeping their heads well down, the crews pulled away from their stricken vessel. In apprehensive silence they watched as the raider steamed up to within a few hundred yards of them. Then to their horror the Japanese opened fire on the boats with machine guns. The tanker's chief engineer and three of the Chinese crew died under the merciless hail of lead. The others threw themselves flat on the bottom boards expecting every moment to be their last.

After a while the Japanese gunners ceased fire and the raider moved off. Then she turned broadside on to the tanker and fired two torpedoes at her. Both torpedoes struck and, with smoke and flames gushing from her forepart, the tanker heeled slowly over to port. Seemingly satisfied that the vessel had been dealt her death blow the raider then steamed away at high speed to the spot where her consort had sunk. For forty minutes she cruised slowly around, obviously picking up survivors, while the *Ondina*'s men plugged the bullet holes in their boats and bailed out the water they had shipped.

Then once again they dived precipitously for the bottom boards as they saw the raider turn and head in their direction. But this time she ignored the boats and fired another torpedo at the listing *Ondina*, evidently intending it as the *coup de grâce*. But the torpedo missed. To the infinite relief of the tanker men the Japanese captain apparently decided to waste no further time. The raider swung round to the north-east and made off at high speed.

Alone on the heaving sea save for the abandoned tanker, the *Ondina*'s men rowed back and lay off her listing hulk debating their best course of action. A few shattered timbers and other debris floating amid a vast oil patch marked the grave of the *Hokoko Maru*. Of the little *Bengal* there was no sign. She had probably gone to the bottom with all her company. Except for her steep list due to the torpedo hits the *Ondina* showed no sign of sinking. If they went back aboard they might be able to keep her afloat. But there was always the chance that the raider might return, or that another Japanese warship would find them and finish off the *Ondina*.

But as the afternoon wore on and the horizon remained empty the *Ondina*'s men grew bolder. Led by Second Officer Bakker, Third Engineer Leys, Bert Hammond, the Australian naval reservist, and Chinese quartermaster Ah Kong climbed back on board. While the Second Officer and the two seamen scouted round to make a quick examination of the deck damage, Leys went below to inspect the engines. To his joy he found them intact. All four then set to work to correct the list. After they had laboured for more than an hour the tanker was once more floating on even keel. The rest of the crew then clambered aboard. By ten o'clock that night the fire in the *Ondina*'s forcastle had been extinguished, her engines were turning and the battered tanker was on her way back to Fremantle. She arrived there safely ten days later.

When the full story of this extraordinary action had been received by the Admiralty they forwarded a copy to the India Office.

'My Lords,' ran their covering letter, 'have read with great interest the report on this noteworthy success against a much superior enemy force, and they would be glad if the Secretary of State would convey to the Government of India an expression of their deep admiration for the gallant part played by H.M.I.S. *Bengal*.'

Her gallantry was further recognised by the award to Lieutenant-Commander Wilson of the D.S.O., while six Indian D.S.M.s and two Indian Orders of Merit went to the officers and men of the little minesweeper. All the D.E.M.S. gunners of the *Ondina* were awarded the Netherlands Bronze Cross.

## CHAPTER X

## A GREAT AND DANGEROUS JOB

PHENOMENALLY severe weather again in 1943 afflicted our ships at sea. No fewer than one hundred and sixteen gales of force 10 and over were recorded. Larger vessels suffered equally with the ships of the Lilliput Fleet. One month's crop of casualties in the North Atlantic alone included a 6,000-ton merchantman carrying a Convoy Commodore overwhelmed and sunk with no survivors; a destroyer whose bridge structure was bodily torn off by gigantic seas and hurled overboard, taking her captain with it; and a convoy rescue ship capsized with the loss of all hands; while escort vessels came limping into port with bows and gun turrets buckled and decks and superstructures coated with ice up to ten feet thick!

Escorting a convoy from Iceland during continuous gales, the trawler *Northern Spray*'s wardroom was flooded to a depth of five feet and the officers had to swim out to avoid being drowned at their own mess table. On the crew's mess-deck a heavy iron stove was wrenched from its cement base and hurled bodily against a bulkhead eight feet away. At one period during this nightmare voyage the trawler listed over almost to her beam ends and remained there for fifteen agonising minutes while the coal and ballast shifted dangerously and all the ships lights were put out. The lifeboat was smashed to matchwood, deck ventilators were flattened by blows from a giant's fist, and cabin drawers washed into the scuppers. Clinging to the binnacle on the top bridge, forty feet above the deck, Lieutenant Downer, the trawler's captain, could at times see nothing of his ship below, which appeared to be almost entirely submerged. But the *Northern Spray* survived and brought her charges safely into harbour.

Trawlers spaced along the convoy route to Russia as rescue ships heeled over in terrific seas as much as 58 degrees. These fantastic gyrations could be measured by the apparently gravity-defying movements of the blackout curtain covering the wardroom door. As the ship rolled the lower hem of the heavy curtain rose slowly to the level of the table top and remained stiffly suspended there for seconds at a time. Twenty-five degrees of frost were frequently recorded, and axes and steam hoses had to be continually wielded to lessen the dangerous top hamper of ice which persistently formed on decks and superstructure and threatened stability. Even so, two of a small group of ex-Norwegian whalers manned by Patrol Service personnel which were sent to Murmansk to instruct the Russians in our latest minesweeping methods capsized due to becoming top-heavy with ice en route. There were few survivors of these disasters.

But if bad weather added to our misfortunes afloat it combined with poor seamanship on at least one occasion to add to the casualty list of the Nazi U-boat fleet.

Towards the end of April nine German submarines were ordered by U-boat Headquarters to concentrate on a line roughly abreast of Cape Finisterre where they could expect to encounter some rewarding targets. Among the vessels instructed to join up with this wolf pack were *U.439* and *U.659*. Both were 500-ton craft of the Type VII.C class, well armed and equipped with five torpedo tubes. The former was commanded by Oberleutnant zur See von Tippelskirch who, although having made three previous patrols, had not yet been lucky enough to fire a torpedo at a live target; the latter by Kapitänleutnant Hans Stock, a more experienced commander with a total of 31,000 tons of Allied shipping sunk to his credit. By May 1st both U-boats were in position but invisible to each other and others of their consorts who might have arrived.

Two days later *U.439* was informed by a patrolling Focke-Wulf of a convoy of some fifteen ships proceeding southwards and escorted by only two trawlers. Excitedly von Tippelskirch set off at high speed on the surface in the direction of this juicy target. At last he could strike a blow for the Führer. Then to add a positive surfeit to the feast in store the obliging Focke-Wulf reported a second southbound convoy approaching which comprised no less than twenty-eight ships, also weakly escorted by a pair of trawlers. Unknown to von Tippelskirch, Stock in *U.659* had also been acquainted with this information and was steering for the hapless vessels as fast as he could.

The smaller convoy was in fact made up of fifteen coastal-force craft escorted by the trawlers *Bream* and *Coverley*, Admiralty designed vessels of the 'Fish' and 'Dance' classes. The larger convoy was composed of landing craft escorted by the ex-Grimsby trawler *Huddersfield Town* and the Nor-wegian-manned *Molde*. Since all were warships both groups were well able to look after themselves, hence the 'weak' escorts.

The converging courses of the scurrying U-boats and their intended victims met shortly before midnight on the 3rd. *U.439* sighted the coastal-force convoy first and quietly took up station astern of it. But the weather was very unkind for the time of the year. There was a high sea running and visi-bility was poor. Von Tippelskirch decided to dive, push on ahead of the slow-moving convoy, then surface and pass back through the lines of the advancing ships wreaking havoc with guns and torpedoes set to run shallow. as he went.

The first part of his move was carried out according to plan. He surfaced, and with *U.439*'s first lieutenant, Ober-leutnant zur See Gerhard Falow acting as port lookout in the bridge cab, the U-boat increased speed and altered course to port to close the convoy. It was at that precise moment that *U.659* appeared practically alongside. Even if Falow had sighted their sister ship when she loomed up there was little he could have done to avert disaster, for by then the U-boats were too close to each other. With a scream of rending metal *U.439* rammed *U.659* hard amidships.

At once von Tippelskirch stopped engines and then went full astern. But his vessel was mortally stricken. Miniature Niagaras were spouting into the bow compartment and water flooded through before the compartment could be sealed off. The action of going astern drowned the diesel exhausts and the submarine was filling up with choking fumes. Frantic efforts were being made by the engineer officer to trim the wallowing U-boat, but her ballast tanks were too badly damaged, and she began to founder.

All hands were thereupon ordered up into the conning-tower and a signal flashed to the nearby *U.659* asking her to stand by to take off survivors. If Kapitänleutnant Stock made any reply to this it was probably unprintable since with a ripped-open pressure hull his own boat was rapidly filling with sea-water and oil fuel. In a few moments she sank.

On the crowded bridge of the floundering *U.439* a nice point of etiquette was being hotly argued. Oberleutnant zur See Falow vehemently insisted that since it was he who had failed to spot their sister submarine in time to avoid a collision he alone was responsible for the disaster and must therefore go down with the ship. Fiercely he thrust away a proffered lifebelt. While the argument was still in progress a large uncaring wave broke heavily over the U-boat and washed the Germans into the sea.

Meanwhile, unaware of the suicidal mêlée that had taken place in the darkness ahead of them, since the escorts were not fitted with radar, the fifteen-ship convoy continued to approach. Prowling up and down the columns of her flock in a periodical hunt for intruders the captain of the trawler *Coverley* felt a slight bump as though his ship had met some floating obstruction. A discreetly shaded light directed over the bows revealed the tattered wreckage of *U.439* bouncing off the stem, to vanish for good following this fresh collision with the steaming trawler.

Subsequently thirteen indignant Germans were fished out of the sea by the convoy and escorts. Four of them were officers, but they did not include Oberleutnant zur See Gerhard Falow. The senior officer of the escort was delighted to learn from these survivors that not one but two U-boats could be written off at a cost to the Patrol Service of a few feet of badly scraped paintwork.

\* \* \*

After the initial Allied setbacks following Japanese successes in Malaya and elsewhere the Navy's Eastern Fleet was gradually strengthened in preparation for the time when it could take the offensive. Not least important of the reinforcements sent out were some minesweeping trawlers of the Lilliput Fleet.

Since passage through the Mediterranean was still closed due to Axis domination these little ships were compelled to make the long voyage to Ceylon round the Cape. Although the average British trawler is sturdy enough to operate in the waters of any part of the world she is not really intended or designed to undertake lengthy ocean passages. Yet many of those who served under the White Ensign in World War II journeyed great distances during their war service. Due to their limited endurance and the appalling weather they encountered the voyages of some of them became at times long-drawn-out nightmares. Take for example, the saga of H.M. Trawler *Lord Grey*.

Taken over by the Navy at the end of August, 1939, and converted for minesweeping, the *Lord Grey* was a vessel of some 346 tons gross. She had been built in 1928 by Cochrane's of Selby for the Pickering and Haldane Steam Trawler Company of Hull. She was 140 feet long with a 24-foot beam, and her main armament as a minor warship comprised a 12-pounder gun mounted on her forecastle. After serving in the 130th M/S Group at Falmouth, during which time her crew had become adept in the use of the latest equipment for coping with all known forms of moored and influence mines, she was converted for tropical service and sent round to the Clyde for a quick work up. The intention was that she should proceed to Ceylon and join the East Indies command as a unit of a new minesweeping group about to be formed.

Commanding the *Lord Grey* was Lieutenant Austin, an officer of the permanent R.N.V.R. Executive Officer and Navigator respectively were Lieutenant Maurice Hampson and Sub-Lieutenant Cobbe, both temporary R.N.V.R. officers. The crew hailed from the Patrol Service Central Depot, and some of them, including their coxswain, Second Hand Murdo McLeod, were fishermen in civil life.

146

On November 18th, 1941, the *Lord Grey*, together with the controlled minelayer *Jay* and the trawler *Aiglon*, for little ships embarking on a voyage of any length were if possible sailed in company for mutual protection, left Greenock for the Azores on the first leg of her journey. The *Aiglon*, formerly a French-owned trawler from Boulogne, belonged to the 158th Mine-sweeping Group of the Mediterranean Fleet and was returning to her station after refit. But by mid-day on the 19th the two latter vessels were suffering from engine troubles and the *Aiglon* had begun to turn back. During the night the *Jay* disappeared and was not sighted again by Austin in the *Lord Grey*. Later it transpired that she too had been forced to return to harbour.

The weather was about to treat the trawlermen to a sinister foretaste of what was in store for them later on. When daylight came on the morning of the 22nd the *Lord Grey* was cavorting crazily in tremendous seas whipped up by a south-westerly gale. While struggling to secure the sea boat which had broken adrift Sub-Lieutenant Cobbe had one of his legs broken by a blow from the wildly swinging griping-spar. After lying hove to for some hours Austin managed to turn the trawler and the *Lord Grey* made for Campbeltown, where the injured officer was landed and sent to hospital. From there she was ordered to Ardrossan where Lieutenant Austin, required for another appointment, handed over command to an R.N.R. lieutenant. Sub-Lieutenant John Challis, R.N.V.R., also joined as a relief for Cobbe.

On December 19th the *Lord Grey* sailed for the second time again accompanied by the *Aiglon* whose defects had now been repaired. But once more the weather gremlins pounced and soon the trawlers were rolling and bucking in beam seas lashed to fury by vicious squalls. Losing his footing during one of the *Lord Grey*'s wilder lurches the new captain, a big-ship man, was thrown heavily against the binnacle and fractured several ribs. There was no option but to return to harbour at once so that the injured officer could receive medical attention.

Back at Greenock Hampson coaled, stored and watered ship in readiness for their third take-off while his commanding officer was being examined at the naval hospital. Then, since the latter had not returned, Hampson took his place at the customary pre-sailing conference held in the Admiral's office. There to his surprise he was told that due to his injuries the captain of the *Lord Grey* would not be rejoining his ship, and as there was no more experienced officer available Hampson would have to take her to Ceylon.

'Your ship is urgently required on her station,' the grey-haired flag officer told the startled lieutenant. 'Do you think you have the confidence and ability to take her out there?'

Lieutenant Hampson had every right to feel nervous. Prior to joining the Navy as a 'hostilities only' seaman in 1939 he had had no seafaring experience whatever. As a good West Countryman, however, he showed plenty of aptitude for the sea and soon obtained a commission. In August, 1941, sporting the wavy gold stripes of a lieutenant on his sleeves, he joined the trawler *Lord Grey* as Executive Officer. Now, four months later without ever having held seagoing command he found himself called upon to sail one of his Majesty's minesweepers across hostile seas to a point halfway round the globe. But what Hampson lacked in experience he more than made up for in enthusiasm. He was anxious to get on with the war, and he had been keenly disappointed and frustrated by the succession of delays that seemed continually to hold them back.

Temporarily unmindful of the exalted rank of his questioner, he blurted out impulsively: 'I'll get her there, sir, or bust!'

On his way back to the ship he began to wonder how the crew would react to the notion of himself in command. The men were, he knew, equally unhappy and unsettled about the series of accidents and delays. To be saddled with yet another, and this time inexperienced, captain might prove to be the final straw. Well, they would have to put up with him for he was determined to go through with the job. Arrived on board he ordered all hands to be mustered on deck where he spoke briefly and to the point.

'The captain will not be rejoining,' he told them. 'Instead I have been put in command, and this time we're going to get the ship out to her station or sink on the way. There

148

will be no, repeat no, turning back.'

To his surprise there seemed to be unanimous approval of his appointment, not unmixed with enthusiasm. Nevertheless it was with a good deal of inward trepidation that he mounted to the bridge and prepared to take the *Lord Grey* to sea.

This time there were three other trawlers in company: the *Rosemonde*, also an ex-French-owned trawler and now a unit of Minesweeping Group No. 171 in the East Indies command; the *Rosalind*, on her way out to join the 3rd Trawler Group of the Eastern Fleet; and the *Aiglon* whom we have already met. When we learned that two of the vessels were coming all the way with him Hampson felt considerably relieved. But of these four little ships the *Rosemonde* never even got as far as Gibraltar; somewhere in the anonymous wastes of the Atlantic she fell victim to a U-boat. The *Lord Grey* was in fact to meet with only one other of her consorts during the whole of her thirteen-thousand-mile voyage.

On the way down the Clyde Hampson's doubts as to his own capabilities for ship handling were by no means comforted when, over-anxious to avoid collision with a fussy little tug and her charge, he ran the trawler aground. Fortunately the stranding was slight and temporary. The *Lord Grey* was soon backed into deep water without damage to her hull and continued on her way. Two days later the four ships arrived at Milford Haven, where they topped up with coal ready for the run to the Azores. Gales delayed them further, but on January 13th – fortunately for the peace of mind of the superstitious, a Tuesday – the group, now reduced to three, for the *Aiglon* had developed yet more engine defects, finally sailed.

Straight away they ran into their old enemy, foul weather. Heaped up by a strong to gale-force west-south-westerly wind, the seas soon became mountainous. By midnight on the 15th the *Lord Grey* had completely lost touch with her consorts. Two hours later wind and sea were so violent that Hampson was compelled to heave to. A massive wave carried away the lifeboat's griping-spar, but by the light of torches this was secured and lashed back in position. Next morning Hampson confronted a fresh crisis: Second Hand Murdo McLeod was stricken with illness and unable to rise from his bunk. The captain diagnosed influenza.

All that day the trawler lay hove to with great waves breaking over her. Around noon the navigational lights were washed overboard, and a few minutes later the troublesome griping-spar was first broken, then swept away altogether. A fresh spar was contrived from the boat's mast with a number of planks to strengthen it and lashed in position. Then in the late afternoon the wind shifted and fell slightly and it began to rain. Cautiously Hampson increased speed and the trawler began to make headway on her course.

But this improvement in the weather was only temporary, and soon the *Lord Grey* was forced to heave to again. When daylight came on the 16th the trawler was once more labouring in terrific seas. Hampson had managed to take star sights during the night which had fixed their position well to the west of Land's End. By midnight the wind had risen to gale force and the *Lord Grey* was being flung about viciously. Due to bad coal steam pressure had dropped to such an extent that the trawler was scarcely able to keep way on.

A vast army of rollers marched in from the Atlantic to smash successively down on her reeling bows and cascade over her decks in a ceaseless flood. At every moment Hampson expected the 12-pounder gun to be torn from its mounting and flung bodily backwards through the flimsy bridge. There were times when it seemed that the shuddering trawler would never rise from the wave troughs, but somehow she always managed to recover from one savage assault in time to meet the next onslaught. Even the fishermen among the crew vowed that this period was the worst they had ever experienced at sea.

As the hours dragged by the trawler laboriously inched her way onwards, with the unsleeping Hampson clinging grimly to his wave-swept bridge. He had decided to ignore the route orders which instructed him to proceed to Gibraltar by way of the dog-leg route via the Azores, and to make for the Rock direct. Thus he hoped to edge round the storm belt.

By now the severe strain was telling on the crew. Everyone was seasick and some were too ill to move. Water leaked in everywhere and swirled about the messdeck and wardroom inches deep, soaking clothing and bedding. Coxswain McLeod was in a bad way, and the cook, too, had been stricken with a mysterious malady which caused him to vomit blood. Yet despite their sickness and discomfort all hands remained cheerful and inspired by the determination of the captain to pull them through their troubles. With the cook out of action there were no proper meals. But the young steward did his best to fill the breach, although sometimes officers and men felt they would rather face unadorned bully beef than the weird concoctions the amateur chef insisted on preparing by way of variety.

By the 19th little more than coal dust remained in the trawler's bunkers, bread had to be rationed and there was no fresh meat, But, blessedly, wind and sea had eased and the *Lord Grey* was making better progress. Hampson felt able to leave the bridge and go below for a spell. But it was not to rest. Instead this indefatigable man retired to the galley where he mixed, slapped and kneaded dough, and produced a creditable batch of fresh bread for his worn-out crew.

Then at last with Cape St Vincent on the beam grey skies gave way to sunshine. Three days later, with her ensign tattered almost to shreds and the scars of her stormy passage woefully apparent, the *Lord Grey* crept into the shelter of the Rock. Secured alongside the Mole they found the *Rosalind* which had arrived twenty-four hours previously, but of the *Rosamonde* there was no sign, nor would there be ever again. Her loss was the chill reminder of a fate which might befall all of them.

For the next leg of the journey, Gibralta to Freetown, a 2,000-mile run through an area notorious for U-boat activity, there was important work to be done by the trawlers. A tanker had to be escorted to Freetown. On the 29th the *Lord Grey* and *Rosalind* sailed with their valuable charge. Since the *Lord Grey* boasted no asdic set, however, Hampson felt a trifle inadequate as a convoy escort. Whenever his consort began zigzagging as though she had smelt out a

U-boat the little minesweeper prepared for the worst by hastening up to the tanker and remaining handy ready to pick up survivors if she was torpedoed. But to his infinite relief the worst that did happen was a verbal rap over the knuckles through the loudhailer of a lordly British destroyer for making an incorrect recognition signal when challenged by her off Freetown.

The trawlers spent a week in the steamy heat of the West African convoy staging port, boiler cleaning and making good various defects in preparation for the next 1,190-mile lap to Lagos. This time their sailing date was the 13th of February, and it was indeed a Friday. But by now Hampson felt confident of being able to cope with whatever else Fate might have in store. And at least there could be no turning back at this stage in the journey. Except for losing the *Rosalind* en route – due to engine defects she had to continue her voyage later on – the *Lord Grey* arrived at Lagos without untoward incident.

From Lagos the next stop was Walvis Bay, another 2,000-mile run. But Fate had by no means wearied of harassing the *Lord Grey*. Less than two days out Second Hand McLeod collapsed with a severe pain in his side. *Ipso facto* doctor as well as captain, Hampson apprehensively diagnosed appendicitis, and decided to make for the Portuguese island of São Thomé in the Gulf of Guinea where the coxswain could receive proper attention. Here the trawlermen met with much kindness and hospitality. A civilian doctor ran his professional eye over the sick man, assured Hampson to his infinite relief that no operation would be necessary, and prescribed and supplied the appropriate medicine. Before the trawler sailed to resume her voyage the islanders sent her gifts of flowers, fruit, pigs, chickens and ducks. At Walvis Bay they met the *Rosalind* again and celebrated the reunion with an inter-ship cricket match.

The short run from Walvis Bay to Capetown, a mere 750 miles, was by no means the easiest leg of the voyage. For four days and three nights the trawler crept along shrouded in dense fog. Lookouts were required to be doubly alert, for to the wartime hazards of a possible encounter with a floating mine, a U-boat or a surface raider, was added the risk of being run down by a blind-steaming convoy. But Capetown was reached safely and for three weeks, while the *Lord Grey* was given a thorough overhaul, her weary officers and men basked in South African sunshine and hospitality.

Capetown was only a halfway house, however; there were still some five thousand miles of ocean to be faced. At the beginning of April the *Lord Grey* sailed for Durban. But at sea their old foe was lurking in wait. Barely had Table Mountain dipped beneath the horizon than a gale came shrieking down and the trawler was soon floundering in heavy seas. It was cold, too, and the trawlermen were glad to don their heavy winter clothing once more. The waves grew mountainous and the old familiar pattern of flooded mess deck and wardroom brought a renewal of the discomforts they had endured in the early days of the voyage.

They had to remain at Durban for four days while repairs were made to various deck fittings which had suffered from the brusque caresses of the South Atlantic. Then on April 9th the trawler sailed for Mombasa, her last African port of call before tackling the 2,300-mile haul north-eastward to Ceylon. This was to be made with one stop, at the Seychelles.

Despite all the vicissitudes through which they had passed Hampson had kept his men up to scratch at gunnery and other exercises, although if the *Lord Grey* had encountered an enemy submarine or surface warship she could not have put up much of a showing with her little 12-pounder. But the weakness of his armament did not deter the lieutenant from carrying out his duty as a British warship, and he boldly closed and investigated any passing merchantman whose identity seemed doubtful.

At Mombasa the trawler at last fell in with some of the larger units of the Eastern Fleet in harbour there. On April 29th, coaled stored and watered and once again 'in all respects ready for sea', the trawler sailed for the Seychelles. One little *contretemps* occurred to enliven her farewell to her bigger sisters. On the way down river to the open sea, with crew in tropical shirts and shorts properly fell in at their stations for leaving harbour, Coxswain McLeod sounded the 'Still' on his boatswain's call as the bows of the *Lord Grey* came abreast of the flagship's quarterdeck. Hampson turned to salute, then to his horror he saw that the battleship was herself under way. Caught in the grip of the fast-flowing current the little minesweeper was rapidly overhauling the admiral and would thus, contrary to all tradition and regulation, precede her out of harbour. Astern the other ships of the squadron, with their anchors up and down, were also on the move.

Swiftly Hampson made his decision. He could not haul out of the way of the flagship without causing complications, for the trawler could not easily be manoeuvred in the swift tideway. After all, he comforted himself, a minesweeper's job is to sweep ahead of the Fleet. He rang down 'Full Ahead' and, expecting every moment to be blasted off his bridge for his impudence, led the fleet to sea.

Once clear of the land and heading into the Indian Ocean his worries returned in full measure. The trawler was now entering a theatre of war wherein the Japanese still roamed practically unopposed. Certainly their submarines would be active, and without asdic the *Lord Grey* would remain blindfolded to the stealthy underwater approach of a U-boat until it was too late for her to avoid the lunging torpedo. Once again he had his mattress and bedding taken up to the bridge and prepared for a protracted vigil. And now Challis, the young Navigating Officer, suddenly went down beneath a severe attack of bronchitis and was unable to stir from his bunk. The First Lieutenant, Colin Martin, a young Australian Volunteer Naval Reserve sub-lieutenant, took over his duties.

The trawler arrived at Mahe just in time, for when she tied up alongside most of the crew were ill with dysentery. Since the sick men included three out of the four stokers who comprised the *Lord Grey*'s 'black squad' the trawler was now unable to steam. So at Mahe they had to stay until the invalids recovered. It was here that Hampson himself became a casualty. In playing a game of football for the ship's team he broke three ribs.

But their long and eventful voyage was nearing its end. On May 18th the *Lord Grey* set out on the last 1,400 miles to Colombo. This time the Indian Ocean's weather god frowned on them and the voyage was rough and uncomfortable. Steaming blacked out at night in the moist enervating heat was eerie and trying to nerves and bodies. One unexplained occurrence gave them a sharp scare. With their goal only a few hours steaming away a submerged object suddenly crossed the trawler's bows leaving behind a spreading wake. It was too big and slow to have been a torpedo, but it could have been a submarine. Mystified but unprepared to inquire further into the phenomenon they pressed on, to arrive at Colombo on May 25th, 1942.

Soon after the trawler had secured at her berth in the harbour Lieutenant Hampson, newly shaven and immaculate in white tropical uniform, was ushered into the office of the Rear Admiral, Ceylon.

'H.M.S. *Lord Grey* come to join the station, sir,' he reported.

'Good. Glad to have you here at long last,' smiled the admiral.

It had been a long time. Counting her two false starts the *Lord Grey* had been on passage for seven months!

And the epic of the *Lord Grey* was only one of many. A sister ship, the *Lord Irwin*, sent round the Cape to become the first 'LL'[1] minesweeper in the Mediterranean, took six months and five days on the voyage. Commanded by Chief Skipper Cyril Sutcliffe, R.N.R., an experienced trawlerman from Grimsby, the *Lord Irwin* suffered her full share of bad weather and other misfortunes. At one period in the voyage Sutcliffe and his second skipper, Jasper Pidgin, like himself a Grimsby fisherman, were left to run the ship by themselves; the entire crew had been laid low by fever. Yet as proof of her quality the gallant little *Lord Irwin* celebrated her arrival in the Mediterranean by disposing of eight enemy mines in her first sweep.

These men and others of the Lilliput Fleet who daily faced and overcame all hazards and difficulties well deserved the tribute paid to them at the time by the First Lord of the Admiralty when he told the country they were doing 'a great and dangerous job'.

[1] 'Double longitudinal', a method of sweeping magnetic mines.

## CHAPTER XI

## 'DOENITZ MUST BE FEELING AWFUL'

THE Allied landings in Sicily and at Salerno in 1943 promised ripe pickings for German submarines. Accordingly a number of U-boats were hurried round to the Mediterranean. Among them was *U.732* commanded by twenty-four-year-old Oberleutnant zur See Klaus Peter Carlsen, an ardent Nazi. Unfortunately for him he was to encounter en route a particularly alert unit of the Lilliput Fleet.

Built at Danzig in 1942, *U.732*, also known as 'U-Carlsen' after the name of her commanding officer, as was the custom in the U-boat fleet, was a 500-ton vessel of the Type VIIC class. She was armed with one quadruple 20-millimetre gun, a pair of twin 20-millimetre guns, and also mounted two machine-guns on the bridge. She was fitted with one stern and four bow torpedo tubes. During her two previous patrols she had sunk four Allied ships totalling 25,000 tons, and when she left Brest on October 17th, 1943, at the start of her third and final cruise Carlsen looked forward to adding considerably to this total. Painted on the bridge of *U.732* and sported on the caps of her crew was Carlsen's chosen symbol, a red devil carrying a trident.

Soon after sailing Carlsen received orders from U-boat Headquarters to proceed down the Portuguese coast and through the Straits of Gibraltar into the Mediterranean for an undisclosed destination. Cruising submerged, *U.732* had reached the entrance of the Straits when, soon after one o'clock in the afternoon of the 31st of October, propeller noises were suddenly detected on her hydrophones. Before Carlsen could take avoiding action all hell was let loose.

Above them in the sunshine a convoy of six Allied merchantmen had been peacefully steaming on its way from Lisbon to Gibraltar. Shepherding the flock were a pair of trawlers belonging to the Gibraltar Trawler Force. They were the *Imperialist* and *Loch Oskaig*, commanded respectively by Lieutenant-Commander Bryan Rodgers, R.N.V.R., senior officer, and Lieutenant George Clampitt, R.N.R. Approaching the searched channel leading into the Gibraltar anchorage Rodgers formed the convoy into two columns with his own ship leading and the *Lock Oskaig* bringing up the rear.

At sixteen minutes past one in the afternoon of October 31st Seaman William Jeffrey, in civil life a Cornish stonemason and now a Higher Submarine Detector Rating in the trawler *Imperialist* – a man so single-mindedly concerned with the faultless operation and maintenance of his precious asdic set that his shipmates dubbed him pernickety – obtained a submarine contact. The echo as he reported it to his captain bore 'Red 40 degrees', which was ahead and to port of the convoy. Rodgers himself donned the headphones to check on Jeffrey's report purely as a matter of routine. An asdic operator as keen as the Cornishman was not likely to be mistaken. Nor was he indeed, and Rodgers noted that the contact was distant about a thousand yards. A moment later the trawler captain pressed the alarm button and, while the crew of the *Imperialist* were pelting excitedly to their action stations, he rang down to the engine room for maximum revolutions.

In the little wardroom Rodger's Number One, Lieutenant Agnew of the Royal Canadian Naval Volunteer Reserve, who was censoring the ship's company mail ready for despatch on arrival at Gibraltar, had just read a sentence in one letter which began, 'Things are very dull here these days,' when the clangour of the alarm bells galvanised him into activity. With a wry grin he dropped the letter he was censoring, grabbed his steel helmet and leapt for the door.

The *Imperialist* was a fine little ship. She grossed 520 tons, was of part-welded construction and measured 175 feet overall. She had been built in 1939 by Smiths Dock Company for the Hull Northern Fishing Company Ltd, and taken over by the Navy in August of the same year. Com-

157

pared with most other ships of the Lilliput Fleet she was well armed indeed. In addition to depth-charge rails and throwers she mounted a 4-inch gun forward, a Bofors and a pair of point-fives abaft the funnel, and two Oerlikons amidships mounted on sponsons placed to port and starboard of the bridge structure.

Not only was the *Imperialist* well armed for a trawler, she had an exceedingly enthusiastic crew. Leading Seaman Evans, gunlayer of the 4-inch, and Seaman Sam Barrett, a Newfoundlander who was trainer of the Bofors, were as fanatical about the superlative qualities of the respective weapons as any dyed-in-the-wool Whale Island gunnery instructor. Chief Engineman Riley ran his department with the clockwork efficiency of a Fleet destroyer, doing all his own maintenance, and the depth-charge crews under Sub-Lieutenant Marc, R.N.V.R., had brought their drill to a high state of proficiency. Compared with his own submariners, however, Oberleutnant zur See Carlsen would probably have dubbed the trawlermen blundering amateurs, and he would not have erred more gravely.

Ordering Clampitt in the *Loch Oskaig* to take care of the convoy Rodgers steamed at top speed towards the target. As the trawler bounced over the sunlit waves the depth-charge crews stood by alert and ready to put their drill into deadly practice. To obviate any possibility of a mistake or delay Rodgers had instituted a duplicated system of communication with Marc. Two ratings stood by the telephone and loud-hailer to repeat all depth-charge instructions from the bridge.

'Set pattern D for dog,' would be the order from Rodgers.

'Pattern D for dog set,' came the reply from his A/S officer.

'Out pins,' would be the next order, followed by the prompt echo of 'Pins out.'

Then after the cautionary 'Stand by' the final order to fire would be given by both the depth-charge bell and orally through the loud-hailer.

Such was the speed of reaction and manoeuvre on board the *Imperialist* following the initial contact report that a bare four minutes later the trawler fired her first depth-charge pattern. Ten amatol-packed cylinders sank into the sea, and inside U-boat Carlsen, nearly two hundred feet beneath, their thunderous detonations sounded like the crack of doom. The U-boat whipped and shuddered, sending the crew sprawling in all directions; lights snapped out as the bulbs exploded, particles of cork, flakes of paint and dust showered in clouds, and thick choking fumes filled every compartment.

While the trawlermen in the *Imperialist* were gazing awe-struck at the sea's furious turmoil caused by their bursting depth charges the dark-grey hull of a submarine surfaced abruptly at its centre. Grabbing up his binoculars Rodgers noted with considerable satisfaction that the U-boat had been badly mauled by the shattering blows he had dealt. The barrel of one of her guns was bent and twisted grotesquely, her conning-tower was buckled and torn and the jumping wire had been ripped off. With no way on, the submarine's fore-casing was dipping beneath the surface while her stern canted upwards. The periscope remained housed, the conning-tower hatch battened down, and there was no movement of engines or hydroplanes. She lay like a great stunned whale.

But despite her lifeless appearance Rodgers was taking no chances. In making a submarine attack you had to get your blows in first and give the enemy no chance to retaliate. The U-boat had surfaced on the *Imperialist*'s starboard quarter and the trawler's engines, attaining under Riley's skilful coaxing a higher rate of revolutions than ever before, were thrusting her round to starboard so that the 4-inch gun could be brought to bear. Already the Bofors was pumping shells at the silent target, and the twin point-fives were hammering rhythmically; then the starboard Oerlikon came into action, to be followed at last by the deeper crash of the 4-inch, firing on an extreme bearing.

For ten minutes the trawler's guns banged away in this weird one-sided duel. Shells from the Bofors blew one of the U-boat's machine-guns clean out of the conning-tower, tracers from the point-fives bounced and ricocheted off the sleek whaleback, the starboard-side Oerlikon gunner played a devil's tattoo along her pressure hull. The steamer

*Fylingdale*, on the extreme wing of the passing convoy, enthusiastically joined in with a couple of bursts of machine-gun fire which endangered the men in the *Imperialist* more than the wallowing U-boat.

After the first two sighting shots the trawler's 4-inch had begun ranging on this oddly quiescent target. The third round scored a direct hit at the base of *U.732*'s conning-tower which was followed by an explosion and a gout of greenish-yellow gas from the riven hull. Then slowly the submarine began to sink.

Keeping the target dead ahead as the trawler steamed towards the U-boat Rodgers ordered a temporary cease fire. As the noise of the bombardment died away he noted that there was still no movement of the submarine's engines, no alteration of trim, no sign of life. It was vastly mystifying and somehow macabre. The trawlermen gazed fascinated at the spectacle of a slowly foundering enemy who refused to come out and fight.

When the *Imperialist* eventually reached the submarine's position *U.732* had disappeared beneath the waves. Grimly Rodgers hastened her on her death dive with another pattern of ten depth charges. Set shallow, the thudding detonations of this pattern put the trawler's own dynamo out of action, and Chief Engineman Riley resignedly chalked up another repair job. Having crossed the target to drop the ten-charge salvo the *Imperialist* turned, came back to the spot and let go a further eight charges, this time set deep. That ought to finished off this peculiar opponent, thought Rodgers, as he moved away towards the *Loch Oskaig* who had now come up to lend any additional aid needed.

Nevertheless, while his own men took a breather Rodgers ordered his junior to try to obtain asdic contact with the sunken U-boat. But after half an hour's search Clampitt reported 'no contact'. Rodgers instructed him to drop a full depth-charge pattern set deep then to carry on with the search until dusk when he should return to harbour.

As he led the convoy into Gibraltar Rodgers felt certain in his own mind that the U-boat with its red devil symbol had been destroyed. Probably his first pattern of depth charges had put her out of action completely and her surfacing had been involuntary, the crew already struck down by poisonous fumes in the form of the greenish gas which had gushed from the submarine's hull after the 4-inch shell had opened it up. Nevertheless his formal report to the Flag Officer Commanding North Atlantic was meticulous in detail and summing up, and he modestly claimed only a 'probable' kill. There was, after all, a total absence of fuel oil and the usual wreckage to provide tangible evidence. F.O.C.N.A. was pleased, for the naval authorities at Gibraltar had learned that a number of U-boats were moving south, and an augumented sea and air patrol had been ordered.

But U-Carlsen was not in fact finished. It has been emphasized that U-boats were tough and hard to destroy, and the action between *U.732* and the trawler *Imperialist* is a striking case in point. When the trawler's first salvo of depth charges exploded beneath her keel the U-boat was very badly shaken indeed. In addition to the external damage noted by Lieutenant-Commander Rodgers when the submarine had surfaced under his gunfire all her compartments had suffered severely, her wireless was wrecked, compass smashed, periscopes badly damaged, the saddle tanks were pierced and water was entering the pressure hull. She had been literally blown to the surface by the force of the explosions.

As she lay there apparently helpless while enduring the bombardment from the trawler's guns Carlsen and his men were striving frantically to get the boat down to the exiguous safety of the sea bed. Answering the controls sluggishly *U.732* had at last consented to slip downwards. But due to the hammering she had received it was difficult to regulate the speed and angle of her dive, and she hit the bottom at five hundred and eighty-five feet with such a force that her hydroplanes were jammed in a hard-up position. Carlsen ordered the motors to be shut off and told his men that they must lie doggo where they were for as long as possible in the hope that the hunter above would eventually go away believing she had sunk them. Periodically the weakened hull trembled and shook to the detonation of further depth charges, but at last the attacks ceased.

As the long hours dragged by the U-boat crew lay gasping and sweating in the fetid darkness of their steel prison. At irregular intervals the eerie silence was broken by a strange rustling noise from outside the boat which heightened their fears and stretched their nerves to snapping point. Although they did not know it this terrifying sound was caused by the submarine's hull brushing against the sea bed as a powerful current trundled them along the bottom like a huge tin can.

By nine o'clock that night the air in the stricken U-boat had become so foul that Carlsen decided they would have to surface and take their chance. Oberleutnant Ingenieur Gunther Feist had managed to check over the diesels before movement became too much of an effort and he felt fairly confident that they were undamaged and would still function. Accordingly the motors were started and put to full ahead, and with the hydroplanes still immovable in the 'up' position, *U.732* corkscrewed to the surface.

One by one the sailors thankfully dragged themselves out on to the crumpled casing to gulp the lifegiving fresh air, while Carlsen took a cautious sweep around with his glasses. The wind was westerly and the sea slight. Away on the port quarter twinkled the lights of Ceuta and ahead lay Cape Spartel. *U.732* was in the middle of the Straits heading for the Atlantic at sixteen knots. If they could only find somewhere to lie up and effect emergency repairs, thought Carlsen, they might be able to get back to base. But the trawler *Imperialist* had struck the submarine a mortal blow even if U-Carlsen's death throes were a trifle delayed.

On anti-submarine patrol off Gibraltar on that Sunday night cruised the British destroyer *Witherington* (Senior Officer), *Douglas, Wishart* and *Active*. Since the trawler's afternoon attack on *U.732* the *Douglas* had also visited the spot to probe the position of the reported sinking, but with negative results. This was not surprising, for the current had in fact carried the crippled submarine to a point six miles away before Carlsen had finally been forced to surface.

Thirty-four minutes after *U.732* started her forlorn dash for the Atlantic a searchlight beam suddenly stabbed out and held her in its glare. At the business end of this merci-less dagger of light was the destroyer *Douglas*. This fresh misfortune, as Carlsen realised only too bitterly, signified the beginning of the end, and he ordered his men into the conning-tower in preparation for abandoning ship. In the absence of any identifying signal from the speeding sub-marine the *Douglas* opened fire and shells began to burst all around her.

Through his night glasses the destroyer captain could see that the U-boat's conning-tower was packed with men wav-ing their arms and shouting, while others appeared to be falling or jumping into the sea. But since she continued on her way and ignored his signals to stop he had no option but to shoot at her although this seemed to be plain murder. Then, sickened by the slaughter, he swung round and came in to ram.

As he approached at high speed *U.732* suddenly turned away to port and the destroyer passed just ahead of the submarine. But as she did so she dropped a pattern of shallow-set depth charges. Straight into the boiling inferno of their explosion slid the straining hull of *U.732*. When the smoke and spray had cleared away the submarine had vanished. Twenty-two survivors were eventually picked up, among them Oberleutnant zur See Klaus Peter Carlsen.

That same night the destroyer sank another U-boat, and in reporting these successes to the Captain (D) at Gibraltar Lieutenant-Commander Tennat, senior officer in the *Wither-ington*, felt justified in adding an unofficial postscript. 'Doenitz,' he signalled, 'must be feeling bloody awful!'

## MISSING, PRESUMED LOST

DURING the war if a vessel belonging to the Royal Navy was reported missing, presumed lost, the Admiralty's assumption that the worst had happened was usually only too sadly justified. When, therefore, in January, 1944, the relatives of the twenty-two officers and ratings serving in one of the smaller ships of the Lilliput Fleet received a telegram from the Admiralty conveying just such ominous news there can have been few of them who dared to hope that perhaps somewhere, somehow, their loved ones might yet be alive. So much can happen to a little trawler in wartime.

At four o'clock in the afternoon of January 11th, 1944, Convoy UR.105 and escort left Loch Ewe, on the north-west coast of Scotland, bound for Iceland. Three merchant ships comprised the convoy, and escorting them were the trawlers *Northern Spray* and *Veleta*. The former was a 650-ton turbine-driven vessel built at Bramen in 1936 and originally owned by Northern Trawlers, Ltd; the latter an Admiralty designed trawler of the 'Dance' class. The *Veleta* displaced some 530 tons, could steam at 15 knots and had an endurance range of 3,000 miles. Attached to Convoy UR.105 as additional escort for the voyage was H.M. Trawler *Shrathella*.

While by no means the oldest ship in the Patrol Service – at least one vessel of 1906 vintage rendered yeoman service under the White Ensign throughout the war – the *Strathella* could nevertheless be classed as a veteran. She was a little steel-built trawler of 210 tons gross, 115 feet long with a 22-foot beam. She hailed from Aberdeen where she had been built in 1913. Ever since her take-over by the Navy in 1940 the *Strathella* had been employed as a Harbour Defence

Patrol craft at Akureyri, in Iceland. She was armed with two 6-pounder guns, one on the forecastle and the other on a sponson immediately before the bridge. For air defence she mounted two Browning machine-guns. Since she had to be on the lookout for U-boats the *Strathella* was also fitted with an asdic set and carried depth charges. A roofed-over structure had been added to her original bridge to function as a 'monkey island', and this gave her the look of having an old-fashioned bathing cabin built amidships.

In January, 1944, the *Strathella* was commanded by thirty-year-old Temporary Lieutenant Osmund Lee, R.N.V.R., in peacetime an accountant, who had joined the Navy in 1941. His previous ship had been an Examination Vessel stationed at Londonderry. Although he claimed no nautical experience before joining the Navy his rapid promotion to lieutenant was proof of a natural bent for the sea. His First Lieutenant was Temporary Sub-Lieutenant Alan Bateman, another wartime entry who, after serving for a time on the lower deck, had been commissioned in the previous August. The *Strathella* was the latter's first seagoing ship as an officer. The trawler carried a crew of twenty, a number of whom, including both enginemen, had served in fishing trawlers in civil life.

After months of arduous service in Iceland the little trawler became badly in need of a thorough overhaul. Accordingly she had been sent down to North Shields for a refit. From there she had sailed south-about to Tobermory for a quick work-up at the Atlantic Battle School in H.M.S. *Western Isles*. While there she had developed certain engine defects which necessitated a visit to the repair yard at Oban for these to be doctored before returning to Iceland. Passed as fit once more the *Strathella* had travelled on to Loch Ewe where she was ordered to join up with Convoy U.R.105. To maintain her normal service speed of eight knots she needed to consume some eight tons of coal a day which, with a bunkering capacity of sixty tons, gave her a maximum endurance of range of about a week. Prior to departure from Loch Ewe she topped up her bunkers to their limit.

When Convoy UR.105 reached the open sea the *Strathella* was ordered to take station on its port beam, with the

*Northern Spray* leading and the *Veleta* on the starboard beam. For the first twenty-four hours of the voyage the weather remained moderate, but towards dusk on the 12th conditions began to deteriorate. A deepening swell set the ships pitching and rolling awkwardly, while periodic rain squalls frequently curtained them from one another in the lessening visibility. Soon after midnight Bateman, who was on watch on the bridge of the *Strathella,* lost sight altogether of the ships in the convoy, which had fallen some way astern. But by now the little trawler had plenty of worries of her own.

To start with, the engines were giving trouble again and she was difficult to handle in the heavy seas. There was worse to come. A full gale was now developing from the south-west and, with the trawler crazily corkscrewing to a wind and sea fine on the port quarter, there was continuing danger that she might ship a big sea which would poop her. Somehow they managed to get through the night without serious mishap, but the grey dawn brought no relief in the weather.

The wind was blowing at near hurricane strength, marshalling endless battalions of long foaming combers with crests over thirty feet high. Clinging to his reeling bridge that morning Lieutenant Bryant, R.N.V.R., captain of the *Veleta,* caught a single brief glimpse of the *Strathella* through his binoculars as she topped a wave far to the west of the straggling group of ships. That was the last anyone in the convoy saw of the little trawler.

For forty-eight hours the gale continued to pound Convoy UR.105. When it finally blew itself out Lieutenant Downer, R.N.R., senior officer of the escort in the *Northern Spray,* was able to take stock of the situation. But when he checked over his flock there was no sign of the third trawler. Closing the *Veleta,* Downer asked Bryant over the loud-hailer if he had seen anything of the missing vessel. But Bryant could only report the fleeting glimpse he had caught of her through the flying spindrift and driving rain on the morning of the 13th. The masters of the merchantmen had not sighted her at all. Accepting the risk of attracting the attention of a patrolling U-boat, both the *Northern Spray* and the *Veleta* now tried to raise their missing consort by wireless. But no answer came to their repeated calls; no reassuring chatter of morse from the *Strathella*. The two larger trawlers dared not leave the convoy unguarded to go in search; they could only push on to Iceland and hope that the *Strathella* would turn up later.

When they arrived at Reykjavik on the 19th Downer reported the disappearance of the little ship to the Admiral Commanding. Although the weather was still very bad the admiral promptly ordered a sea and air search. He knew that the *Strathella*'s wireless set was weak, which was probably why she had not been able to make contact with either of the other two escorts or answer their signals. He was also aware of her limited steaming endurance. Since the convoy itself had taken eight days to make the passage from Loch Ewe the trawler's fuel must be running low, if it were not entirely exhausted. He warned the Admiralty by signal that the *Strathella* was missing.

Four days later the search for the vanished ship having proved abortive it was reluctantly abandoned. On the 23rd the Admiral Commanding Iceland informed the Admiralty that H.M. Trawler *Strathella* was still missing and must now be presumed lost. Then followed a list of the names of her officers and men. A few hours afterwards the stricken eyes of their relatives were desperately seeking a grain of hope in a tersely worded telegram which began 'The Admiralty regrets...'

But the cranky little *Strathella* had neither floundered through stress of weather nor had she fallen a victim to a prowling U-boat. Her crew were alive and well and their vessel was still afloat. But they were indeed in a hazardous plight.

For the best part of the forty-eight hours that the gale which had sprung up on January 12th continued to rage the *Strathella* had been compelled to heave to. She was rolling to an alarming degree and heavy seas were breaking over her. One solid wall of water crashing aboard wrecked her solitary boat in its davits, unshipped both machine-guns and whirled them overboard, shattered the ten-inch signalling searchlight on the port bridge wing, and tore two of the depth charges free of their lashings. After a nightmare chase in pursuit of the heavy canisters of high explosive as they went crashing and bounding around the spray-swept decks, both were eventually captured and jettisoned.

Barely had this emergency been overcome than another towering greybeard smashed down on the staggering trawler. The irresistible flood burst open and cascaded through the door of the wireless cabin and burned out the transmitter. Thus the *Strathella* was deprived of her only means of communication with the other ships, for she carried no spare parts for the set.

On the 15th the tired overstrained engines staged a series of calamitous breakdowns that taxed all the ingenuity of Engineman James Harkness and his colleague Harry Heap to cope with. Machinery parts actually dropped off and had to be lashed in place with seizing wire; more than a score of the boiler tubes were leaking and steam pressure fell disastrously. Due to the violence of the storm the trawler had been swept considerably off course and fuel was now running low. By the 21st barely three tons of coal, most of it dust, remained in the bunkers. Because of the bitter cold Lee decided to husband this tiny stock of fuel for heating and cooking; otherwise they could only hope to accomplish a bare half-day's steaming which would scarcely improve their position, and leave them in a worse plight when it was exhausted. The naval authorities in Iceland would, he knew, institute a search as soon as the convoy arrived and reported them missing.

He despatched Second Hand Victor Anderson in search of some canvas to use as a spanker to try to keep the ship's head to wind. Anderson and his men duly fashioned a crude sail from the boat's cover and this was rigged up on the mainmast. But due to the trawler's high bow the sail had little effect.

Lee now made a careful inventory of the provisions and water on board. Their stock was slender enough, for as a harbour defence vessel the *Strathella* had no reason to carry a large supply of emergency food nor had she the necessary stowage space for it. A system of rationing was introduced, but since both officers and men confidently expected that they would soon be found, the allowance was fairly liberal at two meals a day per man with two cups of tea. Distress signals were hoisted and watches set, with extra air lookouts posted.

While Harkness and his men laboured in the trawler's dank and silent engine-room to patch up their defective machinery, Sub-Lieutenant Bateman, the telegraphist and the asdic operator tried a little cannibalising in an endeavour to get the wireless set working again. They opened up the asdic and extracted a condenser and transferred it to the wireless transmitter. But after hours of work all that the set could be persuaded to emit was one miserable signal of such weak strength as to be inaudible at any but the shortest range. Then it refused to function again. They were now permanently cut off from communication with the outside world.

Meanwhile the *Strathella* had become the plaything of certain ocean currents which were bearing her helplessly out of range of searching aircraft. The chief culprit at first was a flow known to oceanographers as the Irminger Current. An offshoot from the eastward-flowing North Atlantic Drift, the Irminger Current recoils cyclonically from the land mass of Iceland and swings westward, where it is joined by a chilly flow from the Arctic. Known as the East Greenland Current this stream sets south and west around the coast of Greenland. Thus the Irminger Current had first borne the trawler away from Iceland and into the orbit of the East Greenland Current, which was now sweeping her to the westward at a speed of some five to ten miles a day.

The days dragged past with nothing to be seen but the empty expanse of the North Atlantic stretching to the horizon all around. Not even the brief flight of a seabird broke the monotony of the dull grey sky which hung overhead like a pall. But with Lieutenant Lee's cheerful confidence to encourage them the men of the *Strathella* remained in good spirits. Those off duty played 'Huckers', slept or wrote letters just as if they were out on normal patrol, although they sometimes wondered if these would ever be mailed. The men on watch cleaned their guns, worked about the ship at routine tasks and kept a keen eye lifting for a glimpse of land, a patrolling warship or a scouting aircraft. Hopes that a search for them was continuing had faded, for the trawlermen realised that by now they must have been given up for lost. Their chief worry was the thought of the anxiety their absence was causing their wives and families.

When daylight came on the morning of the 27th an excited yell from the lookout brought all hands rushing on deck. Land was in sight some thirty miles away to the northwest. But without proper charts Lee could only guess that this was the east coast of Greenland. He decided to squander the remaining coal, add all the wooden fittings that could be stripped from the ship and used for fuel and try to reach the shore. By three o'clock that afternoon the trawler's engines were once more turning and the *Strathella* began her slow approach. When darkness fell Lee decided to lay to until the morning. Tired and hungry the trawlermen turned in full of hopeful anticipation.

Next day however brought bitter disappointment. Steam was raised and the *Strathella* was under way again by ten o'clock. But as they closed in the trawlermen found themselves entering a vast field of brash ice dotted with floating icebergs. All approaches to the land were completely blocked by this impassable barrier as far as the eye could see. With only two hours of steam left in the boiler Lee edged the little trawler back to the comparative safety of open water. Then the engines ceased to turn, the ashes cooled in the furnace, and the *Strathella* resumed her slow heart-breaking drift to the westward, firing distress rockets at regular intervals.

Daily the cold grew more intense for they were within only a few degrees of the Arctic Circle. The trawler's deck, gun platforms, bridge and superstructure were soon heavily coated with a thick mantle of ice. Icicles hung pendant from the gun-barrels and festooned the rigging in glittering clusters. The trawlermen set to work with a will to chip away this dangerous top hamper, for at least the exercise helped to keep the blood circulating in their numbed bodies. And the ice was useful, for by now they had run out of fresh water and were forced to melt down some of it for drinking.

Rations were cut to one meal a day and a half a pint of water per man.

After their brief tantalising glimpse of the land, which had soon receded from sight once they were caught up again by the current, the days marched in barren procession. If any one of the men of the drifting *Strathella* was secretly beset by fears that they would all ultimately starve to death, leaving a ghost ship peopled by crumbling skeletons doomed to drift endlessly about the oceans, he kept them to himself. Lee, Bateman, Anderson the Coxswain, Harkness the senior Engineman, all of them in fact, were constantly cudgelling their brains in search of a way out of their predicament. But always in the end they were driven back to the inescapable facts. With no fuel to drive the engines, no boat with which they could try to tow the ship or send a party away for help, and without wireless to tell of their plight they could only drift and hope for the best.

On February 8th land was sighted again. Lee now set all hands to work to fashion a jury trysail from the scant material available with which they could endeavour to head the ship in the right direction. By sewing together the remnants of their original spanker and adding the ship's blackout screens and the bedcovers from their bunks they managed to contrive an area large enough to catch the wind effectively.

The work took them four days to complete during which they were pounded by more bad weather. Icy squalls swept down on them and snow storms frequently blotted out all trace of the distant shore. Icebergs, too, were becoming numerous, menacing neighbours to have around, for if the helpless *Strathella* should be thrust on to an underwater spur projecting from one of them and holed, her end would be swift and certain.

On the morning of the 12th the patchwork sail was finished and hoisted. To the delight of all hands its effect on the *Strathella* was immediate and at last they could begin to steer for the shore. But the sail could only be hoisted in a very moderate breeze for a stronger wind would soon have ripped it to shreds. Then occurred an incident which caused their hopes of rescue to soar steeply. High in the sky they spotted an aircraft, their first sign of life for more than four weeks.

They rushed about the deck shouting and waving their arms. They fired salvoes of flares and rockets. Signalman Turrel flashed away with his Aldis lamp until his fingers ached. But it was all in vain. Thousands of feet above them, unseeing and unheeding, the plane droned steadily on its course. Gradually it dwindled to a speck, then finally vanished from sight.

The spirits of the trawlermen slumped to zero, but hope flooded back when their captain reminded them that the aircraft must have a base and that base was probably not far distant. They had obviously drifted into a regularly patrolled area. Also the current that had borne them along for so many days was now definitely edging them towards the land. Next day, the 13th, the *Strathella* had drifted to within four miles of the shore. But icebergs were even more thickly scattered about and the trysail had frequently to be brought into use to haul the trawler out of the path of the chilly monsters which periodically bore down on her.

Then, at about five o'clock that evening, they heard the engines of another aircraft. This time Lee determined to go into action in a big way. He sent the 6-pounder crews to stand by their loaded guns and stationed all spare hands with rockets at vantage points round the ship. Turrell clutched his Aldis ready to start signalling. Steadily the plane approached, and through his glasses Lee saw that it was a Catalina bearing U.S. Navy markings. As soon as he judged the airmen were close enough to see their signals he gave the order to open fire and the trawler erupted in an impressive display of gunfire and exploding rockets. Turrell's lamp winked continuously as he kept the light trained on the flying boat.

To their joy the big aircraft suddenly banked, lost height and swept low over their mastheads. While the airmen circled the trawler Turrell flashed brief details of their odyssey. Presently the Catalina's signal lamp began to blink in reply. They had informed their base in Greenland, said the Americans, and help was already on the way. Then with a final flirt of her wings the aircraft skimmed off towards the land, while the trawlermen settled down to wait. Shortly before dawn next day the U.S. Coastguard Cutter *Madoc* surged alongside the *Strathella*. Her long ordeal was at an end.

## CHAPTER XIII

# A NAVY WITHIN THE NAVY

As the war progressed the composition of the Patrol Service changed both in ships and men. By 1943 many of the original requisitioned fishing trawlers had been sunk, but their places had been taken by Admiralty-built trawlers specially designed for the job which were being turned out under the various war-time shipbuilding programmes.

Differing from each other only in minor constructional details the new ships were built in ten classes, nine of these being designated by the names of trees, lakes, Shakespearian characters, dances, British islands, hills, Knights of the Round Table, fish and military ranks. The tenth class, of twelve vessels built in Portugal, were known as the 'Porta-downs', and bore such names as *Product*, *Professor*, *Protest* and *Probe*. It is appropriate that during their widely separated war travels H.M.S. *Romeo* met H.M.S. *Juliet* at least once!

The new trawlers came off the stocks in a steady stream every year, the largest number of them being commissioned for service during 1942. Of roughly similar dimensions, their displacement averaged up to 650 tons, they measured some 164 feet long with a beam of 27 feet and a draught of 12 feet 6 inches. They were fitted with radar and asdic, could steam at a top speed of fifteen knots and had an endurance range of three thousand miles. Their complement was 33 officers and men, and they were armed with a 4-inch gun, two twin .5 inch machine guns and some smaller weapons. They were generally classified as A/S-M/S ships, which meant that they could be employed either for minesweeping or anti-submarine duties. A few were designed specially for

174

danlaying, dans being special buoys for marking cleared areas in minesweeping.

Along with the new trawler fleet hundreds of smaller craft were also being built for this Navy within the Navy. Next to the trawlers in size and importance were B.Y.M.S., or British Yard Minesweepers. Of wooden construction throughout to render them impervious to magnetic mines with a strengthened oaken apron aft, these were sturdy little ships displacing some 334 tons gross. They were about as large as the average fishing trawler, measuring 136 feet overall and 24½ feet in the beam. They were diesel engined and could steam at fifteen knots for two thousand five hundred miles. Their complement was 30 officers and men, and they were armed with a 3-inch gun, two 20-millimetre guns and a couple of Lewis guns. Built in American ship-yards under Lease-Lend, many of these little ships crossed the Atlantic alone and unescorted; others voyaged distances to reach their war stations which in peacetime would have been considered remarkable.

There was, for example, *BYMS.12*. Built at Seattle in the State of Washington, U.S.A., this little ship was com-missioned in her American yard by Skipper Lieutenant Cyril Watson, R.N.R., in peacetime a Hull trawlerman, and his Patrol Service crew who had been shipped over for the purpose. *BYMS.12* was then ordered by the Admiralty to proceed direct to her station in the Mediterranean, a voyage of sixteen thousand miles.

The route for vessels built in yards on the western side of the United States was down the Pacific coast, through the Panama Canal and across the Caribbean to Natal in Brazil. From this point on the South American coast to Freetown in West Africa the extent of the Atlantic crossing is re-duced to something less than two thousand miles. From Freetown *BYMS.12* would sail northwards to Gibraltar and the Mediterranean.

The voyage took five months. The first bad stretch en-countered was when crossing the Gulf of Tehuantepec, off the Pacific coast of Mexico. This area is notorious for its fierce northerly storms which rage for five days at a time. After battling for ten hours with wind and sea in the Gulf,

175

during which she rolled as much as forty degrees and advanced only a few miles, the little minesweeper had to give up and run for shelter. The Atlantic, too, gave them a rough time. For most of the way they had to head into huge seas rolling before the fresh south-easterly trade winds. The passage took so long that fuel ran short and water had to be rationed.

*BYMS.26*, another Seattle-built vessel captained by a temporary R.N.V.R. lieutenant, suffered an engine breakdown on her run down the Pacific coast of America and had to put in to San Diego for repairs. But this misfortune had its compensations. The late Sir Alexander Korda who happened to be in Hollywood at the time heard of the British ship's arrival in San Diego and, with great generosity, arranged for half the crew to be flown to Hollywood at his expense. The minesweeper men were accommodated at a luxury hotel, and spent a crowded day at the studios of several of the big film companies. Here they were lionised by a number of prominent film personalities and amassed an unrivalled collection of pin-up photographs personally autographed in lipstick by the film lovelies. One happy encounter was with our own Gracie Fields, then in Hollywood, who afterwards kept her promise to write personally to each of their families to say she had seen them. *BYMS.26* then continued her interrupted voyage without further mishap, and, joining up as a unit of the 153rd Minesweeping Flotilla of the Mediterranean Fleet, led in the initial assault convoy to the beaches of Sicily in Operation Husky.

*BYMS.39* was built at Beloxi on the Mississippi River and commissioned by her Patrol Service crew in August, 1943. She sailed from Mobile, near New Orleans in the Gulf of Mexico to Halifax, Nova Scotia, and thence to St Johns in Newfoundland for her ocean passage to Britain. At dusk one evening in mid-Atlantic a U-boat suddenly surfaced close beside her. At once the minesweeper men manned their guns and the little ship turned to attack. But the U-boat commander lost his nerve and promptly crash-dived. Although equipped with neither asdic nor depth charges the minesweeper nevertheless cruised hopefully round waiting for the submarine to reappear. But when it became apparent that the U-boat had made off, *BYMS.39* reluctantly abandoned the prospect of battle and resumed her voyage. On the last leg of her journey, from the Azores to Plymouth, bad weather struck. At one period during her long drawn-out battle with raging seas all hands were ordered on deck in case she foundered. But although *BYMS.39* was carrying a weighty deck cargo of American diesel oil, lubricating oil, flour and sugar, despatched to Britain under Lease-Lend, she came safely through her ordeal.

Patrol Service crews sent over to commission the American-built B.Y.M.S. as they slid down the ways found them complete in every detail from guns to blankets, and the store rooms fully stocked with top quality provisions. Even the ships' life-saving rafts were lavishly equipped down to harpoons and collapsible fishing tackle. Many were built on the shores of Lake Michigan and in the other Great Lakes by small shipyards that before the war had produced only pleasure yachts. They then travelled hundreds of miles through inland waterways to receive their salt-water baptism in the Atlantic Ocean. Only six of these sturdy little vessels were lost during their war service, all by mine explosion.

Throughout the war minesweeping remained a task of vital importance, for the enemy's prime objective against these islands never faltered. This was to destroy our shipping faster than new construction could replace it, to dislocate vital traffic and render ports and channels unusable not only by laying minefields but by sinking ships so as to block the fairways and harbour approaches. By D-day in 1944 no fewer than 57,000 officers and men of the Royal, Dominions and Allied Navies were employed in minesweeping. Sixty per cent of them belonged to the Royal Naval Patrol Service. Nine hundred and forty-seven minesweeping vessels were operating in home waters, and five hundred and forty-seven overseas.

Thus, in addition to the B.Y.M.S. the new Lilliput Fleet included large numbers of motor minesweepers, minesweeping motor launches, motor fishing vessels, and even minesweeping landing craft for work in clearing shallow waters, rivers and narrow channels. Generally speaking the motor minesweepers were 300-ton craft, 105 feet long, diesel driven, with a speed of ten knots and carrying a crew of 18. But some were larger, and displaced as much as 428 tons, and boasted an endurance range of 4,000 miles. The motor launches were 85-tonners, carrying a crew of 16, and armed with a Bofors or a 3-pounder gun. The landing-craft were little more than open motor lighters, and carried a crew of six.

These then formed the bulk of the vessels spearheading the Allied landings that marked the turn of the tide of war in the Mediterranean and elsewhere. At Sicily twelve trawlers of the 'Fish', 'Isles', and 'Dance' classes were among the warships that escorted and supported the vast Allied invasion armada. B.Y.M.S. and motor minesweepers manned by Patrol Service personnel swept close to the beaches for the landing craft to move in. At Salerno twelve A/S-M/S trawlers worked with the larger Fleet sweepers to clear the way for the Allied invasion fleets to assemble in the assault areas with clockwork timing and precision. Nine of the trawlers belonged to the 'Dance' and 'Isles' classes but three were veterans of earlier days; the *Visenda, Stella Carina* and *Reighton Wyke*. Sweeping closer inshore under continuous shellfire from the enemy were flotillas of Patrol Service-manned B.Y.M.S., motor minesweepers and minesweeping motor launches.

At home, too, the new ships, both trawlers and smaller craft, were coming into service in increasing numbers. But, in the words of the official naval historian, 'It should not be forgotten that for nearly four years it had been the converted fishing vessels, mostly manned by Reservists and by men of the Royal Naval Patrol Service, which had kept the channels swept and our vital east-coast harbours open.'[1]

The personnel of the Patrol Service was also radically changing. Men from many different walks of life had joined the Lilliput Fleet, among them barbers, stockbrokers, taxi-drivers, shop assistants, farm labourers, transport workers, office managers, chemists, navvies, journalists and insurance agents. A high percentage of those who had volunteered to serve in the ships that had formed the anti-invasion Auxili-

[1] *The War At Sea* Vol. II, by Capt. S. W. Roskill, R.N.

ary Patrol and the River Emergency Service – the latter largely composed of Londoners possessing their own boats who during the days of the Great Blitzes organised themselves into a kind of floating fire- and mine-watching service on the Thames – had also been subsequently absorbed into the Patrol Service. Among the more famous members of the one-time River Emergency Service was the well known humorist Sir Alan Herbert, who in due course became a Petty Officer in the Patrol Service. Since he was also an M.P., this was surely the first time that the Lower Deck had a serving representative in Parliament.

Even conscientious objectors sought to enrol in the Patrol Service for minesweeping, doubtless considering that their scruples would permit them to engage in this humanitarian work, though apparently ignorant of the fact that minesweepers spent a good deal of their time actively fighting the enemy.

The supply of fishermen and other professional seamen had dwindled considerably. By 1944 most of these had become distributed throughout the Patrol Service so that almost every ship included at least a few in her complement, but the bulk of the crews were men serving for 'hostilities only'. Of the commanding officers of the ships of a unit of five B.Y.M.S., for example, only one was an R.N.R. Skipper; the remainder were temporary R.N.V.R. officers whose individual peacetime occupations had been turkey farmer, bank clerk, schoolmaster and stockbroker. But whatever their former calling may have been, all of them took to life in small ships as if they had been born to it and earned the ungrudging admiration of their professional brethren.

In addition to Dominions naval officers and men, the Patrol Service also included personnel from the Allied navies and from the merchant marine and fishing fleets of countries under Nazi occupation. Thus there were French, Belgians, Dutch, Danish, Norwegians, Poles, Greeks and Yugo-Slavs serving in what might be termed their own offshoots of the Lilliput Fleet.

Belgium had no navy before the war, but when that country capitulated, hundreds of Belgian fishermen, many in their own fishing vessels, and officers and men of the

Belgian State Marine escaped to Britain. Eventually they were formed into a homogeneous naval force known as the *Section Belge*, and the officers were given commissions in the R.N.R., and R.N.V.R. By 1942 the *Section Belge* was manning minesweeping trawlers, motor minesweepers, mine-watching vessels, target towing ships and boom defence craft alongside British-manned vessels. Their ships flew the Belgian flag together with the White Ensign. At the peak period of the war the *Section Belge* totalled nearly 500 officers and ratings whose ships operated from Iceland to Weymouth.

Some of the earliest arrivals from the Nazi-occupied territories were Norwegians. In their van came the crews of the Norwegian whaling fleets who were at sea when Hitler invaded their country, and sailed straight back to Britain. Brawny and tough, most of these men could handle boats almost before they could walk, and all were itching for action. Those who escaped after the invasion came over in fishing vessels, lifeboats and small sailing-craft. One man actually rowed across the North Sea single-handed with only a bottle of water and two loaves of bread to sustain him. Others made their way to Britain via Russia, Persia and India. The youngest, a lad of eighteen who later became a wireless telegraphist in a minesweeper, was brought over in a British destroyer after the Vaagso raid. The Norwegian seamen and engineers went straight into the Patrol Service, and by 1942 they were manning a complete minesweeping flotilla of their own which was responsible for a stretch of the Scottish coast. The flotilla was run by a Norwegian staff and under the charge of a Norwegian commander. By June, 1944, Norwegians were manning more than 120 ships, operating from the Arctic Circles to the Levant.

Although the Free French had their own Navy under General de Gaulle, a number of Frenchmen who escaped from Dunkirk and St Valery found their way into the Patrol Service and stayed there. A Danish section was started for Danish seamen who made their way over here after their country had been occupied by the Nazis. In 1943 Danes were manning a number of their own motor minesweepers, and wore British uniform with a red and white shoulder flash. Dutch sailors manned anti-submarine whalers, mine-sweeping trawlers and motor minesweepers. Yugo-Slav naval forces were trained in minesweeping at Malta, and operated with Patrol Service-manned craft in the Adriatic; and Greek sailors manned B.Y.M.S. and motor minesweepers loaned to them in replacement for the sailing schooners they had been using for minesweeping under British naval super-vision.

Two special naval instructional establishments came into existence during the war at which personnel of the Lilliput Fleet were trained in the technique of their particular jobs. One of these, started in November, 1939, was H.M.S Lochinvar, a minesweeping training school established at Port Edgar, in Scotland. Lochinvar conducted three types of technical course; one for personnel who possessed little or no experience of minesweeping; a refresher course for those who had; and a third for officers intending to become specialists. The curriculum covered all methods of sweeping moored, ground and influence mines, the technique of wire sweeping, the tactical aspects of minesweeping, and in-struction in all types of enemy mines and sweeps.

Eventually all R.N.V.R. officers newly promoted from the ranks of 'hostilities only' seamen and intended for em-ployment in minesweepers were sent to H.M.S. Lochinvar for training. In addition to attending courses of lectures ashore these men, generally aged between thirty and thirty-five, since most of the younger officers were required for service in high speed coastal craft, had to serve afloat for three weeks in a trawler. Living on board as ratings they were required to perform the daily chores of a ship's crew, from scrubbing decks to working the mine sweeps. But it was due in no small measure to this part of their training in H.M.S. Lochinvar that the wartime R.N.V.R. officers who later captained a high percentage of the minesweeping vessels of the Patrol Service owed their skill and efficiency and their ability to understand and handle the men under their command. In all, H.M.S. Lochinvar trained some 4,050 officers and 13,000 ratings during the war years. But many hundreds of others, especially in the early months of hostilities, were sent direct to operational ships and had to learn their jobs at first hand.

Mines, too, had changed. No longer were they solely the comparatively uncomplicated moored contact variety. The Germans had started using magnetic mines in 1939. In the following year they added the acoustic mine. Actuated by means of a sensitive microphone this type of mine is detonated by the propeller noises of an approaching ship when in close proximity. Then the enemy began to fit his magnetic mines with arming delays and period-delay mechanisms which required repeating actuations by the minesweepers before they would detonate. Another type of mine introduced by the enemy was the 'Sammy', which was operated both magnetically and acoustically. Later still came the 'oyster', a ground mine which was actuated by the temporary lessening of water pressure caused when a ship passed immediately over it. Enemy minefields were frequently composed of a mixed bag of all the different types which took days to clear completely.

The Germans also incorporated many anti-sweeping devices in their minefields. One of these was a grapnel attached to the moored mine. When the mine mooring was cut the grapnel hooked on to the sweep wire and was thus drawn in close where it exploded and either sank or severely damaged the unsuspecting minesweeper. Explosive grapnels were used to sever the sweep wires, and a variety of other booby traps employed to add to the dangers of minesweeping. All types of mines were also laid in considerable numbers by aircraft and E-boats.

Anti-submarine vessels also had various unpleasant surprises to contend with, among them the 'gnat'. This was an acoustically homing torpedo which when fired from a U-boat homed on to its target by the latter's own propeller noises. As a counter to this escort ships towed astern of themselves a noise making device known appropriately by the name of 'foxer'.

New minesweeping methods were developed as the different types of enemy mine made their appearance. The most effective sweep for the magnetic mine was the 'LL', or 'Double Longitudinal'. This consisted of two buoyant cables of unequal length with an electrode at the end towed astern of the minesweeper, herself deguassed to provide immunity. LL trawlers usually worked in pairs steaming abreast. Fitted with large storage batteries they periodically sent out through the cables as they steamed along a surge of current strong enough to detonate all magnetic mines in the patch of water between their cables. Another method of sweeping magnetic mines was by means of a wire led through a 'gallows' in the bows of each vessel and towed between a pair of trawlers. Suspended from the wire were a number of wooden floats with magnetic bars hanging from them. For clearing rivers and narrow channels a solenoid towed on a raft, known as a 'skid', was used. Acoustic mines were detonated ahead of the sweeping ship by means of an electrically operated hammer fitted in the bows of the vessel, which worked somewhat after the principle of the hydraulic road drill.

During the first three years of World War I just over 5,000 moored mines were swept up. During the same period in World War II slightly fewer than this number were cleared. But the circumstances were vastly more difficult and hazardous. By September, 1941, 3,360 moored, magnetic and acoustic mines had been swept in all theatres of war, the bulk of them magnetic. Casualties to warships and merchantmen during these two years totalled 452 vessels, of which 56 were minesweepers. Another 53 ships of the Lilliput Fleet were lost by air attack and other causes. But by June, 1942, minesweepers of the Nore Command alone, who were responsible for much of our coast, had swept over 2,000 mines. In a speech at that time the First Lord of the Admiralty told the country.

'We have destroyed around the coasts of Britain more magnetic, acoustic and moored mines than would have been sufficient to destroy the whole of the British Merchant Marine. That is an amazing thing, and it has been done by the men joining the Navy from the fishermen ranks and from civil life.'

One Patrol Service ship, the trawler *Rolls Royce*, had by Christmas, 1941, attained her century of mines swept, the first minesweeper in history to perform such a feat. This little vessel, probably the oldest veteran requisitioned to serve under the White Ensign in World War II, was commanded by Skipper Lieutenant L.D. Romyn, R.N.R., who during the war service won the D.S.C. and Bar for outstanding minesweeping work. Forty-eight year old Leopold Dickson Romyn, an experienced Bridlington trawlerman, joined the R.N.R. as a Temporary Skipper in November, 1939. After commanding minesweeper *Rowan* for a spell he took over the *Rolls Royce* as a Unit Minesweeping Officer in April, 1941.

Built in 1906 by Cochrane's for the firm of B. H. Banister of Grimsby, the *Rolls Royce* grossed only 238 tons; she was 120 feet long and 22 feet in the beam. She was attached to Minesweeping Group No. 110 operating from Grimsby. Her almost equally distinguished sisters included the 234-ton *Ben Meidie*, hailing in peacetime from North Shields, and the *Kastoria* and *Rose of England,* both ex-Grimsby craft, the latter only three years younger than the *Rolls Royce*. During her first day as a minesweeper the *Rolls Royce* detonated three ground mines, and under Romyn's command she began to notch up minesweeping records. On November 30th, 1941, she swept thirteen mines in 79 minutes. On another occasion when E-boats and aircraft had drenched the outer channels of the Humber with their deadly eggs and cucumbers, the weather added to the normal hazards of minesweeping by its extreme severity. Nevertheless Romyn's Group went out as usual and in a week of arduous sweeping detonated thirty-one mines, Romyn himself destroying seventeen of them in the *Rolls Royce*. By the end of the war this remarkable little ship under its remarkable captain, now promoted to the highest Patrol Service officer rank of Skipper Lieutenant, held the record for the largest number of ground mines to be swept by one trawler. The formidable total was 197, each of which represented a warship or merchantman saved from destruction.

Overseas the minesweeping war was equally hard fought. During the first desert campaign in Egypt the small British minesweeping force attached to the Mediterranean Fleet was almost halved by losses from air attack alone. Despite this, by the middle of May, 1942, they had accounted for

360 mines. By the time of the second Egyptian campaign the little ships had been reinforced by others which made the long passage round the Cape. The North Africa landings brought more minesweepers to operate from the western end of the Mediterranean. When, following Alamein, the Eighth Army began its chase of Rommel, the minesweepers of the Inshore Squadron leapfrogged ahead of them, often clearing approaches to enemy-held ports before they were captured.

By May 15th, 1943, less than a week after the Axis surrendered in North Africa, the little ships had cleared the Sicilian Channel, an area some two hundred miles long by two miles wide, enabling the first convoy from Gibraltar to Alexandria to pass safely through the Mediterranean. In recognition of this feat they received the personal thanks and congratulations of the Prime Minister. Subsequently they swept the Allied invading forces into enemy-occupied ports in Italy, France and Greece and established safe traffic routes in support of the advancing armies. In the Dodecanese they cleared heavily mined shore approaches not only to bring resources to our own forces but relief to the liberated population. Outside the harbour of Leros alone a flotilla of B.Y.M.S cleared 91 mines in twenty-one days, while two minesweeping motor launches shared a bag of 90 mines between them.

The other instructional establishment which played no inconsiderable part in training the officers and men of the anti-submarine trawlers was H.M.S *Western Isles*, which subsequently became known as the Atlantic Battle School. H.M.S. *Western Isles*, an old Dutch horse boat converted for her job as headquarters ship at Tobermory, in the Sound of Mull, was under the command of Commodore Sir Gilbert Stephenson, a sixty-five year old retired Vice-Admiral recalled for service. Here newly commissioned ships were sent for two to three weeks training in seamanship, boatwork, gunnery and battle tactics. Depth-charge crews were trained to a high pitch of efficiency, being required to prepare their weapons for action in thirty seconds. Realistic battle exercises were staged using aircraft, submarines, motor launches, and speed boats, which helped to weld ships' crews into first-class fighting units.

Admiral Stephenson, knighted for his services in 1943, was a believer in unorthodox methods, but he certainly got results. It was said that when a newly commissioned trawler arrived at Tobermory for training her captain would be commanded to produce a ship's concert party. If he protested that his vessel did not possess one he would be ordered to produce by the end of the training period ten men who could stand on the quarterdeck and sing 'Good King Wenceslas' in close harmony.

To keep officers and men on their toes at all times Stephenson frequently paid surprise visits to ships under training. On one occasion his barge suddenly appeared alongside a trawler. But he had not caught the trawlermen napping. As the Commodore stepped on to her deck he was piped aboard and greeted by her alert captain in correct Navy fashion. Everyone then stood to attention waiting for the Great Man to disclose the purpose of his visit. Instead he suddenly snatched off his gold-laced cap and threw it on the deck in front of the startled captain and his men.

'That's an unexploded bomb which has just dropped on your ship,' he snapped. 'What are you going to do about it?'

For a moment no one moved. Then a young sailor stepped smartly forward and, to the captain's horror, kicked the cap overboard.

The Commodore's craggy features creased almost into a grin of approval.

'Quite right, my boy,' he said. 'Proper way to deal with it.'

Then the approving look vanished. Pointing to the waterlogged cap now floating alongside in the chilly water, for it was winter, he rapped out:

'That's a survivor who can't swim. Jump in and save him!'

It is little wonder that after such training the A/S crews of the Lilliput Fleet were quick off the mark in action.

*     *     *

Whether or not they had undergone a course at the famous 'Atlantic Battle School' at Tobermory, the officers and men of the little ships which belonged to a Dominions' section of the Lilliput Fleet must have earned Admiral Stephenson's unqualified approval for the smartness during a certain night action which took place in the Pacific in January, 1943. The vessels concerned were his Majesty's New Zealand ships *Kiwi* and *Moa*, a pair of A/S-M/S trawlers belonging to the 25th Minesweeping Flotilla.

Built by Henry Robb of Leith for the New Zealand Government in 1941, these little ships displaced 600 tons apiece, and measured no more than 150 feet in length and 30 feet in the beam. They were armed with a single 4-inch gun mounted on the forecastle, and carried a number of smaller weapons including 40 depth charges. The *Kiwi* was commanded by Lieutenant-Commander Gordon Bridson, D.S.C., of the Royal New Zealand Naval Volunteer Reserve, a big tough individual with a forthright manner, and the *Moa* by Lieutenant-Commander Peter Phipps, D.S.C., also of the R.N.Z.V.R.

Since December of the previous year the ships of New Zealand's naval forces had been working with the American Third Fleet in the Pacific under the command of Admiral 'Bull' Halsey, U.S.N. Based at Tulagi on Florida Island in the Solomons Group, the Americans had landed forces on the neighbouring island of Guadalcanal and were gradually mopping up the fiercely resisting Japanese garrison. Despite the hopelessness of the situation Japanese headquarters in Rabaul was still trying to reinforce and maintain their beleaguered troops in Guadalcanal. Since the American blockade prevented the use of surface ships for this purpose the Japanese were employing submarines as troop carriers. The submarines, large ocean-going vessels of nearly 2,000 tons displacement, sneaked down through the narrow channels between the islands and landed their soldiers and supplies on Guadalcanal by means of barges carried lashed to the deck casing.

On the evening of January 29th, 1943, H.M.N.Z.S. *Kiwi* and *Moa* sailed from Tulagi and proceeded to their patrol area for the night off Kamimbo Bay at the northern end of Guadalcanal.

'Wonder if we'll catch any of the little yellow baskets tonight?' speculated Phipps to Brisdon over the loud hailer as the trawlers steamed slowly past Cape Esperance, near which was a favourite landing place of the Japanese.

'You'll keep your lads on top line,' returned Bridson with a grin. 'Old Halsey might be persuaded to give us a couple of days' leave down home if we can bag one of their subs.'

At five minutes past nine that night Able Seaman McVinnie, the *Kiwi*'s asdic operator, excitedly reported a submarine contact. The trawlers were then patrolling on a line to seaward of Cape Esperance with its dark bulk looming on their starboard hand. With its engines just turning over they were barely making way through the water.

As soon as he had checked the asdic report Brisdon, a wide grin of anticipatory joy splitting his features, altered course to close the echo and jabbed his finger on the alarm button.

'Signal the *Moa* we've got a sub contact,' he ordered Leading Signalman Buchanan, 'and tell her to stand by with starshell.'

Then he snapped up the cover of the voicepipe to the engine-room.

'Chief,' he barked. 'I want every knot you can get out of this tub double quick!'

'Oh now, wait a minute, Skipper,' came the drawled reply. 'What's all the hurry? We aren't going anywhere.'

'Shut up you clot!' roared Brisdon. 'There's a weekend leave in Auckland right ahead of us. Now get cracking and give me all the speed you can.'

There was no further argument from the engine room, and soon the throbbing of the deck beneath his feet told the big New Zealander that the *Kiwi* was working up to full speed. On board the *Moa* her crew had also closed up at action stations, and the ship was beginning to pile up a creamy bow wave as she loped along abreast of her consort.

A mile and a half ahead of the speeding trawlers, snaking along at periscope depth in the shadow of the land was His Imperial Japanese Majesty's submarine *I.1*, of 1,955 tons, and in size almost a small cruiser. Crowding every compartment below deck steel-helmeted Japanese soldiers in full war kit squatted, their sweat-daubed faces impassive as they awaited the moment when they would be launched on their way ashore to join their comrades in the shell-swept foxholes

of Guadalcanal. Every available foot of space in the big submarine not occupied by the soldiers was stacked with boxes
containing stores and medical supplies. Lashed to the deck
casing abaft the conning-tower were tiers of wooden landing barges. *I.1* was carrying out an important assignment,
and Lieutenant-Commander Eiicho Sakamoto, her captain,
was just congratulating himself on having slipped safely
through the American patrol line when a thunderbolt
struck.

From the dark waters to seaward hurtled the straining
hull of the trawler *Kiwi*. As the little warship passed directly
over the phosphorescent-outlined shape of the submarine
gliding below her, a pattern of six depth charges splashed
downwards and the rumbling roar of their explosion shattered the quietness of the tropic night. Then with helm hard
over the trawler heeled in a creaming circle and began to re-
trace her course. But the asdic beam was still groping for
the enemy as she combed her track, and the second pattern
of depth charges remained unfired in the racks. Two and a
half minutes later McVinnie again heard the clicking of the
contact, then it faded and died.

Cursing, Bridson opened the range, steaming at full speed
for almost a mile. Then, just as the *Kiwi* was swinging round
for another vain run in, McVinnie regained contact. This
time the asdic held the jinking submarine, and another six-
charge pattern blew her to the surface with her electric
motors out of action. To illuminate the scene both trawlers
had fired starshell, and in the eerie light shed by these the
big I-boat stood clearly revealed.

Startled by the blaring of the klaxons and the immediate
scurrying response of the sailors inside the submarine, then
thrown to the deck by the explosions of the depth charges,
the Japanese soldiers shed their impassivity as they sprang
up and began struggling through the conning-tower hatch.
On deck the sailors had manned their 5-inch gun and their
shells screamed closely over the *Kiwi* and *Moa*, who were
both now firing every weapon that would bear.

Sakamoto was on the bridge with some of his officers, but
his efforts to control the situation were hampered by the
wild mêlée in progress as soldiers and submariners fought to

get out of each other's way. As the *I.1* reeled under the lashing impact of the trawlers' fire the dark bulk of the *Kiwi*, thrusting forward at the full extent of her straining engines, suddenly loomed high above them. There was a grinding crash and a chorus of screams and shouts as her stem tore into the pressure hull of *I.1* abaft the crowded conning-tower.

As the big submarine spun over to starboard, shedding soldiers and sailors alike into the foaming water alongside, Bridson on the bridge of the *Kiwi* rang down 'Full astern'. Yelling with the excitement of battle his machine-gunners flailed the wallowing hull of the I-boat with a whiplash of lead as the trawler broke clear. Unable to depress his weapon sufficiently to fire at the submarine the gunlayer of the *Kiwi*'s 4-inch fingered his trigger and blasphemed impotently.

Bridson backed the *Kiwi* to a distance of no more than 500 yards from the rapidly slowing submarine. Then he opened deliberate barrage fire on her with the 4-inch, noting several bursts around the *I.1*'s conning-tower in the beam of the searchlight kept trained on the enemy by Leading Signalman Buchanan who, though mortally wounded by an enemy bullet, remained at his post throughout the action. The landing-barges stacked on the submarine's after-casing were also hit and set on fire. In the light of further starshell put up by the *Moa* some of the yelling Japanese soldiers could be seen hurling themselves into the sea.

'Here we go again, Chief,' bellowed Bridson exultantly down the engine-room voicepipe as he jerked the telegraph over to full speed ahead. With machine-guns hammering ceaselessly the little *Kiwi* launched herself across the flame-dappled water and smashed her steel bows like a battering-ram into the groaning hull of *I.1*. Then, wrenching free of the twisted junk which was all that remained of the submarine's port hydroplanes, the *Kiwi* drew astern again, like a boxer stepping back a pace to take another swing at his opponent. With her engines rapidly checking way at a range of 150 yards, the *Kiwi* paused to drench the *I.1* with a cascade of lead and steel. Carefully hosepiping his weapon, a New Zealand machine-gunner saw his bullets cut down a

Japanese officer in the conning-tower. It was Sakamoto.

While the furious British bombardment was scything the enemy, the water beneath the trawler's counter boiled and swirled as the *Kiwi*'s engines began thrusting her forward in a third fierce lunge. This time her buckled stem struck the reeling submarine close to the conning-tower, slicing through and riding high over the riven hull. Fuel oil spouted upwards from the bowels of *I.1* like blood from a stricken whale. To the accompaniment of shrieks and yells from the Japanese who were still clinging to the submarine's broken hull, and the harsh grinding of metal, the bows of the *Kiwi* slammed back into the water as her racing engines tugged her astern. But by now her guns had become too hot to fire, and Bridson grabbed the microphone of the loud hailer.

'Okay, Peter,' he shouted to Phipps manoeuvring anxiously close by. 'He's all yours. Finish the bastard off!'

But despite the savage punishment the Japanese vessel had taken her diesel engines were still functioning, and she began rapidly drawing away. The gallant little *Moa* sped in pursuit with all guns blazing. Phipps zig-zagging her from side to side to prevent the Japanese from bringing their 5-inch to bear. But the end of this fierce two-hour combat was near. During the action the three ships had been closing the land. Now suddenly the *I.1* impaled herself on the sharp fangs of an under-water reef jutting out from the shoreline, and with her hull ripped apart in a dozen places she rolled over and disappeared in a flurry of foam and spray.

The *Kiwi* and *Moa* hauled off to await daylight. When dawn came the New Zealanders closed in to behold the battered forepart of the big submarine projecting grotesquely from the creaming surf at an angle of 45 degrees. There was a sign of movement on board and the itching trigger-fingers of the *Moa*'s gunners sent in a quick burst which hurled a tottering figure overboard to join the drowned and shell-torn bodies bobbing alongside the wreck. Then as the victorious trawler turned away, a solitary swimming Japanese was fished out of the sea. He, perhaps more than anyone else on board the submarine *I.1*, could appreciate to the full the speed and hitting power of the British Navy's little ships. He had been her gunnery officer.

CHAPTER XIV

IN AT THE DEATH

FOLLOWING the Allied landings in the Mediterranean in 1943 the enemy was at last forced on the defensive. But there was no relaxation of the war at sea. Everywhere the little ships of the Lilliput Fleet were busy, minesweeping, convoy escorting, salvaging damaged vessels, ferrying supplies to invasion landing ships and their supporting craft and aiding the army inshore.

One small group of trawlers, none of them grossing more than 300 tons, operating as supply ships in the Mediterranean called themselves Walt Disney's Navy; but they might with justice have appropriated the name of a famous British transport firm. They were H.M. Trawlers *Transvaal*, *Quercia*, *Lapageria*, *Wythan Braes* and *Triton*, in peacetime well known in the fishing fleets of Hull, Fleetwood and Grimsby. For months they chugged up and down the Mediterranean ferrying stores and mail for warships and troop transports. Working stripped to the waist in the grilling heat their crews, few of them professional seamen, humped aboard drums of water, fuel and lubricating oil, cases of provisions and stores, and sacks of parcels and letters from the mail offices ashore and set off from the base area ports for the invasion beaches.

On passage to their destination half the crews at a time had to keep closed up at the guns ready to repel enemy attack in any form, while those off duty tried to rest on their tiny messdecks in oven-like temperatures of more than a hundred degrees; the only deck awning in the group, incidentally, consisted of an Italian army tent which had been 'captured' by the *Quercia*. As soon as their welcome cargoes were offloaded in the anchorage, frequently under air attack, they started back to port to repeat the process all over again. Of Walt Disney's Navy only the *Transvaal* failed to survive the war. She foundered in heavy weather on her way home in 1944.

Normally all small vessels were scheduled to go into dock for minor refit and boiler clean after every thousand hours steaming. But in the urgency of quickening events periodic overhaul programmes went by the board. One little ship, the 'Isles' class trawler *Eday*, steamed continuously for ten thousand hours before her protesting machinery could receive the attention for which it noisily clamoured. When she was finally taken in hand for overhaul the dockyard engineers gaped unbelievingly at her propeller. The stout metal blades had been worn down to no more than paper thickness. Strange marine growths inches deep clung to every foot of her underwater plating. During her seventy thousand miles of voyaging the little *Eday* had taken part in the landings in North Africa, in Sicily and in Italy, and had been the first Allied ship to enter the liberated ports as they were captured in support of the Army.

Four of her sisters, the *Rysa, Hoy, Inchcombe* and *Mull*, boasted an almost equally impressive record. From the time of the landings in North Africa they had guarded convoys, swept up enemy minefields, carried out anti-submarine patrols, towed bomb and mine-damaged ships to safety and acted as tugs and ferries in harbour. But no amount of work or hardship could get the trawlermen down. Perhaps as a result of the training they had undergone at Commodore Stephenson's Atlantic Battle School, the little *Rysa* boasted an extraordinary talented concert party which was greatly in demand whenever the trawler had a few hours in port; they called themselves the *Rysa* Ballet Company. The trawler's First Lieutenant, a ballet enthusiast, was producer, manager and, under the appropriately Slavonic pseudonym of Serge Jumper, also the male star of the show. The prima ballerinas who were guaranteed to bring the house down in every programme staged by the *Rysa* Ballet Company were two lusty trawlermen rejoicing in the exotic stage names of Marlene Spike and Belle Bottom, and they were backed up by a sprightly corps de ballet hailing from the engine-room billed as Les Stokerettes. Sadly enough the gallant little *Rysa* was later blown up by a mine off Sardinia.

Among some even smaller units of the Patrol Service employed in the Mediterranean at this time, whose crews were apt to describe themselves somewhat sadly as the Cinderellas of the Navy, were the motor fishing vessels. Sixty feet long, built of wood and diesel-engined, with a crew of one officer and eight ratings, a flotilla of these little ships made the 2,500-mile journey from the United Kingdom to take part in the landings in Sicily. Loaded to the gunwales with diesel fuel, petrol and lubricating oil, they acted as floating filling stations for the landing-craft. When they had fulfilled their prime purpose of fuel replenishment they turned themselves into maids-of-all-work, ferrying stores, equipment and troops where these were most needed. Their roll may have been humble but it was not unimportant. Only three of the many hundreds of these stout little craft, mostly built in back-garden shipyards up and down Britain, became war casualties.

In home waters the ships of the Lilliput Fleet, the minesweepers and the convoy escorts, continued to battle against undiminished odds. The German U-boat fleet was being added to at the rate of twenty every month; E-boats were now attacking coastal convoys in packs to overwhelm the escorts and sink the merchantmen they guarded; off Dover minesweepers and convoys alike came under shellfire from the German long-range guns mounted on the French coast; the enemy continued to lay mines in our swept channels; air attacks on the little ships, although less frequent than formerly, had still to be reckoned with.

Early one August morning in 1943 the trawlers *Red Gauntlet, Mary Hastie* and *Lord Melchett* belonging to the Harwich Minesweeping Groups were engaged in searching the swept channel off that port when out of the dawn mists darted the swift grey shapes of a pack of E-boats. Although they were on the alert, the minesweeper men had their sweep gear out and were therefore caught at a disadvantage. The fight was short and sharp; guns barked, machine-guns hammered and chattered, and spears of red and green tracer stabbed the air. Then came the deeper roar of an explosion and a surge of flame-shot smoke billowing briefly above the calm sea. Then the E-boats had gone, the heavy smell of their exhausts mingling with the acrid smoke of gunfire, while debris and unnameable fragments showered down into a vast swirl of water where before the enemy torpedo struck her the trawler *Red Gauntlet* had been steaming.

A month later the same stretch of sea in this important convoy area was the scene of another bloody skirmish. Steaming tirelessly up and down on their unending task were the ships of another small Harwich minesweeping unit. They were the trawlers *Franc Tireur, Stella Dorado* and *Donna Nook*. Suddenly an E-boat pack hurtled upon them, roaring through, past and around the trawler group with guns spitting. Then as the E-boats swanned outwards the bubbling tracks of torpedoes arrowed from the fast-moving hulls. There was a heavy explosion and a tall pillar of smoke and flame momentarily obscured the doomed *Franc Tireur*. When it cleared the little ship was sinking fast. Manoeuvring under helm at all the speed they could muster the two remaining trawlers altered course simultaneously to avoid the running torpedoes. But they were collision-close and, with a rendering crash, the bluff steel bows of the *Stella Dorado* tore into the side of the *Donna Nook*. Flung on to her beam ends the rammed ship began rapidly to founder. By the time the *Stella Dorado* had hauled the struggling crew of her sister ship inboard sixteen of the men of the *Franc Tireur* had died with their vessel.

Farther north off the Humber a pack of four E-boats sneaking in from the North Sea to launch their thrusts at a coastal convoy encountered the minesweeper trawler *Cap D'Antifer*. But the trawler was patrolling with no sweep gear out and her men were waiting at their guns with itching trigger fingers. As the E-boats came drumming out of the darkness the *Cap D'Antifer* erupted into a storm of fire. Flailed by shell bursts and viciously aimed streaks of tracer the E-boats turned tail and fled. But a few weeks later the Nazis took their revenge. Another E-boat pack from Ymuiden slunk through the winter murk until they were within a few hundred yards of the fighting minesweeper. A well-aimed torpedo sent the little ship to the bottom, and the enemy craft proceeded to shed their load of mines undisturbed.

With the increase in the numbers of corvettes and frigates the Admiralty decided that anti-submarine trawlers were unsuitable for the task of escorting ocean convoys, and many of them were employed instead in a process known as 'buttoning' and 'unbuttoning'. This procedure consisted of leading away portions of convoys into intermediate ports, or joining groups of merchantmen sailing from intermediate ports on to the ocean convoys in their assembly areas. During these shuttling operations the little trawlers drove off many enemy air attacks aimed at their charges and towed any casualties back to harbour.

On just such a buttoning job south-west of Skerryvore the A/S trawler *Kingston Beryl* ran on to two floating mines, blew up and sank with all hands. Tragically, the mines were British.

Escorting a convoy section from the Bristol Channel round to Plymouth the 'Isles' class trawler *Wallasea* was sent to the bottom by enemy attack along with two of her flock. Near the Isle of Wight three groups of E-boats pounced on another unbuttoned convoy section guarded by the 'Tree' class trawler *Pine*. For a time the trawler success-fully defended her charges against their crowding enemies. Then one group of E-boats managed to creep between the convoy and the shore and loose their torpedoes among the ships. Two merchantmen were hit and a third torpedo blew the bows off the trawler. Nevertheless the *Pine* remained afloat with her remaining guns in action until aid arrived, and the E-boats fled. She was taken in tow, but turned over and sank on her way to harbour.

Off the coast of Africa the French freighter *St Basile* was being escorted from Takoradi to Freetown by the trawlers *Inkpen*, *Birdlip* and *Turcoman* of the West African Escort Force. Boldly moving in at night on the little convoy, *U.547* torpedoed the *Birdlip*, the only ship in the escort whose radar and asdic were working properly and which was turning to attack her, then sank the merchantman. Gathered together on two small rafts by a young R.N.V.R. sub-lieutenant, the only officer left alive from the *Birdlip*

– her captain had succumbed to his injuries when they fished him from the sea – the fifteen wounded survivors of the trawler managed to reach the shore. Then the sub-lieutenant set out on a treck through the jungle to find and bring help to his men.

H.M. Whaler *Maaloy* of No. 177 Minesweeping Auxiliary Group of the East Indies Command, based on Ceylon, failed one day to return from patrol. Evidence subsequently discovered by searching vessels transformed speculation concerning her fate into ghastly certainty. For a single drifting life-raft bearing her name was hauled from the sea, bullet-riddled and bloodstained. That dead men cannot very well report the presence of an enemy submarine was a fact well known to certain U-boat commanders, German as well as Japanese.

While these day-by-day casualties of late 1943 and early 1944 were being logged great events were portending. At a certain planning headquarters in London a foolscap book more than three inches thick and marked 'Operation Neptune – Most Secret' had been compiled, in which the forthcoming movement of hundreds of Patrol Service vessels as well as larger warships of the Allied Navies were carefully mapped out. And Operation Neptune – appropriate code word – was itself only a part, albeit a most vital one, of a greater conception: 'Operation Overlord, the long-awaited invasion of Europe. Originally planned to be proceeded by twelve flotillas of minesweepers from the larger 'Fleet' class down to the smallest Patrol Service motor minesweeper, in the event no less than twenty-five flotillas of these vessels swept the great invasion fleet into the beaches of Normandy. Eighty anti-submarine trawlers were also included among the 1,102 warships that eventually participated in the assault on Hitler's 'West Wall' on that historic day in early June, 1944.

This was the greatest minesweeping operation in history. Stretching along the whole length of the Channel coast the Germans had laid an extensive anti-invasion barrage of moored mines through which a path had to be cleared. Since it was vital that the landing-craft and their support vessels should follow immediately in the wake of the minesweepers timing was of the utmost importance. In order to stream her sweep effectively a minesweeper must proceed at a certain minimum speed. But although this was not great it was a knot or so faster than the average landing-craft could travel, and if maintained would result in the minesweepers arriving off the assault area more than an hour before the invasion fleet. This problem was eventually overcome by arranging for the minesweepers to carry out a series of intricate turning movements en route.

As the world now knows, the invasion of Europe by the Allies in 1944 had to be postponed for one day due to bad weather. On June 4th, a flotilla of minesweepers sailed from an east coast base in accordance with operational orders so as to arrive in the specially cleared area off the Isle of Wight, dubbed Piccadilly Circus, ready to commence the operation. But when approaching Piccadilly Circus the flotilla discovered a newly laid field of enemy mines and began to sweep them up. Soon afterwards the postponement signal was received. Due to the stringent orders forbidding the use of wireless at that tense period the signal could not be acknowledged; nor could the unexpected presence of the minefield be reported. The flotilla continued to sweep.

A few hours later the ships were sighted by a British destroyer on patrol. Thinking that the minesweeper men were unaware that the invasion had been postponed the destroyer steamed over to them to pass the news. But before she had gone very far a winking signal lamp flashed urgently from the leading sweeper:

'You have entered a minefield!'

Appalled, the destroyer captain instantly stopped engines, and for what seemed aeons she lay gently heaving on the surface of a patch of sea sown with potential destruction until the little minesweepers could clear a path and guide her to safety.

Then in the afternoon of June 5th the great operation began. Following in the wake of the huge fleet of minesweepers steamed the danlaying trawlers marking the edges of the ten cleared approach channels with illuminated buoys, so that they resembled lighted thoroughfares on land. When the first waves of invasion troops were safely ashore the minesweeping fleet turned to the business of widening the channels to the beaches and clearing the anchorages. That night the enemy struck back. Large forces of aircraft and packs of E-boats strove to penetrate our defences and lay mines amid the dense mass of shipping.

These attacks on the anchorage off the invasion beaches swelled in strength and virulence as the build-up for the armies ashore proceeded. A defensive ring around the anchored merchantmen was formed by destroyers, frigates, corvettes, trawlers and coastal craft, which fought day and night battles with German destroyers, E-boats and midget submarines. The Luftwaffe dropped parachute mines in the anchorage and launched circling torpedoes. Electrically driven, these torpedoes were capable of charging round in diminishing circles for as long as ten hours, afterwards transforming themselves into mines. It was the particular job of the little B.Y.M.S. to watch for parachute mines and mark their point of arrival.

Every convoy of ships bringing fresh troops and material from Britain had to be swept across to the French coast, for the cleared channels were sown with new mines by the enemy as fast as they were swept. The little minesweepers constantly came under the fire of enemy shore batteries and, since they could not break the formation of the sweep, were frequently hit. Coastal forces and destroyers laid smoke screens to protect them.

In addition to the attacks by midget submarines, human torpedoes and explosive motor boats, every type of enemy mine was shed on and around the assault area. They included moored contact, ground contact fired by snagline, moored magnetic, ground magnetic, ground acoustic, and magnetic/acoustic fitted with delay mechanisms. Even the smallest of these was capable of wreaking extensive damage. At times mines were sown so thickly that one morning when a flotilla of B.Y.M.S. switched on their sweep gear to test circuits before starting work 23 exploded all round them. One mine, dropped close to a British cruiser, yielded to treatment only after 52 actuations in eleven days! In their efforts to hamper the work of the minesweepers the Germans even scattered garbage and other flotsam in the anchorage to foul their propellers. Frequently an innocent-seeming 'empty' wooden box drifting along concealed beneath it a floating mine. To combat this peculiar menace the officer in charge of the patrol area ordered all his ships to scavenge floating garbage every morning, the ship collecting the largest bag daily to be presented with a prize of a special brand of 'nutty' – nauticalese for chocolate!

But despite all the hazards sixteen convoys comprising an average of fifteen ships apiece entered the assault anchorage daily. By July 10th over a million men had been safely landed in France, and the little ships of the Patrol Service had swept up 674 mines in the anchorage. Nor was minesweeping their only task. As well as trawlers Patrol Service crews were manning fuel and water carriers, smoke floats, motor boats, aircraft safety launches, tugs for towing parts of the Mulberry harbours, cargo lighters, air lighters, aircraft tenders, balloon-servicing craft and wreck-dispersal vessels.

As the Allies advanced the minesweepers went along clearing the liberated ports and harbours. At Cherbourg they set up new records. Thirty magnetic mines were swept in one day, 19 of them in six minutes. The clearance of the port of Brest entailed 900 miles steaming by one flotilla of B.Y.M.S. The first Allied ships to enter the Scheldt were six small Patrol Service craft. They forced their way in under the guns of a heavy German battery at Knocke and swept five mines on the way. With the enemy active on their flanks the minesweepers swept the shallow unbuoyed waters in twenty-four days, clearing 241 ground and 42 moored mines. They swept the 73-mile stretch of the River Scheldt despite constant attacks by E-boats and shelling by shore batteries, and topped off a non-stop run by clearing the 3,600,000 square yards of dock basins in the great port of Antwerp then under heavy bombardment by 'V' weapons. From the yardarm of their senior officer one signal had flown continuously, 'Onward chums!'

In August the little ships swept in yet another invasion fleet, this time in the south of France. British, Canadian, American, Dutch, Polish, Greek and Belgian ships took part in the landing, and with them were forty small mine-sweepers manned by French crews. The net was tightening around Nazi Germany.

In May came the surrender at Luneberg; hostilities ceased in Europe. But the sea war died hard. On May 2nd the minesweeping trawler *Ebor Wyke* patrolling off Iceland was torpedoed and sunk. There was only one survivor. In the last hours of hostilities *U.1023* expended her remaining torpedoes in Lyme Bay. She sank two merchant ships and their escort, a little Norwegian-manned motor minesweeper. Then the U-boat calmly surfaced and hoisted the black flag of surrender.

In eastern waters ships of the Patrol Service with their sisters of the Royal Indian Navy, the Australian and New Zealand Navies, formed part of the Allied fleets now closing in on the forces of Japan. But the long tough struggle that had been envisaged was not to be. Two mushroom-shaped clouds billowed successively over Hiroshima and Nagasaki, and the fighting was over.

\* \* \*

Nine days after the official Japanese surrender on board the American battleship *Missouri* in Tokyo Bay, a small, grey-painted warship flying the Australian flag entered Datu Bay on the west coast of Borneo. Her meagre deck space was crowded with bronzed, slouch-hatted soldiers fully armed with rifles, grenades and bren guns. Their officers shared the bridge with the ship's captain, Lieutenant Callow of the Royal Australian Naval Volunteer Reserve. The warship was his Majesty's Australian minesweeper *Kapunda*.

As the warship approached the shore the sailors and soldiers on her deck saw that the banks along the entrance to the Sarawak River leading to the town of Kuching were thronged with people cheering and shouting and waving flags. Among them were many figures wearing clean new khaki uniforms. But although these men were laughing and cheering as excitedly as the rest their features were gaunt and haggard, their bodies thin and bony. They were Allied prisoners of war of the Japanese, newly freed from their prison camps and wearing uniforms dropped to them by

201

parachute from British planes to replace the stinking rags to which their own had been reduced during their long confinement.

In the centre of Kuching landing-stage, isolated and indifferent to the excited crowds about them, stood a company of Japanese soldiers. At their head, with his scabbarded Samurai sword hanging from his belt, bespectacled face impassive, a Japanese colonel watched the approach of the warship. When her anchor splashed down the colonel followed by his aides marched to the head of the landing stage, descended the steps and boarded a waiting harbour launch. As it cast off and headed out towards the *Kapunda* Lieutenant Callow and the Army officers left the minesweeper's bridge and walked aft to her tiny quarterdeck. In its centre was placed a small table covered with a green baize cloth upon which rested some typewritten papers. In a few minutes the launch bumped alongside and the Japanese colonel stepped on to the deck of the *Kapunda*. A brawny Australian bluejacket conducted him aft, where he saluted and bowed to the assembled officers. The Australian brigadier spoke a few words, then the Japanese seated himself at the baize-covered table and a pen scatched briefly as he signed the documents placed before him. Then he rose, saluted again, unbuckled his sword, and bowing, proffered it to the brigadier.

The date was September 13th, 1945, and, with the exception of the rounding up on September 24th by Australian troops landed from the minesweeper *Gladstone* of a small number of Japanese soldiers who had overrun Portuguese Timor, the last enemy in the Pacific had surrendered.

Strictly the *Kapunda*, like the *Bengal* of the Royal Indian Navy, was not a Patrol Service ship. Yet her tonnage was small her armament slight, and she ranked as a very minor warship. It was fitting that a little minesweeper, representative of all her smaller sisters who had ranged the seas in the struggle for freedom should be in at the death.

*    *    *

On a grey October day in 1953 a large crowd was gathered in Belle Vue Park at Lowestoft. The summer had fled, and the visitors who thronged the walks and gardens, lounged in deck chairs and sprawled on the grass in the sunshine had long departed. At the foot of the cliff below, Belle Vue's companion park, Sparrow's Nest, was deserted. It was seven years since the White Ensign of the Royal Navy that had floated from the flagstaff in its midst had been hauled down for the last time and H.M.S *Europa* formally paid off. A chill wind blew from the north-east bringing with it an occasional spatter of rain. Low clouds scudded over the grey North Sea and white horses gleamed briefly amid the sullen waves rolling in to the foreshore. On countless such days during the war the little trawlers of the R.N. Patrol Service had put to sea minesweeping, escorting, guarding our shores; many had never returned.

Today, on October 7th 1953, the eyes of the waiting crowd were fixed on a monument newly erected in Belle Vue Park; a tall fluted column of stone rising from a circular stone plinth some forty feet in diameter, surmounted by a golden bronze ship device. Symmetrically arranged around the sides of the base hung seventeen White Ensigns, their folds ruffling in the wind. The war memorial to the officers and men of the Royal Naval Patrol Service was about to be unveiled.

In rows of chairs facing the memorial sat two thousand men, women and children, relatives of those who had served in the little ships and would never come back. To one side stood a group of forty men bearing wreaths. A trifle weather-beaten of countenance but otherwise bearing scant outward sign of their calling, they were fishermen representing every fishing port in the United Kingdom from whence had come many of those who had manned the ships of the Lilliput Fleet. Flanking them was a bluejacket guard of honour, collars fluttering, pipe-clayed belts and gaiters gleaming whitely, rifles with fixed bayonets held stiffly in the 'at ease' position. In their white helmets and blue and red uniforms, the band of the Royal Marines, Chatham Division, fingered their instruments.

In her robe of office the Mayoress of Lowestoft stood with her male Deputy; the white-surpliced Bishop of Norwich; the Lord Lieutenant of Suffolk representing the Queen;

Mr Clement Attlee on behalf of the Government; the Parliamentary Secretary to the Ministry of Agriculture and Fisheries for the fishing fleets; members of the Royal Naval Old Comrades Association; the blue-and gold-uniformed figures of Admiral of the Fleet Sir Philip Vian, Sir Geoffrey Oliver, Commander-in-Chief, The Nore, and Vice-Admiral Anstice, the Fifth Sea Lord, and Sir John Lang, Secretary of the Admiralty. A few paces in front of them, alone, stood a short slight figure clad in naval uniform. He was Admiral of the Fleet Sir Rhoderick McGrigor, First Sea Lord and Chief of the Naval Staff, who had come to Lowestoft to honour the dead of the Lilliput Fleet.

After a service of dedication conducted by the bishop, Admiral McGrigor spoke a few words. Then he pressed a button and the seventeen White Ensigns fell away from the base of the memorial to reveal seventeen bronze panels, bearing the names of 2,385 officers and men of the Patrol Service who died in the defence of their country and have no grave but the sea. At that moment the clouds parted and blue sky appeared overhead. On the horizon to seaward a thread of smoke trailed from the funnel of a passing freighter. And as the Marine buglers sounded the Last Post the words of the First Sea Lord lingered in the minds of those who had listened to them.

'In two world wars Lowestoft became the centre of the Patrol Service who manned the small ships which played an invaluable part in the struggle for victory. The world will little note nor long remember what we say here, but it will never forget what they did in the cause of freedom that ships might pass on the seas upon their lawful occasions as they do today.'

# PQ17 – CONVOY TO HELL

## by Paul Lund and Harry Ludlam

In June, 1942, Convoy PQ17, consisting of thirty-five merchant ships, set out for Russia with an escort of cruisers and destroyers. They had a reasonable chance of success until the order came to 'Scatter!'

What followed represents one of the most terrible and tragic blunders of the Second World War.

Authors Ludlam and Lund give a first hand account of the horror and despair that faced the men left to the mercy of a cruel enemy. From thousands of sources and recollections they have built up an unforgettable picture of what it was like to be in PQ17 – and survive . . .

NEW ENGLISH LIBRARY

# TIRPITZ
## by David Woodward

The *Tirpitz* was the biggest warship in the Western Hemisphere and her influence on the war was immense. The British did not dare leave her alone for fear that she would break out into the Atlantic and repeat the terrible havoc of her sister ship *Bismarck*. This gripping and authoritative book tells the dramatic story of how the British achieved the seemingly impossible task of sinking the *Tirpitz*. First came the torpedo bombers, then the R.A.F., then the frogmen. Yet still the *Tirpitz* survived and it was not until the R.A.F. had carried out three attacks with 10,000 bombs that she finally, but slowly, turned over, taking the lives of all but seventy of her crew of a thousand.

'A first-rate story of adventure' – **Daily Telegraph**

On sale at booksellers and newsagents everywhere.

**NEW ENGLISH LIBRARY**

# NEL BESTSELLERS

**Crime**

| | | | |
|---|---|---|---|
| T017 095 | LORD PETER VIEWS THE BODY | Dorothy L. Sayers | 40p |
| T026 663 | THE DOCUMENTS IN THE CASE | Dorothy L. Sayers | 50p |
| T021 548 | GAUDY NIGHT | Dorothy L. Sayers | 60p |
| T023 923 | STRONG POISON | Dorothy L. Sayers | 45p |
| T026 671 | FIVE RED HERRINGS | Dorothy L. Sayers | 50p |
| T025 462 | MURDER MUST ADVERTISE | Dorothy L. Sayers | 50p |

**Fiction**

| | | | |
|---|---|---|---|
| T018 520 | HATTER'S CASTLE | A. J. Cronin | 75p |
| T027 228 | THE SPANISH GARDENER | A. J. Cronin | 45p |
| T013 936 | THE JUDAS TREE | A. J. Cronin | 50p |
| T015 386 | THE NORTHERN LIGHT | A. J. Cronin | 50p |
| T026 213 | THE CITADEL | A. J. Cronin | 80p |
| T027 112 | BEYOND THIS PLACE | A. J. Cronin | 60p |
| T016 609 | KEYS OF THE KINGDOM | A. J. Cronin | 50p |
| T029 158 | THE STARS LOOK DOWN | A. J. Cronin | £1.00 |
| T022 021 | THREE LOVES | A. J. Cronin | 90p |
| T001 288 | THE TROUBLE WITH LAZY ETHEL | Ernest K. Gann | 30p |
| T003 922 | IN THE COMPANY OF EAGLES | Ernest K. Gann | 30p |
| T022 536 | THE HARRAD EXPERIMENT | Robert H. Rimmer | 50p |
| T022 994 | THE DREAM MERCHANTS | Harold Robbins | 95p |
| T023 303 | THE PIRATE | Harold Robbins | 95p |
| T022 986 | THE CARPETBAGGERS | Harold Robbins | £1.00 |
| T027 503 | WHERE LOVE HAS GONE | Harold Robbins | 90p |
| T023 958 | THE ADVENTURERS | Harold Robbins | £1.00 |
| T025 241 | THE INHERITORS | Harold Robbins | 90p |
| T025 276 | STILETTO | Harold Robbins | 50p |
| T025 268 | NEVER LEAVE ME | Harold Robbins | 50p |
| T025 292 | NEVER LOVE A STRANGER | Harold Robbins | 90p |
| T022 226 | A STONE FOR DANNY FISHER | Harold Robbins | 80p |
| T025 284 | 79 PARK AVENUE | Harold Robbins | 75p |
| T027 945 | THE BETSY | Harold Robbins | 90p |
| T020 894 | RICH MAN, POOR MAN | Irwin Shaw | 90p |
| T017 532 | EVENING IN BYZANTIUM | Irwin Shaw | 60p |
| T021 025 | THE MAN | Irving Wallace | 90p |
| T020 916 | THE PRIZE | Irving Wallace | £1.00 |
| T027 082 | THE PLOT | Irving Wallace | £1.00 |

**Historical**

| | | | |
|---|---|---|---|
| T022 196 | KNIGHT WITH ARMOUR | Alfred Duggan | 50p |
| T022 250 | THE LADY FOR RANSOM | Alfred Duggan | 50p |
| T017 958 | FOUNDING FATHERS | Alfred Duggan | 50p |
| T022 625 | LEOPARDS AND LILIES | Alfred Duggan | 60p |
| T023 079 | LORD GEOFFREY'S FANCY | Alfred Duggan | 60p |
| T024 903 | THE KING OF ATHELNEY | Alfred Duggan | 60p |
| T020 169 | FOX 9: CUT AND THRUST | Adam Hardy | 30p |
| T021 300 | FOX 10: BOARDERS AWAY | Adam Hardy | 35p |
| T023 125 | FOX 11: FIRESHIP | Adam Hardy | 35p |
| T024 946 | FOX 12: BLOOD BEACH | Adam Hardy | 35p |

**Science Fiction**

| | | | |
|---|---|---|---|
| T016 900 | STRANGER IN A STRANGE LAND | Robert Heinlein | 75p |
| T020 797 | STAR BEAST | Robert Heinlein | 35p |
| T017 451 | I WILL FEAR NO EVIL | Robert Heinlein | 80p |
| T026 817 | THE HEAVEN MAKERS | Frank Herbert | 35p |
| T027 279 | DUNE | Frank Herbert | 90p |
| T022 854 | DUNE MESSIAH | Frank Herbert | 60p |
| T023 974 | THE GREEN BRAIN | Frank Herbert | 35p |
| T012 859 | QUEST FOR THE FUTURE | A. E. Van Vogt | 35p |
| T015 270 | THE WEAPON MAKERS | A. E. Van Vogt | 30p |
| T023 265 | EMPIRE OF THE ATOM | A. E. Van Vogt | 40p |
| T027 473 | THE FAR OUT WORLD OF A. E. VAN VOGT | A. E. Van Vogt | 50p |

## War

| | | | |
|---|---|---|---|
| T027 066 | COLDITZ: THE GERMAN STORY | *Reinhold Eggers* | 50p |
| T009 890 | THE K BOATS | *Don Everett* | 30p |
| T020 584 | THE GOOD SHEPHERD | *C. S. Forester* | 35p |
| T012 999 | PQ 17 – CONVOY TO HELL | *Lund & Ludlam* | 30p |
| T026 299 | TRAWLERS GO TO WAR | *Lund & Ludlam* | 50p |
| T025 438 | LILLIPUT FLEET | *A. Cecil Hampshire* | 50p |
| T020 495 | ILLUSTRIOUS | *Kenneth Poolman* | 40p |
| T018 032 | ARK ROYAL | *Kenneth Poolman* | 40p |
| T027 198 | THE GREEN BERET | *Hilary St George Saunders* | 50p |
| T027 171 | THE RED BERET | *Hilary St George Saunders* | 50p |

## Western

| | | | |
|---|---|---|---|
| T017 893 | EDGE 12: THE BIGGEST BOUNTY | *George Gilman* | 30p |
| T023 931 | EDGE 13: A TOWN CALLED HATE | *George Gilman* | 35p |
| T020 002 | EDGE 14: THE BIG GOLD | *George Gilman* | 30p |
| T020 754 | EDGE 15: BLOOD RUN | *George Gilman* | 35p |
| T022 706 | EDGE 16: THE FINAL SHOT | *George Gilman* | 35p |
| T024 881 | EDGE 17: VENGEANCE VALLEY | *George Gilman* | 40p |

## General

| | | | |
|---|---|---|---|
| T017 400 | CHOPPER | *Peter Cave* | 30p |
| T022 838 | MAMA | *Peter Cave* | 35p |
| T021 009 | SEX MANNERS FOR MEN | *Robert Chartham* | 35p |
| T019 403 | SEX MANNERS FOR ADVANCED LOVERS | *Robert Chartham* | 30p |
| T023 206 | THE BOOK OF LOVE | *Dr David Delvin* | 90p |
| P002 368 | AN ABZ OF LOVE | *Inge & Stan Hegeler* | 75p |
| W24 79 | AN ODOUR OF SANCTITY | *Frank Yerby* | 50p |

## Mad

| | | |
|---|---|---|
| S006 086 | MADVERTISING | 40p |
| S006 292 | MORE SNAPPY ANSWERS TO STUPID QUESTIONS | 40p |
| S006 425 | VOODOO MAD | 40p |
| S006 293 | MAD POWER | 40p |
| S006 291 | HOPPING MAD | 40p |

NEL P.O. BOX 11, FALMOUTH, TR10 9EN, CORNWALL.

For U.K.: Customers should include to cover postage, 18p for the first book plus 8p per copy for each additional book ordered up to a maximum charge of 66p.

For B.F.P.O. and Eire: Customers should include to cover postage, 18p for the first book plus 8p per copy for the next 6 and thereafter 3p per book.

For Overseas: Customers should include to cover postage, 20p for the first book plus 10p per copy for each additional book.

Name ..................................................................................................................................

Address ..............................................................................................................................

..........................................................................................................................................

..........................................................................................................................................

Title ..................................................................................................................................
(JANUARY)

Whilst every effort is made to maintain prices, new editions or printings may carry an increased price and the actual price of the edition supplied will apply.